DAMON ALBARN
BLUR, GORILLAZ & OTHER FABLES
MARTIN ROACH & DAVID NOLAN

Published in 2007 by
INDEPENDENT MUSIC PRESS
Independent Music Press is an imprint of I.M. P. Publishing Limited
This Work is Copyright © I. M. P. Publishing Ltd 2006

Damon Albarn – Blur, Gorillaz And Other Fables
by Martin Roach and David Nolan

All Rights Reserved

This book is sold subject to the condition that it shall not, by way of trade or otherwise, be lent, re-sold, hired out or otherwise circulated without the publisher's prior consent in any form of binding or cover other than that which it is published and without a similar condition being imposed on the subsequent purchaser.

No part of this publication may be reproduced, stored in a retrieval system, or transmitted in any form or by any means, electronic, mechanical, photocopying, recording or otherwise, without the prior permission of the copyright owner.

British Library Cataloguing-in-Publication Data.
A catalogue for this book is available from The British Library.
ISBN: 0-9552822-8-4 and 978-0-9552822-8-7

Cover Design by Fresh Lemon.

Printed in the UK.

Independent Music Press
P.O. Box 69,
Church Stretton, Shropshire
SY6 6WZ
Visit us on the web at: www.impbooks.com
and www.myspace.com/independentmusicpress
For a free catalogue, e-mail us at: info@impbooks.com
Fax: 01694 720049

Damon Albarn

Blur, Gorillaz And Other Fables

by Martin Roach and David Nolan

Independent Music Press

ACKNOWLEDGEMENTS

Many people have been instrumental in completing this book and our gratitude is warmly extended to Eddie Deedigan, Nigel Hildreth, Lucy Stimson, Pat Gilbert, John Dower, Andrew King, Philip Glassborough, Biffo, Rets, Ric Blaxill, *Top of the Pops*, Chris Twomey, Wiz (RIP), Chris Charlesworth, Hilary Donlon, Paul Mortlock, Nikki Russell, Brendan Coyle, Karen Johnson at EMI, Ellie at Food Records, Andy Linihan and the National Sound Archive, Dave Crook, Paddy at Badmoon, Roselle Le Sauteur. Where possible, the authors have tried to trace the owners of the memorabilia, photographs and ephemera, but some were unobtainable. To this end, they would particularly like to talk to Eddie Deedigan, Lucy Stimson, Nigel Hildreth. Early parts of this book have previously been published under the title, *Blur: The Whole Story* by Martin Roach.

Martin Roach: Dedicated to Kaye for her inspirational and unswerving support and to Alfie Blue and Korda Ace, my very own great escape.

David Nolan: Dedicated to the PSL, Jake, Scott and Bonnie ... my boys and girls.

CHAPTER 1

ALL THAT YOU CAN DO IS WATCH THEM PLAY

"No single person here can change the philosophy of this college." The sentence rang out over the large class of first year drama students. Towards the back of the room, an 18-year-old Damon Albarn glanced across at his friend Eddie Deedigan and raised a sceptical eyebrow. After all, this was East 15, a notorious champion of the method acting school of drama, supposedly a cauldron of latent talent and artistic potential. However, in recent weeks, student dissent and absenteeism had risen in protest at the increasingly strict courses and under-funding. Damon and Eddie had been amongst those refusing to go to tap dancing for example, convinced it was not how they wanted to progress. Matters had come to a head and the director was strolling back and forth at the front of the class warning of the grave consequences for any student who didn't tow the line. She repeated her opening statement. As she did Damon leant across to Eddie and whispered: "No single person here can change the philosophy of this college, eh? What if that single person is right?"

* * *

Damon's somewhat Bohemian upbringing had influenced him in a multitude of ways, but it was this strong-minded self-belief that was his childhood's greatest legacy. His father's family was part of a long line of Lincolnshire Quakers and Damon's grandfather had served time during World War II for his conscientious objection. Paradoxically, his mother's parents were farmers who accommodated prisoners of war to work on their land during the conflict. Despite their different backgrounds, Keith and Heather married and soon gave birth to Jessica, followed by Damon three years later on March 23, 1968, in Whitechapel Hospital. Outside in the big wide world of pop, the swinging sixties were in full effect and The Beatles had just scooped four Grammy Awards for their latest album *Sgt. Pepper's Lonely Hearts Club Band*.

It was a great time to be in London, and the Albarns were deeply involved in the cultural melange of flower power. Damon's mother was an accomplished stage designer who worked for the revolutionary Theatre Royal Stratford East company of Joan Littlewood. She worked on many productions, including one, *Mrs Wilson's Diary*, whilst pregnant with Damon. She later went on to have several collections of her art exhibited and even made the glass bead necklace which Damon frequently wears around his neck.

Damon's father was also creatively talented. Having trained as an artist, he was the first person to show Yoko Ono's art exhibition in London in 1966. Yoko was a highly acclaimed and controversial conceptual artist of ten years standing in her own right before she met her future Beatle husband. By exhibiting her work, Keith was placing himself at the centre of progressive art culture. Keith Albarn was more than happy to work in an environment where Yoko would ask people to "communicate with the other members by mental telepathy." He later presented a BBC2 arts show with some aplomb, which became the pilot production for *The South Bank Show*. He also ran a shop in Kingly Street, just down the road from BBC Broadcasting House, in the heart of psychedelic London. The store was crammed with weird and wonderful furniture, decorations and other design creations of the flowering hippy culture. Like his wife, Keith Albarn also enjoyed a keen interest in stage design which was put to good use in his role as manager of 1960s jazz rock warlords Soft Machine. Founded in the year England lifted the World Cup, Soft Machine's early art rock soon evolved through various personnel changes into a fine jazz rock fusion which, for many people, is still the standard against which all future forays in this field must be measured. Robert Wyatt, the mercurial singer who left in 1970, provided perhaps the band's highlight with 'Moon In June' which mixed his distinct humour with a half-spoken, half-sung vocal, delivered in his very English accent.

The band was a progressive theatrical outfit and Keith was

therefore heavily involved as their residential concept stage designer. The most famous of Soft Machine's various dadaist 'happenings' was one called 'The Discotheque Interplay' in Saint Aygulf, in 1967's Summer of Love. Perhaps not surprisingly, the event achieved much notoriety after the local mayor banned it for making his coastline look like a "pig-sty". Back in the family home in Leytonstone, east London, the Albarn's immersion in the psychedelic 1960s was fully visible when Damon arrived a year later. Outwardly a small Victorian terraced house, Chez Albarn was hardly *Terry and June*. The lounge was painted silver and all the rooms were full of the bizarre conceptual furnishings that his father sold in the shop. In amongst the fascinating clutter were presents from the various artists and performers who would visit, including some odd blue chairs presented by Cat Stevens after he renounced all his worldly goods and converted to Islam. From an early age, Damon and his sister were treated as young adults rather than small children and they were both always welcome at the many parties held at the house. On these occasions, their home would be filled with strange characters, musicians, artists and performers. As befitting the period, drugs were inevitably present, but the Albarns kept them strictly clear of the children and avoided hard drug use themselves. Years later at a Blur gig, journalists were surprised to see Damon smoking a joint whilst talking to his father – for Damon, this was never an issue, as he told Q magazine: "Pop culture was never something new to me. It never served as a reference point for rebellion. I was always allowed to stay up late around at parties with people smoking dope and getting pissed and taking drugs." Damon also said, "I had a very open childhood, in many ways, which didn't hold me back or fill me with masses of angst."

As Damon's first ten years were spent in this liberal atmosphere, his impressionable mind quickly developed and greedily absorbed the colourful environment. Attending the George Thompson Primary School in Leytonstone, Damon was a perfectly normal, ordinary young child. He played football, occasionally listened to music, collected fossils and stuffed animals, enjoyed bird watching and avoided girls. He went to his first musical, *The Point,* at the Camden Roundhouse aged seven, which was a similar production to the hugely successful *Hair.* Damon's other key memory of his primary years was watching the silent monks from a nearby monastery walking through the woods near his home in the mornings. Such a progressive upbringing inevitably influences a child, and Damon is quite sure it fuelled his later lyrical obsession with the mundane, as he told *The Face*: "Normal life is fascinating. That's where I want to be. I started my life in a fucking hippy forest with monks and chrysanthemums."

Damon's first real upheaval came in his tenth year. He was taken on holiday to Turkey with some friends of the family for two months and when he returned his parents had moved house to Colchester. His father had landed an excellent job running the local art college, and his strong wage allowed the Albarns to move into a comfortable four-bedroom 14th century house. Professionally, it was a prestigious position and Keith Albarn reinforced his reputation by writing two books on Islamic design, including *The Language Of Patterns*. For Albarn Junior, however, the change was not so immediately beneficial. Having been more than comfortable in the multi-racial, liberal atmosphere of London, where his family's colourful ways were easily accepted, Damon now found himself in an staunchly provincial environment with stifling values and old-fashioned morals. Damon began attending Stanway Comprehensive School, and during his first year found that his extrovert character was not universally liked. A new boy at any school is at an immediate disadvantage, but the combination of Damon's home life and his already expansive interests made him something of a 'weirdo' (or even worse, the ultimate sin, a 'gay boy'). Fellow pupils do not recall him ever being bullied, however. By now, Damon had begun learning the violin, and was reading the works of Karl Marx; he also loved drama, listened to music and sported an ear-ring, none of which are likely to earn you much respect with tough football-playing, hard-drinking, women-chasing 12-year-old hell raisers. Conversely, Damon's pretty features and extrovert nature attracted certain pupils to him, especially those with a similar interest in the arts.

Shortly after Damon arrived at Stanway, the school employed a new Head of Music, Mr Nigel Hildreth, who brought with him an open attitude to music that Damon has since publicly recognised as vital to his development. Hildreth enjoyed a love/hate relationship with the young Albarn throughout Damon's time at Stanway, recognising and encouraging his talent but being frustrated by Damon's frequent lapses: "What is most noticeable from this period," he told one of the authors of this book, "is that Damon's music was very much secondary to his fervent interest in drama and an acting career. I recall his mother telling me that 'Damon's talents are not in music' and he felt the same. Damon [thought] his skills were in acting rather than music and he was always heavily involved

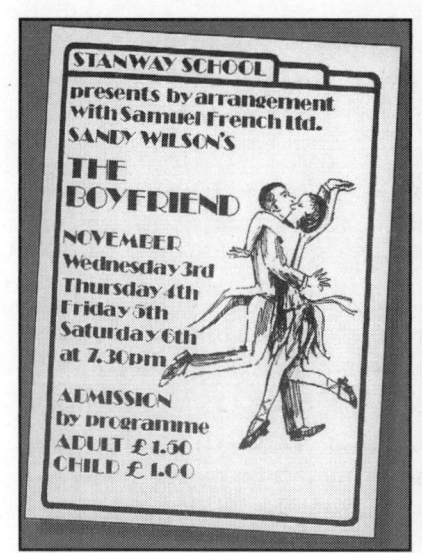

in our school productions. He made his stage debut in a show called *Fist*, which was a rock opera adaptation I had written of the Faust legend. As a third year, Damon was only in the chorus, but he was still very much into it. After that, we did a whole range of pieces in which Damon was always involved, with increasingly important roles. His enthusiasm was such that even if he was not on stage he would find his way backstage to be part of the crew. He played his first lead as Bobby in *The Boyfriend*, a 1920s musical by Andy Wilson, where he had to dance the Charleston. He also went on to play Nathan Detroit in *Guys and Dolls*, and Jupiter, King of the Gods in *Orpheus of the Underworld*, which was his final performance. Interestingly, this particular part showed that although his acting talent was not in question, his singing was not technically up to operetta." However, this production also showed the extent of

Damon's confidence – at one point the weapon he was supposed to be attacking someone with fell apart, but he saved the show from disaster by just calmly ad-libbing the whole of the next scene.

For Damon, the actual performance was everything. This practical approach soon affected his 'O' level music studies, where he found difficulty applying himself to the theory-based course. Even on the preferred playing side, his school instrument – the violin – was soon superseded by his growing interest in the piano. Hildreth saw his talent grow but no more than most competent pupils: "He was quite an accomplished improviser on the piano, although about normal for a good student. It was *never* a case of 'a star is born'. To be honest, he had some problems when playing from written music with timing, with his rhythm. Nevertheless, he played second violin regularly with The Colne Valley Youth Orchestra and with our own Stanway Orchestra, but was frequently chastised for not concentrating. This was particularly frustrating, because when it came to his own music he had no such problems. He took some jazz piano classes of his own volition with a local blind teacher called Rich Webb, and was always encouraged in his artistic endeavours by both his parents, who had an excellent attitude. Having said that, it is very difficult to see any outstanding glimmers at that stage, certainly not in his music – his compositions were good, but nothing outstanding. Where I saw the best of his work was definitely in his acting performance – his stage presence and ability were very definite. He had a tangible magnetism on stage and many of the teachers thought he could make it as an actor."

Gradually, Damon's original compositions did develop: "He was always into composition as well. He developed this ability to extemporise and take from all areas of music, a trait which I feel has always been Blur's major strength. Through a mixture of my encouragement and his own volition, he gained a basic understanding of musicals, classical, jazz, rock, orchestral and many other forms. You could see in his own compositions that he was using all of these reference points."

Away from classes, Damon loved his keyboard and rarely played his violin. The classical proclivity of his course work introduced him to many great writers, of whom Vaughan Williams was a particular favourite. To complement this, his parents' assorted record collection opened his young ears to music that was unusually diverse for his age. Soft Machine were an obvious feature, but Kurt Weill, various jazz masters and even Rod Stewart were regular visitors to the Albarn turntable. At the opposite extreme, Damon spent six months in front of his bedroom mirror at one point pretending to be the dandy highwayman Adam Ant. However, it was the rise of Two Tone that had perhaps the biggest effect on Damon of any popular music and it was thus that he met Graham Coxon for the first time.

Graham had first seen his future Blur cohort next to the music room Porta-kabin, but really took notice when Damon was singing the *West Side Story* number 'Please Officer Krupke' in assembly ("I thought he was a particularly extrovert chap."). Shortly after he was subjected to his first taste of Damon's ebullient confidence. The scene of the crime was the post-punk vacuum at the end of the seventies which gave Two Tone its birthplace. The biggest selling independent single of 1979 was 'Gangsters' by The Specials, released on their own 2-Tone record label, and this heralded a genuine chart invasion of similar Two Tone bands whose music was a curious mixture of modern styles drawing heavily on Jamaican ska. Technically proficient covers of Prince Buster, The Pioneers, The Skatalites and The Maytals were complemented by Two Tone's own intelligent compositions, perhaps most notably when The Specials 'Too Much Too Young' topped the UK charts. Madness, The Beat and Selector were just a few of the classic bands of this period. It was not only the music that mattered either, as Terry Hall of The Specials told the press at the time "The clothes are almost as important. We're not a mod band or a skinhead band, The rude boy thing is a real mixture."

Having the right trousers, the correct shoes and just the right size pork pie hat was crucial to being a cool rude boy. Graham Coxon's brogues were cheap imitations, but luckily most pupils let this pass. But not Damon. Despite hardly knowing Graham, Damon walked over to him during a school trip one day and publicly ridiculed his cheap footwear. Damon, naturally, had the genuine article.

Despite this odd start, the two found they had similar tastes in many things, particularly music, and very soon a close friendship developed. Both boys covered their school books in various Two Tone logos, with Madness and The Specials taking pride of place.

Graham's saxophone, drum and basic guitar playing matched Damon's own musical aptitude and soon they were swapping records and going to youth clubs together in full Nutty Boy regalia. Although many of their female peers were into soul, the two friends were unimpressed. Damon still applauds these bands and cites 2-Tone as a major influence on the material he would later write: "Madness are immensely important folk heroes in British pop music."

At this stage, Graham's greatest gift was his art – his drawing and paintings (which began with him copying Beatles record sleeves) were stunning. He is a genuinely talented artist, a fact which is only overshadowed by his position as one of the finest guitarists of his generation. Back then, although he and Damon were very alike, they had come from very different backgrounds. Whilst Damon's house extolled all the liberal values of the late sixties, Graham's father Bob was in the RAF. It was during one of many postings abroad that Graham was born, in a military hospital in Rintein, in Germany, four years after his sister Hayley. Coxon Senior was a bandsman, and a commendable clarinetist and saxophonist, so the household was a musical one, with Beatles records playing constantly. Graham was given his first instrument – a fife – when he was just six. His infant years were spent on an army estate in Berlin, until aged five, he moved to live with his grandfather next to a flyover in Derby. Life was fairly normal through his primary education until, like Damon, his tenth year brought upheaval. His father left the army and became a conductor for the Essex Constabulary Police Band, moving the family home to Colchester in the process. Bob Coxon also became a visiting music teacher at Stanway, and so that is where Graham was sent to continue his itinerant education.

Damon was a school year older then Graham but that made no difference as they quickly became best friends. The Coxon house ran on to the back of the school playing fields and during many lunchtimes the pair would come home, steam up to Graham's tiny bedroom which had a cheap drum kit levered into it and listen to music, surrounded by posters of The Jam on every wall (indeed, The Jam's B-side 'Aunties & Uncles' was the first song Graham learned to play on his guitar). Other times, they would stay in the music block during the break and play through songbooks given to them by Mr Hildreth, which were full of classic pieces by songwriters such as Simon & Garfunkel and Lennon & McCartney. When they weren't playing music, they would watch Mike Leigh's *Meantime* or *Quadrophenia*, yearning to be Phil Daniels or Jimmy the Mod. Lucy Stimson, a class-mate of Graham's, recalls his other obsession: "He was always going around school talking about Keith Moon of The Who, it was Moon this and Moon that, on and on. He even had a Who video and watched it all the time. He was so into Moon and, of course, this helped his enthusiasm for drumming."

Graham was also studying for 'O' level music, but was markedly less extrovert than Damon, as Hildreth recalls: "Graham was always much quieter. He was always very dedicated and quite serious.

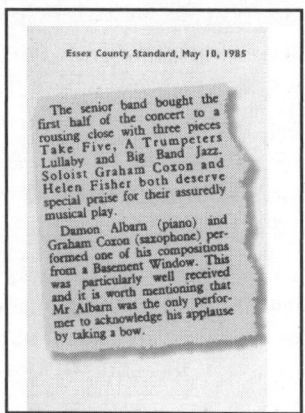

> Essex County Standard, May 10, 1985
>
> The senior band bought the first half of the concert to a rousing close with three pieces Take Five, A Trumpeters Lullaby and Big Band Jazz. Soloist Graham Coxon and Helen Fisher both deserve special praise for their assuredly musical play.
> Damon Albarn (piano) and Graham Coxon (saxophone) performed one of his compositions from a Basement Window. This was particularly well received and it is worth mentioning that Mr Albarn was the only performer to acknowledge his applause by taking a bow.

> STANWAY SCHOOL
> presents
> A SUMMER EXTRAVAGANZA
> Tuesday July 17th Wednesday July 18th at 7:30pm in the School Hall
> Admission £1.00 Adults 75p Children

Whereas Damon's year was not that talented, Graham found himself amongst a very good group of pupils, which he found a little intimidating at times. He always undervalued his own musical ability, which was a shame because he has a very intuitive sense of musicality, he has a lot of skills and a great feel for the music. I remember quite clearly him playing his first saxophone solo, and he played it very musically indeed."

The two boys' enthusiasm for music began to pay off – they became promising classical musicians, who both had original compositions performed by the Essex Youth Orchestra. One of Damon's works was even good enough to win a regional heat in the *Young Musician Of The Year* competition. Damon's non-classical compositions were often aired at school shows. For *The Summer*

Extravaganza, Damon played a piece he had written on his keyboard, with his friend James Hibbins singing. (Cost: £1 to get in, 75p for OAPs).

It wasn't long before Damon and Graham appeared on stage together. Graham was Styx, servant of Pluto, in the aforementioned *Orpheus and the Underworld* whilst Damon was Jupiter, and he was in a minor role for *Oh, What A Lovely War*, again with Damon. Another time, when the school put on *The Bartered Bride* in collaboration with The Royal Opera House, Graham was in the chorus with Damon's sister Jessica, and they both appeared in full make-up on a televised performance for *Blue Peter*. Graham was acutely embarrassed as he had to wear his trousers tucked into his socks all day, but he earned his Blue Peter badge nonetheless. Damon was too busy taking his 'O' level exams and had to make do with helping out backstage. On a few occasions, they actually played in the same band at school. The first occasion was a school show where Damon (keyboards) and Graham (saxophone) were joined by their friends Paul Stevens (guitar), James Hibbins (guitar and vocals), Michael Morris (guitar) and Kevin Ling (drums). They performed two songs that Damon had written, the titles of which have seemingly been lost to posterity amongst the fairy cakes and tombolas. Hildreth remembers the stage magnetism he had noticed in Damon was now clearly growing: "Damon could attract an audience and communicate in such a way that they were literally left screaming for more."

It was around this time that Damon and Graham began to form their first bands outside of school. Damon was as influenced by recent pop events as anyone else: "The Smiths were the best band in the world, we all wanted to dress like Morrissey, give up meat like Morrissey." Damon also claims that The Smiths' singer spurred him on to forming bands himself: "What made me be in a band was seeing a *South Bank Show* on The Smiths and hearing Morrissey say that pop music was dead, and that The Smiths had been the last group of any significance. I remember thinking, 'No-one is going to tell me that pop music is finished.'"

The first real outfit of any note was The Aftermath, which contained Damon, Graham, James Hibbins and another school friend Paul Stevens. Their only real moment of fame was playing

'Hey Joe' by Jimi Hendrix to school assembly. After that, Hibbins left and was replaced by Alistair Havers, and the new band was christened Real Lives (more of which later). All the time, Damon was writing – one of Damon's first pop songs was about a diamond run from Amsterdam to Johannesburg, inspired by a TV documentary he had seen.

As Damon's extra-curricular interests increasingly drew him away from his course work, he frequently came him into conflict with Mr Hildreth: "He could be extremely exasperating, because people knew he had it in him but he had his own agenda. Within any organisational framework that is very frustrating and very difficult to deal with. More often than not, he would be in a world of his own, even during productions and shows. He would regularly not be on stage when he should have been, missing lines or cues, the inevitable slip up. He would be most apologetic, and take the criticism, he realised he was out of line, but he just couldn't help himself and would still do it again. There were times when I really lost my rag with him, he could be a real loose cannon. Interestingly, his fellow students seemed not to mind, they knew he was like that. Also, when he did concentrate, he could deliver the goods." Lucy Stimson recalls that Damon's lack of commitment was not something only the teachers noticed: "At the time he took his 'O' levels, he wasn't famous for his classical music. There was a cruel joke going around about Damon that in the 'O' level paper, the first question was 'How many strings does a violin have?' The rumour was that Damon put 'Six'."

Despite this reputed error, Damon passed his 'O' levels (including music) and decided to stay on at Stanway for the sixth form, studying Music, English and History. The 'A' level music was somewhat harder: "He enjoyed various elements of the course," recalls Nigel Hildreth, "such as the history and the composition, but he struggled elsewhere. He must have enjoyed it to a degree, and he was always incredibly well meaning. He was always very keen on the music, working on it and he contributed a lot, and worked well with the other students. However, by now you could see he had his own agenda."

Real Lives was now firmly established and had already performed several gigs including one at The Affair club in Colchester. Their most noted performance was actually at the school – some sixth formers had to create a limited company for a business project and Graham's class mate Lucy Stimson had the idea that they should put on a live gig for the first and second years. "It was just something different from their normal disco. Real Lives played all original material and the kids went absolutely mad for it, they were a smash hit. Damon in particular had this magnetism on stage. As a fellow pupil, it was absolutely abundantly clear that he was far from ordinary. His presence simply wasn't normal and the teachers and the pupils knew it. He never excelled at classical, but on stage he had that something extra, without a doubt. There are very few people who stand out at secondary school age, but Damon did easily."

Away from school work and bands, Graham and Damon went on summer holiday to Romania with Graham's parents. The remainder of their education was spent snogging their first girlfriends, buying as many records as they could afford and getting drunk on cheap wine and smoking bad cigars. The first time they got drunk was next to the local canal. When the alcohol had really taken affect, Graham crouched down for a desperately needed poo, but forgot to remove his jumper which was wrapped around his waist, and promptly dumped into his rather nice Fred Perry.

Lucy Stimson remembers that Damon was always more successful with girls than his friend: "Damon was very charming and with his acting ability he was very popular, although not really until the sixth form. Lots of girls liked him. Graham meanwhile was much more shy and reserved, but he was always a very sweet character. He did seem to struggle with girls more than Damon because of that quieter nature. Neither of them were yobs, there were no real dirty stories or shady episodes. They were seen by fellow pupils as friendly and sweet."

The inevitable result of the increasingly varied distractions during sixth form was that Damon failed his 'A' level music (as well as his Grade 8 theory), as Hildreth explains: "There were two key factors which led to Damon failing his 'A' level. Firstly, he had decided beyond question that he wanted to go to drama school, and so the discipline needed for the music course simply wasn't there. Secondly, the qualification itself wasn't something he was that keen on – when you really got down to the nitty gritty of 'A' level Music, where he was required to sit a three hour silent harmony exam, he just wasn't interested. He even brought the wrong music scores for one performance exam.

There was inevitably a conflict between us as a result, because I felt he could have achieved the grade if he had tried. He had the potential but he was not using all of his talents. However, in retrospect, I don't hold that against him because to a certain extent he had taken what he wanted from the course – the exam was just unnecessary icing on the cake to him. By taking the course, he had learnt several things – his playing was fine, he had some starting points of composition, he knew about basic harmonies, and had acquired a broad listening base of musical knowledge. That was what the course offered and he took that, [so] the final exam was irrelevant." Having said that, Damon was sufficiently worried about his poor results (he got an E and D in History and English respectively), that he lied to his parents about them.

Lucy Stimson confirms that Damon was frequently distracted from the course work: "If he wasn't interested in something then he just wouldn't apply himself. That is purely and simply the sign of someone with creative talent who wants to spend time working on those skills. My over-riding memory of Damon at school was him crouched over the piano in the music room, completely oblivious to everyone around him, writing and improvising his own music. Sometimes Graham and the other band members would join in, but quite frequently he was on his own."

In the lower sixth, Graham had also started 'A' level Music but struggled more than Damon with the staid theoretical bias of the course. Halfway through the first year, he gave up. Instead, he headed for The North Essex School Of Art to begin a two-year foundation course in General Art and Design, temporarily breaking up the friendship. The connection was still there however, as the college was the one run by Damon's father.

Meanwhile, Damon had already auditioned and been accepted at the infamous East 15 drama school in east London. So, by their late teens, both Damon and Graham were actively pursuing interests outside of music. Damon went to tell Mr Hildreth about his decision, and explained that drama was his first love, as his teacher had suspected. Mr Hildreth suggested that quite often the music comes back to people, but Damon was adamant: "The music means nothing to me, I am really into the drama."

CHAPTER 2

TRY, TRY, TRY

In September 1986, Damon caught the underground heading towards the eastern reaches of the Central line to Debden, where he was to embark on a three-year course at East 15. As mentioned, the school was a stalwart supporter of method acting, whereby pupils have to actually live their roles so as to better understand them. The policy obviously worked, as amongst its ex-students the school boasted Alison Steadman and many of the Mike Leigh group. However, on a practical level, for an 18-year-old Damon travelling to work as a high-heeled tart, or returning home to a flat in Leytonstone as Ayatollah Khomeini, this presented not inconsiderable practical difficulties.

Within a few days of the opening term, Damon had struck up a friendship with a fellow first-year called Eddie Deedigan, who was three years his senior – most drama pupils at the college were older than Damon, who was precociously young to be starting the course. When they discovered they were into similar writers and music, the friendship was really cemented, as Eddie recalls: "If we had group debates with a director, it always used to end up with me and Damon talking. That really interested me, this younger guy talking with great knowledge about all manner of subjects. At that point, his confidence was really striking, he could talk well and always with this great sense of humour." As with all school friends, there was plenty of fooling around, but beneath it all there was an intelligence, tenacity and drive developing in Damon that was very noticeable. Eddie learnt early on that his new friend's knowledge could be most helpful: "We were in this class about the history of music in theatre, and this really boring lecturer was asking a variety of obscure questions about baroque that no-one in the room knew anything about. Except Damon. However, instead of being the class know-all and answering all the questions himself, he started to whisper every answer into my ear, which I then told the lecturer. This guy had previously thought I was a prize working-class twat, but here I was coming out with all these amazing answers. Everyone was stunned. Damon and myself pissed ourselves laughing."

The two shared many more laughs together at East 15. One project was to live as roaming gypsies in the 1500s. The majority of the class toiled away building historically authentic dwelling tents, and living a sparse and frugal life - Eddie and Damon had different ideas however. They decided to be travelling gypsy musicians, christened themselves Marco and Alexandro, and spent five weeks sitting under a blossom tree playing guitar and fiddle. For another project, they were transported 150 years in time to a mid-17th century England gripped by the Black Death, as Eddie recalls: "The college gardens needed re-landscaping, so suddenly we are all supposed to be plague-infested labourers working the land. Like a total twat, I grew a beard and spent six weeks digging, but somehow Damon had managed to get himself cast as the bloody landlord. So he just strolled around with this stupid accent telling us what to do, and we couldn't argue because he was the top man."

Although he was primarily at East 15 to learn drama, many of the assignments involved music, and by now Damon was an exceptionally gifted pupil, particularly on piano. For a project called 'A Night In The Longhorn Saloon', Eddie felt that just churning out the same old tired Western saloon sequence would be too obvious. Instead, he suggested writing a piece about the American Indians' plight, but no-one except Damon agreed. As a compromise, they agreed to do the saloon scene but with original music: "Within minutes, Damon had penned this superb Western theme tune, and I made up some words, a complete piss-take which went, 'I wanna sing in a Western, walk like big John Wayne, I wanna kill a hundred injuns, then shoot myself in the brain.' The rest of the class were gobsmacked because it sounded amazing, but they just didn't get it, it was a total piss-take. Later on we wrote a song for a friend and Damon just slipped into this lovely lilting Irish ballad, easy. It was only fun, but it showed that Damon was already completely versatile. Within a few months he was doing operas, and playing piano for the college musicals, reciting Brecht and Weill, all sorts of stuff, no problem." Damon even played with the visiting Berliner Ensemble for a Brecht Festival, a highly prestigious accolade for the youngster.

Damon soon became known as something of a character at the college, and although not technically proficient as an actor, he was frequently the most watchable during productions. Sometimes this caused friction: "He shone, not as a great actor, just as an immense personality. At a drama college that is quite an achievement. He looked good, had a great voice as well as this amazing aura about him. Couple that with him being so young and I think that intimidated a lot of people.

He even unsettled one of the lecturers, who [had regularly been on various] television shows himself. He was really quite famous but for some reason he just couldn't handle Damon. One time we were performing *The Duchess of Malfi* and Damon was just pleasing himself, and you could see this lecturer getting really irate. Eventually he cracked and said, 'Damon, you think you are a god, and the fact is you probably are, but will you please listen to some direction.' The thing is Damon didn't need direction because he wasn't trying to be an actor, he was just exploring that side of expression.

A few weeks later, we were at a student party and by now this same lecturer was really pissed off with Damon, you could see it in his eyes, he felt really threatened. Damon's confidence is a weird thing, at times it seems almost physically threatening when he looks at you. This lecturer was getting very drunk, and so he decided to sort Damon out because he knew it would be put down to the alcohol. So he started having a go at Damon and he got really out of order, saying how much better and more talented he was. Damon just waited for his chance and calmly said, 'Is that why your wife left you?' The lecturer flew at him, grabbed him by the throat and pinned him to the wall. All the time Damon was just looking at him in this confident way of his, calm as fuck. That really struck me, being on national television every week and still being that threatened by an 18-year-old."

When he was not baiting lecturers, Damon was becoming increasingly prolific in his compositions. Eddie himself was working on what was a promising musical career, but his previous band had split up when he had enrolled at East 15. Eddie kept the monicker of The Alternative Car Park and promised to fulfil a gig obligation that was outstanding in November of the first term. This was a gig he could not afford to miss, a support slot to one of his all-time favourite performers, Nico, formerly of The Velvet Underground, who was on the tail end of a tour to promote her *Camera Obscura* album. "I had this brilliant actor called Oscar Stringer on saxophone, and a guy called Roy playing just snare. On backing vocals we had this girl called Chris who wore a short skirt and fishnets – she was completely wrong for the set up, not least because her powerful voice nearly blew me offstage! I knew Damon was amazing on keyboards, so I asked if he was interested and he said, 'Yeah, no problem, what for?' I casually said, 'Oh, you know, we've got this support slot with Nico,' and Damon said, 'Who's he then?' I said, 'Nico, you twat, you know, the fucking Velvet Underground?' and he said, 'Who are they then?'"

Eddie played him some Nico and Velvet Underground material, Damon thought it was cool and agreed to play the gig. Unfortunately, because he was in big demand for college musical projects, he had to miss the first three rehearsals. When he finally found some free time, Damon sat and listened to Oscar and Eddie play the songs they had been rehearsing. When they had finished he said, "Did you know you're both playing in completely separate keys?" Eddie continues: "He just told Oscar to do this, told me to do that and in five minutes he put us all together. This fucking kid had sorted us all out, and it was my songs!"

The night of the gig arrived and the band travelled to Gold Diggers in Chippenham, followed by a bus full of their fellow students for moral support. The gig went well and, at the end, the rest of the band left the stage so that Damon could play a song of his own which he had been rehearsing with just the fishnet clad singer. He shuffled up to the mike and rather sheepishly apologised in advance: "Sorry, but this is another slow one." Eddie continues the story: "My songs are relatively sad and they were well received. Then Damon came on and did this song of his called 'The Rain' and it just fucking blew us away. There were 300 or 400 people in the audience and they were just amazed, it was a great ballad. That style of song was my vernacular, but 'The Rain' just blew us away." Eddie consoled himself by talking to Nico, who made his decade worthwhile by allowing him to buy her a beer.

Although most of his peers preferred pop, Damon still found huge inspiration in the classical form. Much has been made of his fascination with Bertolt Brecht which he said was "overwhelmingly articulate music. It had more influence on me than any pop record." The influences of this writer – particularly in Blur's music – is clear to see. Brecht wrote contemporary music that was intended to be highly popular, using simple forms and melodies, but with a quirkiness and chromatic nuance that made them unusual. The origins of much of Blur's more unusual material can be traced back to this period. When Damon performed Brecht's *Die Drei Groschen Oper* with the Berliner Ensemble, Damon's old music teacher Mr Hildreth was in the audience, and afterwards he went out for a curry with his old charge: "There was a definite progression at that show, he was by now very accomplished, and technically very assured. When we ate afterwards, the shift in his interests away from drama back towards music was very clear." For his part, Damon thanked Hildreth for shouting at him during school rehearsals and said, "it made me realise that performing was important and it prepared me for the harsh treatment given out at drama school."

After each college day, Damon would return home to the digs he now shared with Eddie and sit in his bedroom writing yet more songs. His hunger for knowledge was already reaping rich rewards in the breadth of his material, and Eddie is in no doubt that Damon's parents should take much of the credit for this: "His upbringing is crucial, being so open, it gave him all these hundreds of influences. Someone like myself and a lot of contemporary writers, who come from a very working-class background, haven't been educated in the same way. I went to comprehensive school just as he did, but my upbringing gave me a far narrower scope of reference. I think his parents' lives were extremely influential – he could learn by their example. That shows – you can talk to him about certain things, such as music, art and books, but then he's off, and you can't really catch him, he's gone. He seems to know so much more about other things." Damon agrees, as he told the press: "I always thought my parents were dead right. I was going against the grain in a weird way, by continually following my parents. It just seems to have worked for generations in my family."

Despite the hilarious experiences they shared, both Eddie and Damon soon became disillusioned with East 15. The overpopulated classes and under-funded resources did indeed fuel student dissent and absenteeism. Shortly after the aforementioned "no single person can change this" statement, Eddie and Damon left. Ironically, Damon had gone to East 15 to pursue his childhood ambitions in acting, but it had turned him into a music-obsessed 19-year-old.

Once he had left East 15, Damon's musical focus sharpened. Various odd jobs were taken to earn money for demos and to buy cheap drink, but Damon frequently got sacked for fooling around. He lost a fruit-picking job for doing wheelies in the farm's tractor. He also worked as a barman at The Portobello Hotel, a famous rock star haunt where he served The Edge and Bono from the Joshua Tree-tastic U2 (all he remembers is that Bono was rude to him). That job didn't last long either and Damon had to rely on shifts at Le Croissant in Euston Station as his main source of income. Fortunately, Damon had some £3000 inheritance money saved and this was spent on new gear and a basic demo. This crude tape was then taken to The Beat Studios in Christopher Place near Euston, whose key client was a post-fame Belouis Some.

The owners Maryke Bergkamp and Graeme Holdaway were immediately impressed and agreed to manage Damon and give him free studio time in exchange for a job as a tea-boy. This was ideal for Damon, because he could work all day at Le Croissant, then head to The Beat Factory and notch up more studio time after-hours. The owners had more preconceived ideas for him – soon after taking the job, he was introduced to a high-pitched singer called Sam, and on the management's urging formed a soul pop duo called Two's A Crowd. The Beat Factory obviously had high hopes for them and a series of industry showcases were quickly arranged. The shows were heavily attended by record company scouts and there were lengthy negotiations over possible contracts. Some sources suggest that Damon sometimes appeared in full stage make-up as a mime artist. Unfortunately, the interest rapidly dried up and the ill-fated group split. This had been Damon's first sniff of possible success, but he wasn't remotely discouraged and just carried on writing.

With the demise of Two's A Crowd, Damon formed a band called Circus with a friend Tom Aitkenhead from Chippenham. This music was much more guitar based than Two's A Crowd, but the band's early progress was hampered by the failure to nail down a firm line-up. After several personnel changes, Damon got back in touch with Eddie, who was now living near Clapham Common, and asked if he would like to renew their previous musical partnership. Eddie was reluctant, as the Two's A Crowd material he had heard did not appeal to him. However, Damon played him a demo of the new songs and Eddie loved them, and so agreed to join on the spot.

The search for new members continued. Eddie roped in a work mate from Dixons electrical store in Marble Arch called Dave Brolan, who was an excellent bass player and superb guitarist. Eddie also recruited Darren Filkins, formerly of The Alternative Car Park (whom Damon had replaced for the Nico support slot), who had just returned from a year travelling around the world, so he took up lead guitar. The drummer's slot was also easily filled. Damon knew of a renowned drummer from Colchester with whom he had some loose associations in the past. A call was made and the affable and charming final member came to his first rehearsal and introduced himself as Dave Rowntree. It was October 1988.

The new Circus line-up immediately started recording the bundles of material Damon had written, and for the next two months worked hard in the studio honing their sound, with the aim of recording an album in the New Year. Everything went brilliantly, the songs sounded great, the members gelled well and the whole outfit was taking shape. Then, just two days before they were due to start recording the album, Darren Filkins announced he had won his first commission as a professional photographer. The band knew he had been trying for this but didn't expect his ambition to remove him from the equation so suddenly. They were all devastated – except Damon, who shrugged his shoulders and said, "That's his choice, I'll phone my friend to do some guitar." Despite Damon's brave face, the band were hugely deflated. Their songs were well-rehearsed, intricate and ready for recording – whoever was brought in at such short notice would only be able to cover over the cracks, and their efforts would be wasted. Damon called his friend anyway, a chap who had done a little saxophone work on some odd meandering instrumentals of his in the past. Two days later, this eleventh hour replacement guitarist walked into the studio, and introduced himself to the rest of the band as Graham Coxon.

CHAPTER 3

COME TOGETHER

Towards the end of his time at Stanway, Graham had become more of an extrovert, something of a common room clown, which was reflected in a school report that politely described him as "a gregarious extrovert who would do well to channel his energies in the future." Those energies were increasingly being used on his guitar. Saxophone was no longer his main instrument, having stopped at Grade Five. Once he moved on to The North Essex School Of Art, his guitar playing continued unabated and completely self-taught. Like Damon, he too worked various odd jobs, including a two month, twice-weekly spell at Sainsbury's, as well as a pea-picking job which he later described as "a human combine harvester." He also became a protest vegetarian for a while, but didn't monitor his diet closely enough and ended up with malnutrition in Severals Hospital in Colchester. This was actually the local mental hospital, so Graham spent seven long days cadging fags from senile old men. It also lost him his job at Sainsburys.

Graham then flitted through various bands, including a largely improvisational outfit called The Curious Band. He graduated from the North Essex School Of Art and enrolled at Goldsmiths College in south-east London, on a Fine Art course. Despite his love of music, Graham was still an accomplished artist, vindicated by the very fact he was admitted to this prestigious course – amongst his fellow art pupils would be the future Turner Prize winner and world-renowned artist Damien Hirst. Damon had kept in touch with Graham regularly since they both left school and Graham had contributed on the aforementioned instrumental demos. He had also gone along to a solo gig of Damon's at Colchester Arts Centre as moral support, where by coincidence Dave Rowntree was in the crowd. Damon had enrolled at Goldsmiths as well, on a part-time course just to get on campus, so the two old friends saw plenty of each other. When Damon asked him to help them out at Beat Factory for that Circus album session, Graham was more than happy. When he turned up at the studio and found Dave on drums, he was even more comfortable – this was not the first time they had played together.

Dave had occasionally called upon Graham's services to bolster the brass section in his own band Idle Vice. One of Graham's own loosely formed bands, Hazel Dean And The Carp Enters From Hell, had even played a small local gig called The Anti-Yuppie Festival in Wivenhoe alongside Idle Vice. The connection went even further back than that – when Dave had enrolled at Saturday morning jazz classes as a teenager, he found himself being taught by Bob Coxon, Graham's Dad.

Now in the studio with Circus, Graham was shown a couple of songs and explained the set up before the new line-up gave it a try. Eddie was stunned: "He fucking licked it, mental playing, unbelievable. He played this incredible guitar, we were completely blown away by it and then he said 'Is that alright?' Fucking hell, it was alright. We couldn't believe what we were hearing. It was easy for him."

After that, Graham slotted in effortlessly, and the band managed to record the entire album live in just four days. The highlights of the record were 'Elizabeth', 'Salvation', 'Happy House' and an untitled track about the Queen. After this unexpected success, Eddie was so convinced of Circus that he left his well-paid administrative job at Wembley Stadium to work on the band full-time: "Graham really had done us a major favour. To this day it still amazes me how easily he took that situation on board."

With the album complete, the band arranged a celebration party – after all, they had got through what could have been a very tricky and potentially disastrous situation. Loads of friends were duly invited and the drinks were flowing, especially as someone had brought a large bottle of Irish moonshine. Graham had brought some friends of his from Goldsmiths College and he hurried one of them over to listen to Circus's great masterpiece. The friend, Alex James, listened to the album patiently, looked at the massed faces waiting for his reply and said, "That's shit." Far from being offended by this, Damon and Eddie were impressed by the nerve it had taken Alex to say what he actually thought. They spent the rest of the night getting drunk on the 100 per cent proof illicit Irish spirits.

Undeterred by Alex's comments, Circus continued rehearsing and producing demos, and were encouraged along the way by Steve Walters at EMI, who advised them to get out there and gig. Shortly after, Circus played their first and only ever gig, in Southborough in Kent. The show was arranged by a friend of Eddie's wife and, supported by Whale Oil, it went very well. After this, and with spirits high, they went back in to the studio to record yet more new material that Damon had written. This time, however, Eddie was in for a shock.

Eddie was flabbergasted to hear that the new Circus material was light years away from anything they had done before. It was effectively a new band. He listened to it several times and came to a painful decision – at the next rehearsal he left: "I was okay with the level we were on before, but this new stuff was above me, I knew that and I had to go." Despite the brave decision to leave his full-time job, Eddie, along with bassist Dave Brolan, left Circus and formed the excellent Shanakies (who went on to become The Apple) whose paths would again cross with Damon, Graham and Dave in some years to come.

Circus was now just the threesome of Damon, Graham and Dave Rowntree. Dave was nearly six years older than Graham, being born in Colchester Hospital on April 8, 1963. He had a sister Sarah who was five years older. His father worked for forty years as a sound engineer at Broadcasting House, just up the road from the site of Keith Albarn's shop. Rowntree Senior even did some uncredited engineering work on the much-awaited *Beatles At The BBC* album. With Dave's mother being in the London Orchestra, it was another very musical household. Dave's first instrument was a simple set of bagpipes given to him by his dad, who also introduced him to the wonders of jazz, and enrolled him at Bob Coxon's weekend class. From there, Dave's musical interest blossomed, and by his teens he was a very keen drummer. His debut was made in 1977 at a street party for the Silver Jubilee where, along with a neighbour's son on piano, he performed an ear-splitting rendition of 'Yellow Submarine'. He also took drumming classes, where he was taught by a gargantuan Scotsman who taped a sixpence to the drumskin and hit Dave over the head every time he missed. Not overly academic, Dave attended a mixed grammar school where he adopted the unused school's drum kit as his own, before heading for a HND in Computer Science at Woolwich Polytechnic.

By the time Damon and Graham were studying for their 'O' levels, a 19-year-old Dave had already donned a kaftan, grown regulation student long hair and earned himself the nickname of Shady Dave. He bummed around Colchester bedsits for a while and finally formed Idle Vice, the three-piece with his friend Robin on guitar and Jim on bass. The band played together well, and decided to move to London, so they switched from a Colchester bedsit to a Crouch End squat. For six months they frequented the London squat scene playing hurried gigs at various parties, mostly centred in and around Kings Cross. By now, Dave's hippy long hair had been cropped into a thick black mohican, and he had developed an impressive tolerance for huge quantities of cider. At this stage, his wanderlust took over, so he upped and left for France, where he earned a meagre living for a while, busking and playing in small clubs. He didn't settle however and, after visiting England for the winter, never returned back to France.

He was now desperately short of money, so took a job as a computer programmer at the council, complete with mohican and shiny suit. During the same period, his girlfriend became pregnant, so he left Idle Vice and his itinerant lifestyle and appeared to settle down somewhat.

That was until Damon asked him to join Circus. Dave liked the music and enjoyed the recording, but was disappointed to see Eddie and Dave Brolan leaving after their first gig. It was a major blow, especially as Damon and Eddie were such good friends, but nevertheless they had to find replacements. It was felt that Graham was more than capable to handle guitar duties alone. All that was missing was a bassist.

Alex James. Tall, dark, louche, confident … and, at that stage, crap on bass. His first guitar, a Fender Precision copy was bought for £50 out of *Exchange & Mart* with his sixteenth birthday money, and was more of a fashion accessory than a musical instrument. His first band, The Age Of Consent, had consisted of Alex splicing a pretend introduction by him on to an actual album, then telling his school friends it was his band – this worked great until one of them recognised four Fleetwood Mac tracks. He never studied music at school, and was even kicked out of recorder class at primary school.

Alex was four months older than Graham, and spent much of his childhood in the grey, seaside dereliction of Bournemouth (years before the resort was re-invented as 'the new Brighton', it was a haven for purple rinses and expiring entertainment careers). He was born four years after his sister, Deborah, in Boscombe Hospital on November 21, to a father who sold fork lift trucks and electronic rubbish compactors, and a mother who did voluntary work, including the local Books On Wheels service. When his grandfather died, the James family moved into the late man's guest house, where they shared their life with a weird menagerie of pets. A £100 piano bought for his eleventh birthday inspired his desire for a keyboard but since he couldn't afford one, he opted instead for the bass.

The quiet retirement resort quickly frustrated the energetic Alex. Despite his boredom, he excelled at school with 13 'O' levels which were easily complemented by three top grade 'A' levels two years later. Before he headed off to more further education, he took a year out which included a job selling cheese at Safeway, where he developed his renowned taste for dairy produce of all flavours. Alex also worked as a labourer at Winfrith Nuclear Power Station, a frightening thought since he was also now experimenting with acid for the first time, and pretty much shagging anything that moved. He also formed an ill-fated band called Mr Pangs Big Bangs (named after his landlord), so by the time he started at Goldsmiths College, he was relatively inexperienced in music.

Alex could have taken any subject at Goldsmiths but he opted for French. On his very first day there, he saw Graham getting out of his parents' car with a guitar case under his arm, and went over and introduced himself. They became good friends, helped by the fact that their rooms were directly under one another in the Camberwell halls of residence.

For some reason known only to himself, Graham plastered his bedroom walls with hundreds of Pixies lyrics on bright pink paper. Alex meanwhile initiated his own school of thought called 'Nichtkunst' into which he dragged Graham – it was an odd clique which largely involved staying up all night and drawing weird pictures, getting increasingly stroppy with each other as the sleepiness swept in and trying to convince themselves they were a movement to rival the Bauhaus era. They weren't, but it was a laugh.

With Damon frequently on campus for his part-time course, it was only a matter of time before Alex was introduced, which was at that party when Alex told him Circus were shit. After this, the group of friends got through loads of gigs, beers and the occasional recreational drug – one show which stood out in all their minds was a legendary performance by The Happy Mondays at London's Astoria. Damon remembers this time well: "I used to go to loads of parties and when I got there Graham was always lying on the ground like a human doormat." One time, a night of especially copious drinking followed a show of Goldsmiths students' work – Alex woke up early the next morning in the middle of a field in Kent, whilst Damon blacked out after two bottles of tequila and fell asleep in Euston Station. The police saved him from a some tramps and slung him in Holborn police cells to sober up, where he was brought round by a Nepalese soldier in full uniform. The tramps had stolen all his money so he had to walk home.

The Circus album had been recorded in January 1989 and by the spring term Eddie and Dave Brolan had left to form The Shanakies. Damon knew Alex played a little bit of bass and that's why he asked if he fancied playing. Alex later said, "I thought Damon was a bit of a wanker but he had these keys to a studio, so I joined." With the completed line up came a new name – Seymour.

CHAPTER 4

SING

Much confusion and uncertainty seems to surround Seymour's first gig. Many have said it was at that Goldsmiths show where their drunken debauchery put Damon in a cell for the night, but at this point Eddie was still in the band. There has always been some mention of a gig at a railway museum near a village outside Colchester, but this was before the Goldsmiths fiasco, so again Alex would not yet have been on bass. What is clear is that the actual line-up that eventually became Blur did not finally come together until the early summer of 1989, during Alex and Graham's second year at Goldsmiths. Uncertainty also reigns about the infamously bad monicker – perhaps it was taken from one of Damon's fictional characters, or indeed from a Salinger story of the same name. Perhaps the latter is the more probable option as many of Salinger's characters, such as Holden Caulfield, are put-upon, alienated teenagers, who remain ever-popular with the entrenched mentality of aspiring art students.

Seymour's life was short, sweaty, but successful – within a year they had signed a record deal. Damon was churning out songs all the time and with a few regional shows under their belts they booked their first gig in London. They were supporting the excellent New Fast Automatic Daffodils and Too Much Texas at Camden's Dingwalls, and in anticipation they plastered the Underground with Seymour stickers. It was a fashionable bill which had attracted many music press and record company types, but the show ended badly for Seymour. After finishing their shambolic set, their drunken high spirits and a friend's willy waving unnerved a bouncer sufficiently for him to panic and spray mace in the band's faces. They stumbled out into the street, smarting from the self-defence spray and ended the night in hospital having their eyes checked. To add insult to injury, *Music Week*'s positive review was incorrectly spelt: "This unsigned and unheard of Colchester band played a blinder which swiftly endeared them to the Dingwalls disaffected. There could well be a gap in the goofy market and Feymour have the charm to fill it."

After this ignominious start, they gigged sporadically around the capital, including a support slot to the Swiss techno-meisters The Young Gods and third on the bill at The Lady Owen Arms to a band with a worse name – Dandelion. At first, the only feedback was from Graham's guitar. At a Brighton Zap Club gig, Seymour even dabbled in performance art with odd-shaped boxes on stage (the support band for the night was an infant jangly Suede, complete with Justine Frischmann on rhythm guitar). At this point, there was nothing to suggest that Seymour would evolve into the musically complex Blur. Graham was firmly immersed in a My Bloody Valentine/Dinosaur Jr fixation and noisy walls of sound smothered everything. Damon was hunched over a second-hand keyboard adding to the racket, occasionally getting up to spiral wildly around the stage. Alex and Dave chipped in with some odd, funky dance rhythms, which made Seymour sound like a weird cross between The Wolfhounds and Sonic Youth. It was shambolic, unfocussed, but not without promise. Damon loved it, and later told *Sky* magazine, "We just worked and worked on making ourselves brilliant. It's great being in a band when you're that age, thinking about what you want to be, doing manifestos, thinking about your image."

One record company man had tried to catch Seymour at Dingwalls, but couldn't get in because of the fashionable nature of the bill. Andy Ross was Head of Food Records, a nascent off-shoot of EMI and home to dance groovers The Soup Dragons and American success story Jesus Jones. The word was round that Seymour was a good live band, and Ross had already received a demo which showed some promise. Amongst the demo tracks were 'Tell Me, Tell Me', 'Long Legged', 'Mixed Up', 'Dizzy', 'Fried' and 'Shimmer' but it was the stand out song, 'She's So High', that grabbed Ross's attention.

Still doubling as a journalist at *Sounds* magazine, Ross finally got to hear Seymour at an Islington Powerhaus gig in November 1989, and he was suitably impressed, as he told *Record Collector*: "They were crap but entertaining. Two better tracks on the demo showed that they had a clear grasp of the facets of simple songwriting. Everything was in the right place and in the right proportion." One thing Ross could not deny was that Seymour was something to watch live – the music may have been ramshackle but by now the band were a live dynamo, and Damon in particular was like a man possessed. Ross saw Seymour twice more and then decided there was enough substance to offer them a contract. When they finally signed to Food Records in March of 1990, Seymour had only played a total of ten gigs.

The deal was simple – Food would put the band's records out and give them a £3000 advance, and in return all Seymour had to do was sign a deal for worldwide rights, change the sad anorak name and burn the grubby pyjama bottoms which Dave always wore at gigs. The first one was done with four signatures, two of which prematurely ended Graham and Alex's nearly complete degree courses – their finals were only two months away but they never went to college again. The second matter was a little more protracted. A proposed list of names discussed in a West End pizzeria included The Shining Path, Whirlpool, Sensitise and Blur. That decision was relatively easy though, especially as one option was a group of Peruvian revolutionaries and another was a brand of dishwasher. Ironically, a few weeks after signing, it became apparent that a band called Blurt already existed whose second album was comically called *Kenny Rogers Greatest Hits: Take 2*, but enquiries could not track them down and a possible name clash was avoided. All that was left was for Dave to vow never to wear his beloved pyjama bottoms again on stage. Record companies expect so much from young bands nowadays.

★ ★ ★

The spring of 1989 had heralded the beginnings of 'Madchester' when the Mancunian corner of the music world once again provided a plethora of bands revolutionising the rock and dance format, following in the tradition of Joy Division, New Order and lesser known acts such as A Certain Ratio. The Stone Roses led the way with The Happy Mondays and Inspiral Carpets following

Damon Albarn

closely behind, as 'baggy' music swept the nation up in a tide of flares, long-sleeved shirts and Joe Bloggs clothing. There was a general air of apathy around these bands, the drugs, the inactivity and the apolitical and abstract dismay towards life which came with the innovative musical territory. By the end of the next year, 'baggy' was creatively dead with the foremost proponents, The Stone Roses, locked in bitter courtroom struggles, spending all their time in the dock rather than the charts. For now though, 1989 was theirs, and

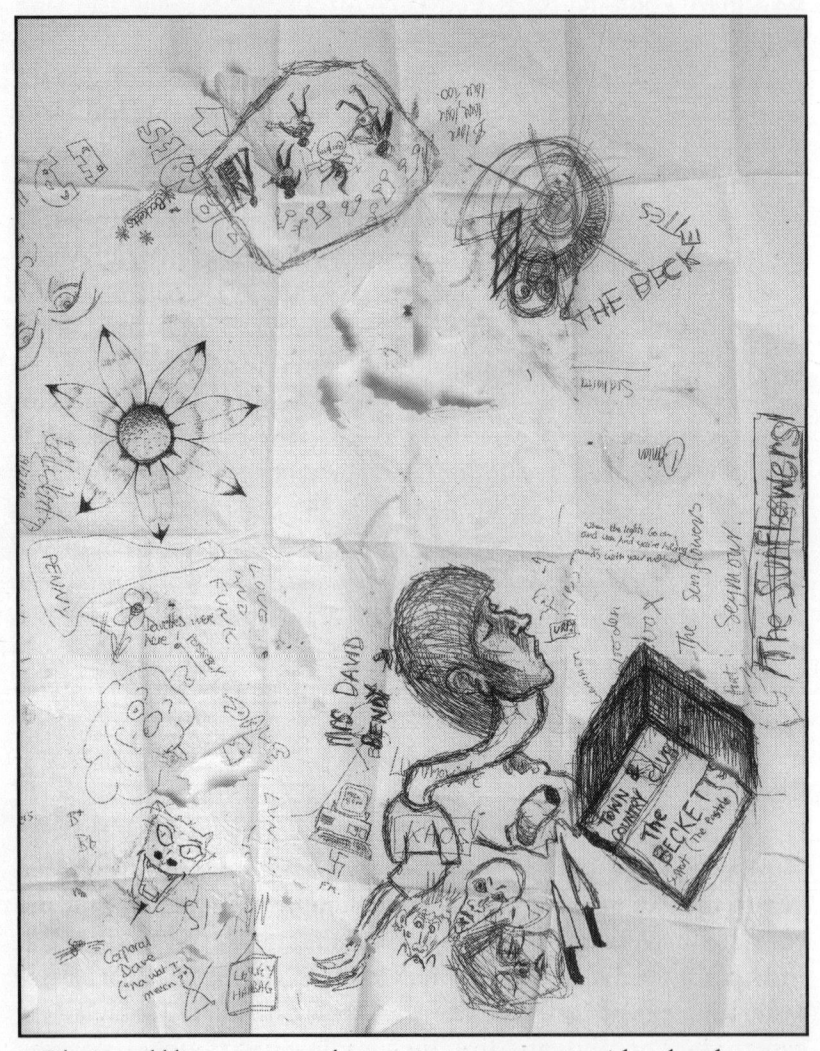

Blur's scribblings on a napkin, trying to come up with a band name

Madchester was a genuine and far-reaching phenomenon. It was impossible for contemporary bands to ignore these surrounding events. Even though the creative death knell of baggy had largely been sounded by the time Blur signed to Food, the repercussions continued for some time to come.

For now, Blur set about making a name for themselves. Initially, the band had wanted to release a single immediately after signing, but Ross convinced them it would be more beneficial to hit the road first to develop a groundswell of support. In July 1990, they headed out on a four-week tour, taking in medium sized venues such as Walsall's Junction 10 and London's Tufnell Park Dome. During this month on the road, the live recklessness that had made Seymour such an attractive band to watch was even more frenzied. Damon's stage antics had become increasingly dangerous. Jumping off speakers had graduated to climbing up lighting rigs and flaky ceilings, and his apparent care-free abandon seemed to border on the suicidal. The word spread and several promoters refused to book Blur, concerned about the legal repercussions should Damon come a cropper. Conversely, the ticket buying public could not get enough of it, as Damon said: "During this tour, I think a lot of people came to see us just in case I killed myself." Musically, Blur was much more accessible than its previous incarnation, as Alex told the press at the time: "Seymour was the more radical, non-bite sized, unfriendly face of Blur." Damon admitted that this transition to a more user-friendly sound was quite deliberate: "Seymour was our obtuse side. I didn't think we'd do well with our obtuse side, so we made less of it. Half our personality is latent."

Damon's destructive abandon set them apart from most of their baggy peers, but many of the songs had that feel to them, which meant Blur were inevitably tagged as succeeding off the coat-tails of baggy. The Stone Roses comparisons were clear, and the legacy of Graham's My Bloody Valentine fixation was also strongly apparent. However, Blur were unimpressed by these parallels and complemented their live shows of the summer with an arrogant and brash press campaign that certainly got them noticed.

Their first public announcement was that they would not release a single until they had secured the front page of a weekly music paper. Their second was that they had no intention of slogging around the toilet venues of Britain for five years, and that their time was *now*. Their third announcement was about their debut album – when asked if this would happen soon, a spokesman for Blur said, "We're going to be huge anyway, so why hurry?" Such a volley of opening comments made it crystal clear that Blur were not short of confidence. Damon in particular was always ready to mouth off about just how unique it all was, as this extract from *NME* shows: "I've always known I'm incredibly special, and if I didn't think we were the best band in the universe, I wouldn't bother." He was particularly dismissive of the baggy scene which Blur were being lumped in with: "The difference is that Blur are going to be hugely successful." With the benefit of hindsight that sounds prophetic, but it is worth bearing in mind that Blur had yet to release a single, and for many people this pretty face was just another self-important upstart shooting his mouth off in the music press for easy headlines.

Whatever the truth was about Blur, it seemed to work: their gigs during the summer were all heavily attended; reviews were frequent and glowing (although littered with various musical comparisons); T-shirt sales were high; and enquiries to Food about the debut single were steadily increasing. In the first week of July, less than four months after signing their record deal, Blur won their first weekly front cover, when *Sounds* heralded them as one of Britain's best new bands alongside the grossly under-rated Ned's Atomic Dustbin and the musically versatile Senseless Things. The combined effect of this excellent press coverage and compelling live shows fuelled Blur's rapid progression from tiny venues like Sir George Robey to a headlining slot at ULU to 1000 people. This big autumn gig made Blur the first band to top the bill there before they had a record out. It was a flying start.

During these dates, Blur had been visiting Battery Studios (where The Stone Roses recorded 'Fool's Gold') in Willesden to begin work on the debut single. The sessions were lengthy, often taking up to 18 hours a day – the best track for release was a choice between 'She's So High' and 'I Know'. Interestingly enough, in contrast to many fledgling bands, Blur were looking for something very different from their records, as Damon told one magazine, "We have no intention of duplicating our live sound, the record should be something great, while live is more of an exhilarating thing."

The choice was eventually made and 'She's So High' nominated as the debut single. Six weeks before its October 15 release, some white label promos were given to select club DJs to whip up underground interest in advance. Produced by Steve Power and Steve Lovell (the latter having worked with Julian Cope), there was some studio friction caused by doubts about the band's musical ability – it took over a week to record just this one track. Power had grave doubts about Alex's playing and on one track he insisted Graham play bass, the ultimate insult to any musician. Damon sympathised with his band mate's predicament: "Us three were as good as classically trained, so that puts Alex at a bit of a disadvantage, as we have that experience of sitting in orchestras and being shouted at and Alex doesn't."

Once released, 'She's So High' was a worthy debut. Very much a product of the time, its languid dance feel and mellower tempo was in stark contrast to Blur live, with the punk edge of their shows being relegated behind treacle guitar effects and sugary sweet harmonies. Graham had written some of the lyrics whilst Damon had been sunning himself on holiday in Spain, and the original nucleus of the song was inspired by a jamming idea of Alex's. As such, this track remains the most democratically created Blur song of all. It showcased much more of Blur's pop side, and this greater accessibility was reflected when it hit No.48 in the charts, despite a relative lack of radio airplay and a critical drubbing by Jonathan Ross on *Juke Box Jury*. Word of mouth was on Blur's side.

The music papers were more impressed than the record buying public, with several 'Single Of The Week' accolades, although *Sounds* writer Leo Finlay was a little over-zealous in saying that "regardless of production, 'She's So High' stands comparison with anything of the last five years, Blur are the first great band of the 1990s." The B-side, 'I Know', was more reminiscent of Seymour and lyrically both tracks were nonsensical, although there were some vague references to drug culture and clubs in the lead tune. The vacuous banality of Damon's early lyrics is something that is curiously at odds with his latter day reputation as a wordsmith of undoubted repute.

Interestingly, much of the attention for the single centred around the sleeve artwork. It was designed by Food's regular collaborators, Stylorouge, a design house who almost exclusively worked on record sleeves, such as those for Jesus Jones and Simple Minds – it was the start of a long relationship that produced some of the most stylish and idiosyncratic band artwork of the period. The cover of 'She's So High' caused something of an outrage. The central image of a naked blonde sitting astride a hippo had been taken from a 1960s painting by American pop artist Mel Ramoff, (who Blur eventually met) but the idiosyncratic style was lost on many people, who took exception to the sexist overtones. During their 21-date tour of universities and polytechnics to promote the single, Blur were frequently bombarded with protests about the sleeve image. At Coventry Polytechnic, The Steve Biko bar banned anyone wearing the corresponding Blur T-shirts, Warwick University students even attacked the band's merchandise stall, Hackney Council complained to Food and, in Brixton, feminists ripped down Blur fly-posters. Some observers saw this as an indication of a much wider scam. With the name change, the designer ethos of Stylorouge and the fashionably lolloping rhythms, they claimed that Blur were just a pre-fabricated Jesus Jones and that a shoddy hype machine was cleverly whirring into action.

This was understandable, but did not allow for the extensive touring which had put Blur in that position in the first place, nor the continued gigging that followed the release of the debut single. The promotional tactics might have stifled a lesser act, but Blur's live show at this time was their saviour – gig after gig was lauded by a largely enthusiastic press. Damon's frenzied performances belied an intrinsic discipline and musicality within the band – Blur appeared always to be on the verge of collapse but they never actually imploded.

The lengthy single tour was topped off at Christmas by a support slot to the fleetingly successful Soup Dragons at the cavernous Brixton Academy. Although Blur had only been together for less than a year, the band took this huge 4000-plus capacity gig in their laid-back stride. The stage magnetism that Damon's teacher spoke of was now equipping him well for Blur's escalating profile. It was a highly fashionable bill, maybe dangerously so, but Blur's punk rock performance was so strong that one music paper only reviewed them, choosing to ignore the headliners. This show was a fitting end to a strong opening year.

* * *

Such was Blur's apparent self-belief that they waited a full, lethargic six months before putting out their second single, in the meantime spending Christmas and the New Year frequenting London social hotspots and writing material for the forthcoming debut album. When the second single finally arrived, any fears that they may have lost the considerable momentum created by 'She's So High' were immediately obliterated when 'There's No Other Way' hit No.8 in the charts. Again, Food had pre-released some white labels on to the club scene some eight weeks in advance, and the band even started their seventeen-date tour for the single over three weeks before its April release date. The song was Blur's most blatantly derivative track but so ultra-modern that it was a massive hit in the pop world. The beat itself was bang up to date, and Graham's snarling riff pieced each stage of the song together well. The infectious melody, superb dance groove and memorable chorus fitted seamlessly into the flow of post-baggy songs that had been riding high in the charts – The Charlatans 'The Only One I Know', had initially been taken by many to be The Stone Roses's new single when it was released just before Blur's debut. With this new song, Blur were also skirting dangerously on the fringes of baggy parody (more of which later). The track was produced at Maison Rouge in Fulham by Stephen Street (who had worked with The Smiths and went on to produce The Cranberries) after the band met him in The Crown public house in the West End. It was the beginning of one of the most celebrated band-producer relationships in recent years.

Lyrically, the single was dreadful. At this stage, the developing musical output of Blur was being let down badly by the inferior lyrics. Damon preferred to see this weakness somewhat more philosophically at the time, when he said to *NME*, "I don't claim that we are stunningly original, I firmly believe in just writing brilliant songs that have an incisive message. I don't like using more than ten words in a song if I can help it, and then I can create a little ball of emotion." Vocally he wasn't excelling either – for "plaintive vocal" you could easily read "weedy and piss-weak". Graham grew to hate the song, and some time later he told *NME*, "it is a monumentally bland record, it's so banal. Its banality led to its being scrutinised when in fact it is about absolutely nothing. Making that record was like deliberately handing in this strange, crappy essay at school just to see what people would think."

The Top 10 success of 'There's No Other Way' earned Blur their debut *Top of the Pops* performance, about which Damon said, "I have been preparing for this moment for years." Graham clearly hadn't – he couldn't get in and had a toe-to-toe row with a doorman. It was a shambolic, chaotic but endearing performance that exposed Blur to a nationwide audience for the first time. In the weeks that followed, with the single still doing well, Blur also found themselves in many of the tabloids, with hilarious features about their private lives. The *Daily Mirror* called them 'Britain's Brainiest Band' (obviously they hadn't seen Damon's 'A' level results) whilst The *Daily Star* chose to pursue the sex, sex and er, sex angle. Blur shagged, drank, drugged, shagged some more and all before breakfast. Even Dave, the unassuming gent of a drummer, was transformed into 'The Dark Destroyer'. Whilst slots on the demonic *Terry Wogan Show* and a feature in *Woman's Own* were turned down, Blur did appear on the kids Saturday TV show *8:15 From Manchester* and in *Mizz, Smash Hits*, and many more nationwide publications and shows.

The teen mags picked up on Blur's good looks and poppy single and hailed them as one of Britain's most shaggable bands. The glossy magazines were crammed with useless and often invented trivia such as Damon and Alex's penchant for starting each day with a bottle of champagne and a shiatsu massage. The band apparently demanded cheese and port for every rider, and had brand new men's underwear delivered from a top London department store for each gig. The front three rows of their gigs frequently had more legs than hair, and the pretty faces of Blur were soon sellotaped on to many a bedroom wall – even a scattering of weathered Bros T-shirts were spotted at some Blur gigs. It was an important commercial crossover in the making, and further fuelled the rumours of a pop scam.

This young following mixed in well with the older audience of the music weeklies, to give Blur's following a very strange demograph. At their smaller provincial gigs, the venues were filled with unusually young fans, with much screaming and general knicker-wetting excitement. For these fans, the repressed punk tendencies of Blur came as a shock to ears used to hearing their sugary sweet pop singles. At the city shows, such as London's Town & Country Club, the more sombre, older audience were nevertheless still a sell-out crowd. Blur seemed to be genuinely straddling across many age and cultural groups. Not bad for a band whose lyrics were, to be fair, largely bollocks.

The single tour itself had to be expanded by another four dates to cope with demand, and was a complete sell-out (as some would say Blur were at this point). The dates were a great success. They toured the UK twice in the next four months and in London tickets were changing hands outside the venue for £50. Inside the gig, the band's famous 'Penguin Classics' T-shirts (aping the front covers of that publisher's vintage novels) were selling by the crate-load. These dates only had one real hitch. At the Woughton Centre gig in Milton Keynes, the band were banned from performing there ever again after Alex jumped into the crowd with his bass and smacked a young fan across the head, sending him to hospital with slight injuries in an apologetic tour manager's car. Despite Damon being a professional madman live, he issued a sensible statement perhaps designed to placate the worried mothers across the country: "We're not a mad irresponsible band. Our gigs don't usually end up in a blood bath. This was an isolated one-off accident and we're sorry about it."

Damon was always the most talkative in interviews, yet also seemed the most sceptical. Concerning the enormous teen success of 'There's No Other Way', he said to *NME*, "I think it's inevitable when you are in our position and you look like we do that you're going to get seen as teeny idols. It's not something that we're keen to cultivate, but what can we do?" Dave was a little more enthusiastic: "I find myself waking up in the morning and realising what's happening to me and just thinking, 'This is fantastic!' I still haven't properly come to terms with it yet."

Dave needn't have got too excited – with the band's third single, 'Bang', they seemed to be trying to burst their own bubble. Perhaps finishing the debut album with Stephen Street distracted them; perhaps the fact it was written in only fifteen minutes showed; perhaps the lacklustre, strained melodies and weak harmonies suggested Blur might be a flash in the pan after all. 'Bang' certainly did little for their cause and barely added to the expectation for the forthcoming album. Its only real plus was a distinct improvement in Alex's bass work. 'Bang' stalled at No.24 in early August 1991, but at least their second *Top of the Pops* performance was more memorable, with Damon parading around the stage waving a plastic cockerel, comically mimicking the theme of the sleeve art work.

★ ★ ★

In 1992, Ride released *Going Blank Again*, which critics saw as an unofficial epitaph for yet another dying music biz movement, the awkwardly christened The Scene That Celebrates Itself. This had centred around a hub of bands who frequented various trendy London watering holes such as The Syndrome Club on a Thursday night in Oxford Street, The Powerhaus, The Underworld and The Borderline. The bands were often seen ligging at each other's gigs – Blur's studio party in Fulham to celebrate completing their debut album was attended by most of the leading lights of 'the scene'. The conglomeration of bands included under this umbrella was wide and varied but was generally given to be listless, apolitical and monosyllabic groups who were fairly inactive live and had little to say in their music, which was often swathed in Dinosaur Jr/My Bloody Valentine nostalgic walls of noise, in sharp contrast to the decidedly bland lyrics. It was different to baggy that's for sure, but it was not exactly life-affirming and eclectic. Bands included in the alternative monicker of "shoe-gazers" (apparently a term christened by Andy Ross of Food to describe all the bands that Blur were *not* like) were Moose, Ride, The Boo Radleys, Lush, Chapterhouse, Telescopes, Slowdive and Blur. This was not a new experience to Blur – at the very start of their career, one writer had laughably tried to christen them as the leaders of 'The New Essex Scene', whilst another tagged them as the 'New Glam Lad Renaissance'.

More often than not, a band's inclusion was more to do with their ability to share a pint with a music journalist than with their musical affinity to the movement, and in this category Blur excelled. Throughout the spring and summer of 1991 whilst recording their debut album, Blur were infallible regulars in both the trendiest bars and the juiciest gossip columns. One week they were pissed and loud here, the next they were, er, pissed and loud over there. Having not yet escaped the "crap baggy" bandwagon jumping accusations, Blur now found themselves accused of joining this dubious bunch as well, and their reputation as professional music biz liggers (and party animals) somewhat undermined their musical credibility. For many cynics, Blur were the Rent-a-Lush of the current crop. Oddly, Damon often seemed more than happy at their inclusion, as he told *Melody Maker*. "We have that idea of deliberate vagueness, of saying nothing and having a point to say nothing. It's that 'Blank Again' generation thing that we started and were talking about nine months ago. There's a whole generation of bands that understand that every musical movement has failed to change anything, so we're deliberately shallow in order to avoid the embarrassment of it all."

After a while, the acclaim afforded to many of these bands began to ebb away and, as it did, their friendly associations often turned into back-stabbing and mutual disregard, as groups desperately tried to avail themselves of the shoe-gazing millstone before it dragged them down with it. Not all of the 'shoe-gazers' followed Blur into the charts, with only The Boo Radleys, Lush and Ride enjoying any longevity. Blur managed to survive through a mixture of sheer persistence and their awareness that any scene is of transitory benefit. Once Damon realised this, he was keen to distance Blur from the dying movement, as he told *Melody Maker*: "Bands like Ride, Chapterhouse and Slowdive had a wonderful pubescent quality, but they were sort of 'the end of indie', it had nowhere else to go."

★ ★ ★

Blur, meanwhile, did have somewhere to go – their debut album *Leisure*. Interest in the record was fuelled just before its late August release by a superb Reading Festival performance (which was unfortunately over-shadowed by Nirvana's triumph). *Leisure* was reasonably well-received and did handsome commercial business, but it was a rather shambolic, unfocussed affair, with two great singles, one poor one, and few other indications of where Blur could go next. They had shown themselves more than capable of storming the singles charts and holding their heads up live, but albums were a different sphere, and with *Leisure*, Blur fell short. It was their debut to be fair, but so was *The Stone Roses*, REM's *Murmur* and Jimi Hendrix's *Are You Experienced?*

One suggested title had been *Irony In The UK*, but Blur plumped instead for *Leisure*, summing up the barely visible theme that tenuously linked the record together. Their celebration of hedonistic youth, the love of life and music, and the self-obsession with enjoyment was something which Blur had shown themselves more than capable of in recent months (perhaps Damon was harping back to his East 15 days of method acting research?!). Lyrically however, there was little clear embellishment of this central tenet. Damon was still producing painfully vague lines; some critics talked of lovelorn angst, poetry and lyrical dreams, but perhaps they were listening to a different album. The I/me focus hinted at the self-centred theme, but there was no real shape, it was all too generalised. Damon himself later admitted that he had actually written most of the lyrics five minutes before recording them − it showed. He told *Q* magazine that "after *Leisure*, I had a very hard time, and rightly so, it was a shit album. There were a few good songs but I was an appalling lyricist, lazy, conceited, woolly."

Musically, the record hardly broke away from the noisey MBV/Dinosaur Jr fixations of earlier material, often filling songs with sustain and feedback at the expense of the tunes. The first two singles were there in all their pop glory, but elsewhere killer melodies were in short supply. Clumsy tracks like 'Fool', 'High Cool' and 'Come Together' cluttered the record and the lazy beats suddenly seemed acutely dated. Backing tracks were largely done live, but the essence and energy of a Blur gig were absent. On the plus side, Graham added touches of flair instead of masturbatory solos − interestingly the backward guitars on 'Sing' were achieved by him actually learning the song backwards note for note. These spatters of psychedelia were everywhere − the backward guitars were joined by phased keyboards and drum samples, which all added an interesting detail. Ultimately, however, you can't polish a turd.

Maybe the lack of shape was due to the mix 'n' match approach to production. Conflicting schedules meant that four separate producers were involved, with some rumours suggesting that Stephen Street was called in to kick the band up the arse and get the lethargic project back on track. Even then, it was still a mishmash, with several ancient Seymour tracks being used, including 'Birthday', 'Fool' and 'Sing'. The latter of these was one of the few more adventurous highlights, a million melancholic miles from what people expected of Blur with its emotionally dramatic solitary piano and climactic harmonies. It was an excellent, even daring ballad. The only other strong tracks were 'Repetition' with its waspy guitar and distorted vocals, and the closing 'Wear Me Down', complete with sugary threats, heavyweight guitars and strong melodies. Much of the record was swathed in noisey guitars which clashed with Damon's lethargic, high-in-the-mix vocals. These swerved from Pete Shelley to Mick Jagger to Syd Barrett – intriguing enough maybe, but not when delivered in a weak Home Counties drawl. *Leisure* was, to be polite, "one for the fans."

There were, however, plenty of those. The album sold very strongly, reaching No.7 and selling out the supporting tour very quickly. The £250,000 spent on the record was quickly recouped, a rare feat for many bands. Critically it was warmly received, although those writers who disliked it did so with a passion – Blur were rapidly becoming a love/hate band. Despite the generally strong reviews, it wasn't about to win any writing awards, but Blur were always very aware of this. Shortly after *Leisure,* Damon said, "We shouldn't be judged on those songs and those performances, but in ten years time. We were a fledgling group having a laugh, but we didn't have a particular agenda." He also called himself "a dyslexic illiterate." Graham's infamous comment that it was their "indie detox album" perhaps sums it up better than anyone. This was Blur enjoying their initial success, not worrying too much about focus, just finding their feet, and in that respect it was engaging enough.

Blur were already giving early hints that their next album might not be so linear, and that they were plundering their own environment for inspiration: "We're all products of our backgrounds and environment, so what we produce is a product of that. We're influenced by adverts and Sunday magazines and slogans around us, things people say in films and certain moments, strange stances and gestures – the madness of human behaviour."

Part of the band's anxiety to suggest they were already moving on was to avoid being dragged down with the carcass of Madchester. With The Stone Roses locked in court room battles and The Happy Mondays about to split, the movement had lost its two leading lights. In the post-baggy vacuum, many bands were accused of jumping on a band wagon that had successfully gelled alternative guitar and dance music and stormed the charts. Blur were seen as one of the main perpetrators, especially with 'There's No Other Way' which sounded distinctly like The Stone Roses 'I Am The Resurrection.' Critics said these groups were probably just keeping The Stone Roses's throne warm during their lengthy sabbatical.

These new bands were in an unenviable position, but those prepared to change and adapt were the only ones with any chance of longevity. Baggy ultimately became a term of abuse reserved for the likes of The Bridewell Taxis, which actually made a mockery of the movement's original brilliance. Damon was obviously acutely aware of this potential and fortunately managed to distance Blur from it, especially in an infamous article for *Select* in which he said, "the next album will be the start of an era. This one is the 'kill baggy' album."

To increase the suspense, Damon also showed sings of a long-term outlook that did not concern itself with the short-term benefits of a smash debut album. "Blur isn't just a one-album phenomenon; it's something that has to develop over five or six years before we can get any sort of perspective."

CHAPTER 5

WEAR ME DOWN

With a commercially successful, recouping debut album under their belts and a sell-out tour ahead of them, Blur might have reasonably expected a clear road ahead. Unfortunately, by the summer of 1992, the band was a shell of its former self, with in-fighting, drunkenness and indiscipline rife. Between now and then it was all downhill.

The 13-date album tour was critically well-received and tickets flew out, even for the bigger shows like Kilburn National. The gigs were now much more punk than sugary pop, as Damon told *Puncture*: "[Live] we're more aggressive and much more sensual than we are on record. We play the songs about four times as fast. It's like we have a mixture of tantrums and ecstasies on stage. It's very violent at certain points, and quite sexy at others." 'Blur live' and 'Blur on record' were virtually two unrelated bands at this stage. Some critics hated them, such as *Melody Maker* writer Andrew Mueller who said, "In a year they will be seen as a Vapour for the 1990s, they really do mark the point at which this year's collective enthusiasm for the new has gone beyond a joke." Others loved them, and most agreed the gigs, if musically erratic, were still strangely watchable.

In addition to their own album tour, they performed on the Radio 1 Roadshow in Skegness in front of 20,000 kids and nine million listeners, they did PA's on several kids TV shows and then rounded the year off with their slot on the Food Records Christmas Party at Brixton Academy, alongside Diesel Park West, the label-named Sensitise and Whirlpool, and headliners Jesus Jones. The first 2000 punters were given a free tape with two tracks by each band, including Blur's demo version of 'Resigned' and a re-mixed 'High Cool'. Special guest on stage for keyboard duties was Natasha of The Bikinis, and Damon managed to badly bruise his shoulder with his customary hands-behind-his-back human pinball routine.

There were also a handful of debut dates in America, where the USA were briefly flirting with 'Madchester', and some French and Japanese gigs as well. Damon was not about to get carried away, however, as he told *Sky* magazine: "All you need to be mobbed in Japan is to have blonde hair and be more than five feet tall. Being mobbed is so ... unrefined."

Blur's live reputation was acknowledged in the New Year of 1992 when they were offered a slot on the so-called 'Rollercoaster' tour. This was the brainchild of The Jesus & Mary Chain, based on Perry Farrell's hugely successful Lollapolooza tour in the USA. The American predecessor had seen a rich diversity of bands such as Jane's Addiction, Nine Inch Nails, Ice T, Living Colour and The Butthole Surfers on the same bill along with performance artists and campaign stalls. The 'Rollercoaster' idea was somewhat more limited, with just four bands and no peripheral activities, but the motive was the same – put on a superb bill of bands for the price of most normal shows.

The Jesus & Mary Chain's first choices were Blur, Dinosaur Jr and My Bloody Valentine, which in retrospect limited the musical variety immediately, but there was still no denying it was probably the most attractive touring line-up for years. Blur were delighted and accepted straight away. Damon told *Melody Maker*, "Without wishing to sound really crap, I think Rollercoaster is the most exciting thing we've done. We usually look to the next two weeks on the road with a sense of dread and loathing, but none of us can wait to get on this tour." He also said, "To be honest, I'm a bit starstruck by it all. I'm delighted that we are gonna be playing with them, even though we're very different to all of them in our outlook and the way we try to present ourselves."

Blur were a relatively lightweight pop band on a rock bill, and several eyebrows were raised at their selection, even those of MBV's Kevin Shields. Nevertheless, Blur's slot also conferred on them a degree of levity and respectability that forced people to listen to them again. The gigs were massive – Birmingham's NEC, Manchester's Apollo and London's Brixton Academy were all sold-out. This was the Mary Chain's first UK dates for two years and all four acts were capable of pulling a sizeable crowd.

However, despite three of the bands being seminal acts, the 'Rollercoaster' quickly became something of a doom-fest. The Mary Chain headlined each night, with the other three bands rotating. This meant that if Blur came on first, the crowd was then subjected to a prolonged blast of Dinosaur Jr/MBV/J&MC, enough doom to out-gloom even the most morbid of music fans. Some dates were all seated and this stultified the atmosphere still further. Also, Blur were the only band seemingly willing to party backstage, and there was always a polite awkwardness between the four groups. Add to that the lack of an agenda, with none of the bands proselytising like Ice T might have, and the dates assumed an air of lethargy, of little historical significance other than value for money. Harshly, this was no new rock dawn. Damon remained buoyant nonetheless and told *Melody Maker*, "I think Rollercoaster is really important, the best thing that's happened to British music in a long time."

During the dates, Blur had been the subject of something of a press backlash, with most reviewers seeing them as superficial pop that was grossly out of place, and Damon's perceived arrogance continued to rub writers up the wrong way. He had only recently said, "We're a band who could completely and utterly change everything. The scale that we are working on is so enormous, we're trying to reach absolutely everybody." At this point in time, this sounded ludicrous. During this tour, Blur also started to plan their first long-form video, a documentary about provincial England to be directed by Storm Thorgerson (who had provided footage as a stage backdrop for each Blur song during the tour). He had conceived much of Pink Floyd's early visual effects along with Syd Barrett, and Blur were delighted to be involved with him. They planned to show the piece on Channel 4 but the actual video never materialised. Within weeks of finishing the 'Rollercoaster' tour, Blur could now see that it had probably done them more harm than good.

★ ★ ★

When a band are playing well and the crowd is lapping it up, constant drinking and debauchery is romanticised into 'partying';

when a band is playing dreadful gigs night after night and arguing all day, it is called self-destructive abuse. When Blur hit the United States in May 1992 for a colossal 44 date, state-by-state tour, their drinking was already dangerously way out of control, and things just got worse.

When they had played The Marquee the previous autumn, Blur had been well-received but in the ensuing six months, America had passed through its minor Madchester fad. Blur were now just a British oddity, and a drunken one at that. Since their last visit, an infant grunge phenomenon had taken hold and Nirvana's *Nevermind* had sold nine million copies – slacker culture was everywhere. Seattle, grunge, Eddie, Kurt, Hole and Sub Pop were the words on everybody's lips. To millions of disenchanted American kids enlivened with the new teen spirit, Damon's cockney charm and Blur's English sound seemed utterly pointless. Blur were about as akin to grunge as Brett Andersen is to weight lifting.

This universal indifference exacerbated Blur's drunken indiscipline such that they became a band just waiting to implode. Three gigs in and Damon's water throwing antics caused the owners at The Venus De Milo theatre to pull the plugs after just three songs. A small scale riot ensued with the band escaping out of a back door, followed by angry fans and even angrier security men chasing them down the street. A sense of impending doom began to suffocate the tour bus, and in-fighting erupted among the friction. Within one three day spell, each member of the band had thumped the other, even Damon and Graham. Damon said to one journalist, "We don't really go into big violent moods with each other, but we're incredibly cruel to each other all the time, non-stop. We are cruel to the point where most people can't believe how awful we are to each other, just vicious, spiteful, it's mental torture, psychological warfare."

This was rapidly becoming an American nightmare. Graham was unwell, with recurrences of the ulcers and bleeding he had suffered on tour before, and Damon was constantly dragging on his high tar banana skin and clove Caravan cigarettes. Even on their way to the now-hallowed grunge capital of Seattle, Blur's tour van broke down and they ended up spending hours in a run-down greasy spoon cafe called The Potato Shop.

Their paranoid state was worsened by their American record company's approach. SBK were determined to break the band state-by-state, and only gave them a meagre two days off in 44. Even when Blur played well, the American press ridiculed them as yet another post-baggy Manchester band well past their sell-by date. The cumulative effect of the drinking, the American public's indifference, the media's ridicule and the record company's exhausting work ethic was disastrous. By the end of the dates, tension in the band was high. Graham was told to lay off alcohol for six months and some rumours even alleged that he had to be committed to a hospital to recuperate. Throughout the tour, most of the band came close to being, or actually were hospitalised. On their return from America, Blur were a pathetic shambles. Damon told *NME* he was bitter about the way some had tried to trivialise their terrible experience: "It makes me laugh when people describe that as rock 'n' roll behaviour. It wasn't an affectation with us. When things area going well, I don't behave like that."

The saving grace in this mess should have been Blur's fourth single 'Popscene', released in March 1992, a song which had been debuted back at the Manchester Apollo the previous year. It was the first fruit of their post-*Leisure* sessions and was produced by Steve Lovell, as Stephen Street was reported to be out of favour with Food's Dave Balfe. It is rather easy to see the brassy, horn-driven chorus, the blazing fast melody and decidedly English feel of 'Popscene' as a long lost sign of great things to come. It was certainly a change in direction. The twitching riffs, choppy dynamics and energy were indeed highly charming, and Blur's first use of a brass section was a distinct Britpop precursor. One could also read in certain native reference points as a hint of Blur's imminent Anglophile preoccupations, with clear similarities to The Teardrop Explodes and The Sex Pistols amongst others. The dog on the cover, taken from *Horse & Hounds* magazine, the lyrical slight on the British music business and the sense of nostalgic Englishness were all there. 'Popscene' was miles away from the ambient abstractions of shoe-gazing or the dated rhythms of baggy. It was a very 1990s song, a big departure, and very possibly one of the first Britpop songs.

However, the single is now mostly remembered because back then it was largely forgotten. Much was made of 'Popscene' in the aftermath of Blur's massive success, but it is important to remember that at the time of release it was absolutely and almost universally reviled. To a press and public similarly fixated with grunge, a 'kill baggy' combo's new single was completely uninteresting and the record was given short shrift in the papers, such as *Melody Maker* who said it was "a directionless organ-fest in search of a decent chorus." Nirvana had just signed to Geffen and grunge was now a worldwide phenomenon – 'Popscene' was lost in the fashionable sea of lacerated vocals and serrated guitars. Blur were not the first to suffer such a fate. The Who had the fantastic but unsuccessful 'Allegal Matter', and even Bowie's 'Space Oddity' reached only No.48 for one week before plummeting out of the charts (only to re-enter when it was used to cover the moon landing).

At the time, the general critical indifference that met 'Popscene' could probably have been tolerated, but the commercial failure of the single was a devastating blow. It was Blur's first single for nearly a year, coming of the back of a Top 10 album and yet it stalled badly at only No.32 and crashed out of the charts after only two weeks. The band and Food Records were stunned. Well-laid plans for the poppier 'Never Clever' to follow up 'Popscene' were abandoned. Worse still, the band had an album almost ready for release on their return from the US dates, but in the face of such indifference, Food said it would now have to wait. Had this album been released, it would have been the majority of the eventual *Modern Life* songs, with some B-sides that finally surfaced on future Blur singles such as 'For Tomorrow'. Damon said to *NME*, "We knew it was good, we knew it was better than what we had done before. We put ourselves out on a limb to pursue this English ideal and no-one was interested." The single's failure coincided with the dreadful American tour and, demoralised, Blur slipped lower into depression. Their media contribution was reduced to lurid tales of Bacchanalian antics in the gossip columns. Having said that, Dave was convinced 'Popscene' was a crucial track: "It was completely ignored by the press, but I think it was the point we realised we weren't going to listen to anything anyone else was saying. We knew then we were capable of making great records."

Despite their disappointment at the time, both the refusal of Food to put the album out in 1992 and the failure of 'Popscene' were very possibly blessings in disguise. Had the second album come out as a total exception to the grunge domination, it may well have lost all its impact and Blur would not have been able to establish the groundswell of support that provided the vital foundation for *Parklife*. Hindsight is however, a very powerful thing – at the time Blur were devastated.

Their misery was compounded by severe financial problems – blamed on one of their inner circle of advisors – that drained most of the funds from *Leisure*. Blur hardly had enough money to pay the rent. Bankruptcy was only narrowly avoided. The Jesus and Mary Chain/Midge Ure manager Chris Morrison was brought in at the last minute, and he secured a Stateside merchandise deal that just about kept the band's heads above water.

There was worse to come. While Blur had been boozing their way around the States, back in Britain Suede had arrived. Heralded by an infamous *Melody Maker* cover announcing 'The Best New Band In Britain', Suede were critically lauded and plastered over every music magazine and paper. While Blur were disastrously flying the flag abroad, Suede had sneaked in and usurped them as the next big thing – it was the start of a long rivalry between the two bands. Blur felt Suede's Cockney slant and camp charm was plagiarised from themselves. There were personal frictions as well, with Damon's girlfriend Justine Frischmann having been both a former rhythm guitarist with Suede (some say she invented the name) and an ex-girlfriend to Brett Andersen, the "bisexual who hasn't had a homosexual experience". Slanging-matches disgraced the music press, with Bernard Butler quoting lyrics from 'Bang' as his worst ever, and Damon constantly ridiculing Brett. Graham said Bernard Butler stole his style of guitar playing and that "he spent hours crying on my doorstep for us to take him on tour as a roadie.". Alex said "Brett got his impetus from Damon coming along and nicking his bird, now he had an axe to grind." A source who worked closely with Suede at the time confirms this: "Many of the songs on Suede's debut album were about Justine and Brett's relationship, that split-up was a big spur to him. 'Metal Mickey', 'Animal Lover', 'Moving' and 'To The Birds' were all highly focussed on that situation. 'Pantomime Horse' was as well, but that has been dramatically misunderstood and misread. Most people see the lyric, 'Have you ever tried it that way?' as some kind of homosexual reference. It wasn't, not at all. It was about looking at losing his girlfriend to Damon and looking at it from the other side of the fence. That central theme did dominate the early work. As far as Suede's material goes, it was miles better once Justine had left, no comparison." Brett Andersen came to personify Blur's difficulties, but that did not excuse Damon's later accusations of Brett's alleged heroin use (whether correct or not), which took this rivalry to a new low.

To his credit, Damon later regretted this statement, telling *NME*, "Every time I got drunk I got very nasty about Suede, I just couldn't see the woods for the trees because of Justine." For now, however, he hated them and his frustration continued to grow and soon encompassed any band who were selling more records than Blur, which at this point was the majority.

To make matters worse, it was a no-contest. Suede were winning all the honours and Blur were just a band in dire trouble. Suede were soon to be *NME* Brat award winners, Brit award nominees, Mercury Music Prize winners and a Glastonbury highlight. Blur were nominated for nothing and were often so pissed they did well to turn up at some gigs. When they did show, as Damon recalls, "it had got to the stage where we were drinking so much we could hardly play our instruments."

The downward spiral could not continue much longer. Things had to come to a head, and they did at a July 'Gimme Shelter' charity gig at London's Town & Country Club. In one night, the tour problems, the drinking, the arguing, the S**** word and 'Popscene's failure burst in one big zit of a fuck-up. Blur shared the bill with guitar noise-mongers 31/2 Minutes, pop tune-smiths Mega City Four and the dreaded Suede. The socially motivated gig should have been Blur's comeback, snatching their crown back from the rival upstarts but things did not start well when Suede played a blinder. Backstage, Mega City Four were waiting to go on after Brett's band when Damon walked in to their dressing room uninvited, swigging drunkenly from a bottle, whereupon he sat down and started mouthing off. MC4's late, lamented genius of a singer, Wiz recalled, "he was really pissed and going on and on about what it's like to be in a band, but especially about how shit America was and how it was great to play the bigger venues there 'cos you are miles away from the punters. He just kept saying he hated the place, he thought all Americans were wankers, and he fucking hated gigs, and he was trying to get us to agree. We just sat there listening, and I remember thinking, "we are not from the same planet as you" and then one of our band just opened the door, pointed him towards his own pissed-up dressing room and shoved him out."

Blur had been drinking copious amounts all day and matters deteriorated when Damon walked on and said, "We're so fucking shit you may as well go home now." A few songs into Blur's poor set and many people did. The band made matters worse for the casual observer by playing several B-sides and weird demo tracks. Those that stayed were treated to the morose spectacle of a band seemingly committing public suicide. While Brett's hammed-up, gender bending Bowie-isms had been rapturously received, all Damon could manage was to pretend the mike was his dick and to bang his head on the speaker. He even got into a scuffle with a security guard – he looked like a prat, and the band played like novices. Blur's arrogant statements of the last two years now seemed to have caught up with them to embarrassing effect. Keith Cameron in *NME* summed it up as "Carry On Punk Rock".

The next morning, Damon was reportedly awoken from his drunken slumber by an angry Dave Balfe of Food Records, who arranged to have lunch with him that day. Balfe told him had seen it all before with his band The Teardrop Explodes, the in-fighting, the excess, the over-indulgence, the bitterness. In short, he thought Blur were over. He gave the band a month to sort themselves out or they would be dropped.

CHAPTER 6

GETTING SNARLED UP IN THE SUBURBS

From this all time low, Damon's band could only improve. During the summer and early autumn of 1992, Blur tried to repair the physical, mental and financial damage they had suffered over the last eighteen months. Gradually, thoughts began to turn to new material and the band holed up in Maison Rouge to try to regain some focus and composure. The resulting second album, *Modern Life Is Rubbish*, actually faired worse than their debut commercially on its initial release, and enjoyed far less media coverage, but it was a watershed release. Even though many of the ideas were not complete, *Modern Life Is Rubbish* was a crucial sign of intent.

At first however, things had to get worse before they could get better. With Blur talking up an English theme for the new record, the quintessential post-punk Englishman Andy Partridge of XTC was chosen to produce the sessions. Ex-Eurythmic Dave Stewart's Church Studios in Crouch End were used for the sessions, but they were disastrous. Things did not start well when Damon introduced himself by telling the producer how brilliant 'Making Plans For Nigel' was – a track actually written by Partridge's ex-XTC cohort and now-rival Colin Moulding. The band was still drinking profusely and they struggled to gel with Partridge's studio approach. When Partridge was asked by XTC biographer Chris Twomey when it all started to go wrong he said, "When they picked up their instruments and started playing! It wasn't totally successful. We didn't seem to hit it off, I think I am a bit dictatorial, I know what I like and I don't think they were delivering what I thought they were capable of. Maybe they thought I was pushing them a bit too hard. Maybe it was the 'difficult second album syndrome' for them."

Only three Blur tracks were recorded at these ill-fated sessions: 'Sunday Sunday', 'Seven Days', and 'Coping' as well as an ill-advised cover of Buggles's 'Video Killed The Radio Star' but none ever surfaced. Blur felt Partridge was trying to mould them into another Jesus Jones, and they were suspicious of Balfe's commercial motives (they later wrote 'When The Cows Come Home' specifically about Balfe's approach). They refused to use the sessions and Balfe – having paid for them – was furious. Meanwhile, Graham had bumped into Stephen Street at The Marquee for a Cranberries gig and Blur began to push for his reinstatement as producer – at least with *Leisure* having recouped, Blur enjoyed a degree of independence many of their peers sorely missed. Balfe eventually acquiesced and so their now famously fruitful relationship was renewed. It was late autumn 1992 by now and recording went so well that the album was complete just after Christmas. However, they still weren't in the clear yet – when Blur took the proposed album tracks to Balfe in the New Year, he rejected them, saying that they needed at least another two singles. Damon was stung by the criticism, but went away and wrote the tracks the next day, calling them 'For Tomorrow' and 'Chemical World'.

Before the public got a taster of the new material, Blur played a low key one-off gig at the Fulham Hibernian, supported by the most unlikely of musical opposites – the fashionably 'PC' Huggy Bear and The Salvation Army Band. At the show, a select number of free one-sided copies of a track called 'The Wassailing Song' were given away to 400 lucky punters. The rest of the nation had to wait until the new single in April.

The importance of 'Popscene' in Blur's rebirth after the debut album has been scrutinised in great depth. However, their next single, 'For Tomorrow', is actually of greater significance, despite also being a commercially muted affair. Without 'For Tomorrow', Balfe refused to accept the album and Blur's difficulties could have continued indefinitely. Musically 'For Tomorrow' was a considerable progression from Blur's previous work, even 'Popscene'. Coming after nearly a year's absence, there was considerable pressure, particularly since their last effort had failed so spectacularly. Damon himself raised the stakes by calling the new single "a 'Waterloo Sunset' for the 1990s", but this time his confidence seemed justified (albeit a little exaggerated). The single was a melancholic tale of London life, complete with killer 'la la la' chorus. It is ironic that someone who had been repeatedly lambasted for banality made his biggest lyrical breakthrough with such a line. Suddenly, Damon was a worthy lyricist – his vision of the contrast between romanticised London and the grim Westway of reality conjured up visions of grey tower blocks and modern day greyness. Damon superbly reinforced his new vision with a spoken piece laid over the closing choruses which spoke of Primrose Hill, London ice, and Emperor's Gate. Vocally he also rose from the plaintive dregs of shoe-gazing and baggy and assumed an arrogance and control that were surprising and highly appropriate. Against this, the music sound-tracked his new theme ideally, with weird twists on music hall melodies, finely detailed guitars and wandering, adept bass lines. The sparse drum structure and string arrangements mixed a sense of lush depth and bare simplicity. When hooked together by that classic pop chorus, it was a blinding comeback single, and probably Blur's first epic record after four years of trying. It was to be a single of pivotal importance.

Oddly enough, on its release in April 1993, 'For Tomorrow' only reached No.28, so in many senses it was as much a commercial flop as 'Popscene'. The video promo was directed by *Absolute Beginners* director Julien Temple but even this failed to incite extra sales. Crucially however, Blur were not plunged into the spiral of destruction they had been after the commercial death of 'Popscene'. They were convinced their new focus was valid and that the already completed album would open a rich new stream of thought that 'For Tomorrow' only hinted at.

The core of this fresh angle was immediately apparent with the photo sessions for the new project, entitled 'British Image No.1'. Blur were no longer the pretty faced, bowl-haired teen idols – instead they wore turned-up jeans, Fred Perry shirts and cherry red Dr. Martens, with sharp suits and trimmed hair, sharing the photograph with a huge Great Dane. When Blur went on a photo shoot for a weekly paper in an old Jag as well, it brought back memories of The Dave Clark 5, but they were casting their net much further than that. There had been hints of the new Blur at both the Reading and Glastonbury festivals of 1992, where the sharp suits and some new songs were previewed. However, the real extent of their new focus only became fully apparent on the release of their second album, *Modern Life Is Rubbish*. They'd had the germ of the idea for some time, and many of the tracks for months – it was worth the wait.

The band set their stall out on the inner sleeve with an oil painting of them on the underground in full 'British Image No.1' regalia. Through a mixture of infectious pop tunes, dark melancholic ballads, and a lyrical progression equivalent to Roger Hargreaves winning the Booker prize, Blur produced an album that made *Leisure* seem like someone else's record. Thematically, lyrically, musically and visually, *Modern Life Is Rubbish* was nothing short of a complete rebirth.

The British focus was the crux of the whole transformation. The album was originally going to be called *England vs America*, and then *British Life 1*, but both were disposed in favour of *Modern Life Is Rubbish* which the band felt was more universal and reflected the themes in the album more accurately (the actual phrase was taken from a piece of graffiti on a wall near to Marble Arch). Yes, there had been elements of that on *Leisure* and more hints with the brassy Englishness of 'Popscene', but it had never been articulated to this degree before. This was a very English record, peculiarly London-centric, and unashamedly so.

Lyrically, Damon was unrecognisable. Some credit for that must go to Justine, his girlfriend, (whose own band Elastica would soon start to take off) who frequently scolded Damon for his lyrical laziness and pointed him towards her enormous record collection. The spoken paragraph that closed 'For Tomorrow' was just the start – the whole record was a London montage full of the underground, the Portobello Road, traffic jams, peeping toms, adverts, commuters, check-out girls and the rush hour. Damon sang about Sunday colour supplements, Sunday roasts, McDonalds and sugary tea, *Songs of Praise* and Mother's Pride. Whilst grunge ranted on about self-loathing and anti-consumerism (even though it had become utterly consumerist itself), Damon was singing about catching a bus into the country, Essex man and the joys of Saturday markets. He was now cramming decidedly awkward language into pop songs such as "carotene tan", "TV guide" and "the Westway". The English suburban malaise was viewed with a mixture of fascination and regret, as he introduced us to a range of characters, relationships and rituals through a predominantly narrative style.

From being a lazy, reticent by-stander, he was now a biting social commentator.

Vocally, Damon dipped into several record collections for inspiration. Julian Cope, Bowie, and every band who had ever sung with a London accent were talked about in the media and those influences are clear to see. At least he had dropped the awful reedy whine of the debut album, with a deeper maturity giving his voice a serenade quality.

Musically, *Modern Life* was a complex yet direct pop album, and a veritable pop encyclopaedia. The array of instruments at last drew on the band's technically trained past with, amongst other things, a Solina organ, timpani, sleigh bells, Casio keyboards, drum box, Moog and melodica being used. To enrich the scenario still more, Blur also used slightly more unusual sonic tricks, such as a shopping PA system, a Butlin's tannoy, a typewriter bell, a triangle and even a Black & Decker. Graham's immaculate guitar work was now free of his MBV fixation, whilst Alex had also developed enormously from the days of their debut. Dave was improving too, and his exact precision nailed down the Blur tracks to an infallible beat. The Duke String Quartet added more texture to the record, but overall the pop elements took second place behind the punk edge, with songs like the storming 'Advert' taking centre stage. There were pub knees-ups with 'Intermission', acoustic moods with 'Blue Jeans' and soft smooches with 'Miss America'. The instrumental variety maintained the level of interest throughout, and was cheekily rounded off by the two daft instrumental tracks ending each side, 'Intermission' and 'Commercial Break'. Both were strong hints of future work and older influences. There were, of course, dull moments such as 'Resigned' and the lyrically questionable 'Villa Rosie' but these were in the minority.

The effect of this musical melange was to create a very parochial sound, which clearly threw up references to a litany of English bands. From hereon, Blur would be plagued for some years by constant but largely justifiable references in the press to peculiar British groups. It is true that some aspects (but not all) of second-album Blur fit neatly into a lineage of clipped British pop. In *Modern Life* you could hear traces of Madness on 'Sunday Sunday', The Kinks on 'For Tomorrow', Buzzcocks on 'Colin Zeal' and The

Smiths on 'Blue Jeans' to name but a tiny few. To claims that Blur were just recycling the past, Damon had a perfect answer. He claimed that as the 1990s had such mountains of precedent, that no band could possibly be completely original, and so it was better to consciously use that past to recreate something new. In doing so, he was cleverly excusing Blur from claims of retrogression, as this extract from *NME* shows: "Modern Life is the rubbish of the past. We all live on the rubbish, and because it's built up over such a time, there's no need for originality anymore. There are so many old things to splice together in infinite permutations that there is absolutely no need to create anything new."

The entire list of reference points has been well documented elsewhere. Suffice to say that *Modern Life* was dramatically at odds with *Leisure* on this point. Whereas the debut record had been very much an album of its time, complete with incumbent baggy beats and phased guitars, *Modern Life* was anything but that. Blur were now scouring the musical past, taking pieces from here and there as required, covering almost everything from music hall to electro pop, as long as it was English. It was a record inspired and heavily immersed in another time and yet, paradoxically, it was a very modern album.

In May 1993, the most unfashionable thing to release was an intensely Anglophile concept record, full of English suburban detail, based around a third person narrative of everyday people's sterile lives, and mixed with a distaste for all things American. That is exactly what *Modern Life* was. It should be acknowledged not because it pays homage to the likes of The Small Faces, The Kinks, and Madness, but because it did *not* draw from Led Zeppelin, Neil Young and all of the godfathers of grunge. Maybe the album will not be remembered as Blur's finest, but it is certainly their bravest.

★ ★ ★

Unfortunately, not everyone was convinced. The album was released to a mixed critical response, although most reviewers did at least acknowledge the progress made since their last long player. As with their previous two singles, the album did not initially fair that brilliantly in the charts either, reaching No.15 then dropping out of the listings three weeks later. By now however, it was almost as if Blur were too involved in their world to notice. Sure, they were disappointed it didn't make more of a commercial impact, but they couldn't help but feel positive. The corresponding press campaign was not exactly ubiquitous, with only one cover feature, but the articles that were published dramatically underlined Blur's new stance. In fact, Damon's increasingly accomplished interview technique meant that he quite often articulated the germ of the idea more proficiently in the media than on the actual record.

He explained that their dreadful American experience had been the creative catalyst for this album, and that the endless shopping malls and bubble culture appalled him almost as much as the Americanisation of England he saw back at home. Damon told *Puncture*: "America wasn't an option, so we concentrated on our own identity. We had started on the long road of odd pop." Through the drunken haze of that terrible US tour, the obscene nature of the States had seemed all the more bloated and superficial, and by the time they arrived homesick back in Blighty, they loathed America, as he told *NME*: "We have stretched our sound considerably. When we were in America, England became this wonderful, fantasy place. The album is a soundtrack for a fantasy London, covering the last thirty years." He also said to *Melody Maker*, "it really fascinates me now. I've really got into the idea of narrowing everything down to the Englishness of everything we do, so everything has much more force because it holds more relevance, you're deliberately focussing on what you know and what you are as a result of your conditioning. It's just an idea of paring yourself down to what you really are. This is a fascinating time to be English and it's great to have things around that focus." Other articles saw Blur spray-painting the album title all over London and a Clacton band stand, and Damon announcing "*Modern Life Is Rubbish* is the most significant comment on popular culture since 'Anarchy In The UK'". Damon was clearly proud of being English, and disliked what he called the "coca-colonisation" of his home country.

Perhaps most controversially of all, in a *Melody Maker* piece by The Stud Brothers entitled "The Empire Strikes Back", Damon said, "I'm not saying that everyone should put on a fake Cockney accent and sing about the Old Bull & Bush, but I do feel that our culture is under siege and we are losing it." This article coincided with the election of BNP candidate Derek Beakon to an east London council and a growing fear of resurgent fascism. Damon carried on undeterred: "We should be proud of being British and not simply follow what comes from America." As examples he cited 'Olde Worlde' pubs saying, "it's just like Britain has become a holiday camp full of cutesy British people. The pubs have become a real plastic replica of what they once actually were." He also slated American music by saying, "don't tell me Nirvana have changed the face of American rock. No-one should kid themselves that anything happens in America unless the establishment thinks there is a buck in it for them. I'm fed up with people taking over the world on the back of that crass nonsense. And what have they got to say for themselves? 'I'm fucked up.' Fantastic." Just in case some people hadn't got the point, Damon also said, "We killed baggy with our first album, this one will kill grunge."

Like it or not, it was gripping stuff. This was all a very long way from the early days of Blur celebrating superficiality as an art form. The dramatic thematic change and contentious statements whipped up yet another controversy around Blur – some sensed the image change was just another thinly veiled attempt to manipulate the media just like the promotional schemes at the time of 'She's So High'. Others were not convinced that such a stylistic change could be genuine, although Paul Weller publicly backed Blur. Elsewhere, the "Empire Strikes Back" article in particular incited a barrage of reader's letters for and against Blur's stance. Many knee-jerk observers myopically talked about Blur flirting with fascism just as Morrissey had done so disastrously at a Finsbury Park support slot to Madness. Others saw it as intended, a genuine attempt to seize back the initiative from the all-conquering Americans. Damon himself recognised the dangers they might be toying with, but felt their sincere intentions would ultimately show through. Still, the band turned down a front cover of *Scooter* magazine and refused offers to play at scooter rallies for fear of inciting the wrong kind of following, a problem that had plagued Madness for years. Besides, the album was not unreservedly pro-Britain anyway, as he told *NME*: "It doesn't hail England as some Utopian place. It doesn't say England is a place of growth and happiness, there is an underlying decay." In many senses *Modern Life Is Rubbish* was as much about a dying country as a vibrant one.

Regardless of commercial success or failure, the underlying premise of the new album was central to Blur's very survival: "We had to make *Modern Life* and we were disappointed when no-one got it. It was certainly the moment when things turned and we pulled ourselves together. We literally had very little to lose." He also revealed to *Select* that "*Modern Life* was the beginning of us having an idea of what we wanted to do. If we hadn't lost all our money, we wouldn't have made the album so quickly but it worked." Damon seems to have an unerring ability to stand outside and observe the current musical climate, and this is possibly one of his greatest strengths. With alarming accuracy, and at a time when Kurt Cobain could do no wrong, Damon recalls that the reserved reaction to *Modern Life Is Rubbish* merely fuelled their resolve: "We were at an all-time low and I remember going to the record company and saying, 'You've just got to let us do it, in six months time you'll be signing bands who sound English because it's going to be what everyone wants.'"

★ ★ ★

Having thrown themselves against a tide of grunge with *Modern Life*, Blur now had to put their music where their mouth was on the road. They were not about to bottle out – the stage was set for the twelve album dates, cluttered with all the trappings of a pantomime modern life – toasters, sofas, flying ducks, lampshades, a greasy cooker and fridge, and a TV playing local news and adverts. If U2 had their global Zooropa, this was Blur's "Shitty bedsit-ooropa". A warm-up date for the national tour at Washington Heights in Reading was warmly received and things got steadily better. The band came on to the bizarre fairground reject 'Intermission' which got proceedings off to a suitably frantic start for many gigs to come. The new album material was delivered as full-on punk for this tour, and Damon's demented stage antics were now revitalised to schizoid heights, after the tiring troubles of the last eighteen months. The band's first ever two singles were still here, but there was a real sense that this was purely a respectful and duty bound nod to posterity. As traditional with Blur, the live set was far more weighty and fierce than on record, unaffected by the more sparse instrumentation that live gigs dictate. There was more here to remind people of '76 than '67. The gigs were all sold out, and an extra date had to be added at London's Astoria through demand.

After initially very quiet sales of only 30,000, *Modern Life* continued to sell gradually over the summer, while the album tour and some festival dates kept the reasonable momentum going. Unfortunately, the response in Europe was pretty poor. Despite covering all the corners of the Continent including a scary excursion aboard a decrepit Aeroflot charter plane to the Soviet state of Estonia, Blur's new angle didn't seem to click, and record sales were disappointingly low. Undeterred, Blur reinforced their creative renaissance at the end of June with the release of the next single 'Chemical World'. This track had originally been written to placate the dissatisfied American label SBK, but they rejected it and eventually put out the original demo version (sorry tales of SBK trying to get Blur to re-record the entire album with Butch Vig are reportedly true. Never mind). With its snarling guitars and stop-start drums, it was one of the album's strongest musical tracks, possibly Graham's finest piece on that record. It was a track that was far stronger musically than vocally, and an odd choice of single perhaps, with clear references to Mott The Hoople and Madness. Damon's vocals were a little odd, vacillating between his new-found depth and his old affected squeak, but the chorus redeemed him somewhat. Many have seen this as another turning point (Blur – and by definition Damon – seem to have had more turning points than a privet maze), but this is patently not so. 'Chemical World' reached No.28 as with 'For Tomorrow', another relatively muted commercial success. Fortunately, the band's slowly building momentum did not stall.

This was largely due to the Blur's continued live renaissance. During the dark days of 1992, Blur gigs were a drunken, unsavoury mess. With the new focus came a new live energy, none more so than with their front man. At the Nottingham Woolaston Park Free Festival they were excellent. At their warm-up for Reading they were superb, and at the festival itself they were blinding, the highlight of the weekend for many. The Reading bill was an oddly sombre affair, with the designer rebellion of Rage Against The Machine alongside New Order, Dinosaur Jr, The The and Porno For Pyros. As Matt Johnson rather unfairly went down like a lead balloon, droves of people walked across to the second stage to see the headlining modern lifers. Damon was in his element. It was a crucial triumph, and possibly the very moment when people started taking Blur seriously and listened to their unfashionable music again. Outside factors were starting to move in their favour and this superb performance perhaps started the momentum rolling that was soon to sweep them off their feet. Damon himself sees this particular show as a triumph, as he told *NME*: "That was amazing. It was the first time I was ever in control of my performance. It was a lovely feeling, and I suddenly realised what we were, I discovered the key, the eclectic quality of gathering lots of different kinds of people together." This gig, perhaps more than any after the album, confirmed Blur's substantial transformation from baggy flop tops and would-be tour abuse casualties to seriously accomplished songwriters ploughing a unique and fertile furrow. In the space of eighteen months, Blur had grown from a fashionable band with no lyrics, musical depth or thematic manifesto to an opinionated, articulate and musically diverse new force. Similarly, Damon had been transformed from a floppy-haired and arrogant newcomer with painfully banal lyrics, to an uber-cool modern commentator and lyrical innovator. It had been an unlikely and intriguing re-invention, but hardly a painless one. Blur were back from the brink.

★ ★ ★

Whilst *Modern Life* continued to sell conservatively but at least persistently, Blur agreed to headline a *Melody Maker* sponsored tour called 'Sugary Tea' (a line taken from 'Chemical World'). For each of the fourteen nights, they were supported by Salad and a local band and, as an added extra, there were three public debates, with Blur giving an open forum to any questions. At these discussions, in Newcastle, Coventry and Brighton, many questions centred around Blur's alleged boot boy image, but Damon defended the band strongly, saying, "we're not crazed patriots, not at all. I'm just not ashamed of using what I've grown up with as a creative aid. Our culture's less embarrassing than America's." He also laughed at the stifling Riot Grrrl movement and belittled excessive political correctness. They talked of embracing their Englishness and how it had given them a new focus and direction, as well as how they had left their drunken, listless days behind. Once again, Damon proved himself to be the most outspoken of the four. A media trump card.

The gigs themselves saw a trimmed down stage set from the cluttered front room of the album tour, with the central prop being a television connected to an archaic space invaders game. The second album material and the dashings of still newer stuff (a song called 'Girls And Boys' was frequently aired during the tour), gave their set a revitalised energy and even tired older songs like 'Popscene' were joyously reborn. Suddenly, Blur seemed to have a set bulging with pop hits, smooth ballads and pure punk stormers. At the Manchester Metropolitan University gig, Damon ended the set by saying, "We were bloody marvellous tonight", a stark contrast to his opening line at the disastrous Gimme Shelter gig of the previous summer.

To coincide with these dates, Blur released a new single 'Sunday Sunday' and a long-form video, *Star Shaped*. The single, one from the sessions with Steve Lovell, was arguably the album's most damning judgement of the hated Americanisation of England. Whilst a Sunday supplement nuclear family take their kids to McDonalds because the Sunday roast has been left too late, an old soldier reminisces about the good old days. The opening drums and clanging guitars are embellished by chirpy brass sections, then halfway through it all goes mental, speeding up to thrash velocity with swirling bingo organs. Dave Balfe hated this instrumental break, but Blur got their own way and it stayed – just as well, because it became a central feature of the song. Interestingly, the B-side finally aired some Seymour demos which had been around since 1989, with 'Tell Me, Tell Me', 'Long Legged' and 'Mixed Up' revealing just how far the band had come since their pyjama-clad beginnings. A second format had odd cover versions of the old music hall classics 'Let's All Go Down The Strand' and 'Daisy Bell'. Blur were now plunging head-first into their English experience, even though not everyone was convinced – yet. 'Sunday Sunday' reached No.26 in October 1993, again not a stunning hit, but another contribution to the band's growing momentum. Damon now had one of the country's most recognised faces.

The *Star Shaped* video was hailed as an impressively honest account of a band slipping into genuine tour psychosis and ravaging themselves with booze and despair. It chronicled the period from mid-1991 to mid-1993 and the disastrous frame of mind the band was in at the time. Amongst the catalogue of excess, we see Graham shooting puke out of his nose, Dave never without a can of beer and Damon vomiting on his shoes and saluting his own sick. In the space of 85 sordid minutes, Blur go from sweet faced bowl haircuts to dishevelled, drunken yobs. The highlight is the now-famous moment when the interviewer asks them what it was like to be in Blur in 1992 and is answered only by stoney silence. This was a genuine fly-on-the-tour-bus account.

Despite the squalid scenes, there were already tentative plans for a sequel perhaps based during a proposed Australian and Japanese tour. Damon later said to *NME*: "Rock musicians have a real fear of embarrassing themselves and that's why *Star Shaped* is quite unusual and interesting. It's good because it's so natural and because we don't act up to the camera." He added, "You couldn't have scripted it, that's for sure." The same could be said for the band's continued recovery – many eyes were now on Blur as a not-so-dark-horse to revitalise English music.

And Damon?

His pivotal role in the landscape of modern British music was only just beginning.

CHAPTER 7

PRETTY ENGLAND AND ME

1993 had been an encouraging year for British music in many ways. Although the slacker hegemony of grunge was still dominant, there had been a few signs of resistance. Suede's much heralded debut album hit No.1 and they swept up the Mercury Music Prize as well as countless other industry media awards. Bands like The Boo Radleys, The Auteurs and, of course, Blur seemed to add to that peculiar English focus. Interesting developments were taking place elsewhere in a multi-ethnic Britain, with bands like Apache Indian, Fun-Da-Mental, Cornershop, Collapsed Lung and Trans-Global Underground all producing exciting new music. Whether the failure of these multi-ethnic bands to break into the mainstream reflected their own inability (doubtful) or the greater prejudicial barriers facing them in a medium still dominated by white guitar bands is beyond the scope of this book. Suffice to say, Blur gigs, and Britpop bands and shows in general were not often graced with many ethnic faces (indeed, perhaps it should have been called Eng-Pop, as the majority of the groups included were in fact English). The future seemed to lay in the hands of a new guard of guitar-based white rock once more.

Blur seemed well placed to be involved in any such renaissance, but Suede were still the leading contenders. *Modern Life* won few end of year polls, although Blur did scoop the *Melody Maker* 'Best Live Act' category. Undeterred, Blur quietly continued to build on their recent progress. A few New Year dates in America were reasonably well received, but Damon's continued criticism of the States was never going to win him too many friends – he lambasted Nirvana's wish to use an 8-track and Steve 'Mr Sparse' Albini's production ethics for their hugely anticipated follow up to *Nevermind* as "a pathetic aspiration." Elsewhere, Blur's musical proficiency was being increasingly recognised. Damon was asked to write the theme tune for a Steven Berkoff film entitled *Decadence*, which he did eagerly: "I've always wanted to go back to my theatrical roots, and it was wonderful to be asked. The producer cottoned on to what we were doing and was confident in us." Also, and much to the band's celebration, George Harrison was seen on MTV saying how he felt Blur were excellent songwriters. A support slot to Siouxsie And The Banshees in Portugal at a stadium gig full of goths was also played with consummate ease.

By early 1994, it seemed the pseudo-mod reinvention for their second album was definitely appealing to increasingly large numbers of people. So, when Blur re-appeared with a new single as a precursor to the next album, eyebrows were raised again with yet another image change. Gone were the turned up Levi's, Dr. Martens and sharp suits; in came the 1984 casual look, complete with Tachini shirts, Ellesse track suits, fawn corduroys (slit at the ankle of course) and coloured suede Puma trainers. To complement the new look, Blur released a single in March 1994 to launch the forthcoming campaign. The song was called 'Girls & Boys' and, for Damon and Blur, things would never be the same again.

Just when we were filing our Small Faces and Kinks records next to *Modern Life*, Blur sent us scurrying back for our early 1980s electro disco pop collection, rooting out our dust-covered Giorgio Moroder and Sparks records. 'Girls & Boys' opened with a rinky dink riff and then a robotic drum machine beat which crashed in with one of Alex's finest bass leads yet. Graham's phased guitar was quirky, piercing and oddly infectious, the keyboards were humourously mechanical and Damon's vocals were as affected as ever, camp yet yobbish. Suddenly, Blur made perfect sense.

If the music was a leap forward, the lyrics took Damon on to a plateau occupied by very few of his peers. This was an ambiguous celebration of the fuck 'n' chuck mentality of the notorious 18-30 style vacations. His words captured the meat market scenarios perfectly. Then there was the chorus with its sexually ambiguous word repetition, sheer pop genius. To complete the package, the sleeve artwork was taken from a cheap packet of condoms. Blur had released a gem of a single that suddenly catapulted them past all their contemporaries. This was unquestionably Blur's finest and most audacious moment so far and easily Damon's most commercial performance.

Backed with four new songs as well, the superb package entered the charts at No.5, and secured massive radio play nationwide as all manner of broadcasting policies found something in the single that fitted with their play lists. 'Single of the Week' awards flooded in and Blur were suddenly splashed across a multitude of magazine covers. It is easy to forget that despite all their traumas and triumphs, 'Girls & Boys' was in fact only Blur's eighth single. By a strange twist of pop fate, Blur's triumph was completely over-shadowed by the untimely and tragic suicide of Kurt Cobain. Whilst the music world was united in its grief, there was a definite sense that the old order had perhaps been irreparably damaged, and whilst wary of disrespectful haste, a new vanguard was clearly about to pounce.

What that new generation wasn't going to be was the clumsily christened New Wave Of New Wave. In the autumn of 1993, two *NME* journalists had listened to the likes of S*M*A*S*H, Blessed Ethel, and These Animal Men and announced that here was British music's saviour: "The concept is New Wave of New Wave. The reality is a lumping together of (at times) vaguely like-minded fresh British bands with ants in their pants and vocabularies laced with shrapnel." The two key players – S*M*A*S*H and These Animal Men – were lyrically astute and articulate in their clarion call to rebellion, and their energetic and vibrant live shows initially seemed to offer the vibrant injection that was so needed. Then, in the New Year of 1994, the New Wave Of New Wave went overground with magazine covers and packed gigs, and a whole host of bands were included, such as Done Lying Down, Action Painting and even Elastica. The movement was as important sartorially as it was for the rather one dimensional, speed-fuelled music, which harped back to The Jam and The Clash, but the NWONW's days were numbered. When Blur released 'Girls & Boys' they effectively killed NWONW. First baggy, then grunge, now this. By the end of 1994, many of the NWONW bands had split and barely any long term success was achieved – in retrospect, the movement had no more cultural significance than shoe-gazing. To add insult to injury, Damon was quite happy to claim that 'Popscene' had actually invented NWONW anyway (Blur briefly considered re-releasing the single as a NWONW cash in). Even Dave, who was used to Damon's espousing by now, was uncomfortable with this one: "Oh no, I think we're going to claim we invented everything again."

Whoever had invented NWONW, with the release of Blur's fourth album, *Parklife*, it was rendered instantly irrelevant. The rest of 1994 was spent in creating new media superlatives for an album that was rapidly recognised as a landmark British record. Things had not augured so well at the album launch party. Having spent much of their careers ligging at everyone else's expense, it was nice to see the compliment returned, with the likes of Pop Will Eat Itself, Sleeper, Elastica, Pet Shop Boys, Carter, Lush, The Cranberries, Jesus Jones, Eddie Izzard and Eddie Tenpole Tudor all turning up at an East End dog track. A riotous evening was had by all, and everything went like clockwork, until the Blur sponsored 'Parklife Stakes', when it all went hilariously wrong. One dog got stuck in the trap then, shortly after, the hare became dislodged and the remaining dogs tried to rip it, and then themselves, to pieces. Pandemonium ensued and the race was declared void – the gold presentation box of *Parklife* and a £90 first prize remained uncollected. Damon was typically philosophical when he told the media: "Slow start, always led, strong finish."

'Girls & Boys' had raised the stakes considerably for Blur and many wondered if they could reproduce that quality across a whole album. *Parklife* silenced all doubters, and the cynics who had dogged Blur since their inception (at times justifiably so) slinked off quietly into the background. Much of the ground work had been done with *Modern Life* and indeed without that record there would have been no *Parklife,* but it was the latter that struck gold. This all-conquering album asserted itself as the year's greatest record – and one of the decade's too – earning Blur a place in pop history in the process. The album was recorded at Maison Rouge between November 1993 and January 1994, with 'To The End' being completed at RAK studios in St John's Wood. Stephen Street was at the controls and Blur worked with customary speed once again. With this being their second album in a twelve month period, Blur were clearly taking the Lieber & Stoller work ethic last seen with Morrissey and Marr to their hearts. They arrived at 11am each morning and worked solidly through until 9 or 10pm, only taking a break in the afternoon for tea.

Progress was quick – after all, songs like 'Parklife' and 'Girls & Boys' had been played in the Blur live set for *Modern Life*, so by now much of the material was well understood by the band. Very soon they had twenty tracks to choose from. Once again, a vast array of instrumentation was used ranging from Hammonds, a Moog, harpsichord, melodica, vibraphone, various percussion, and even clarinet and saxophone, courtesy of Graham. The combination of all this musical texture gave the album a sonic variety unchallenged at this time. The array of styles was enormous, and tied in with what teacher Nigel Hildreth had spotted in a younger Damon's tastes. The record was full of the last thirty years of pop – there was splashes of electro pop on 'Girls & Boys', punk rock for 'Bank Holiday, Gary Numan appears for 'Trouble In The Message Centre', and The Kinks, The Small Faces, Buzzcocks, Madness and The Jam gate-crash all over the record. It swept effortlessly from punk rock to the finest ballads. Clanging sing-alongs sat uncomfortably next to robotic instrumentals and lush string laden epics. The Germanic 'oompah' of 'Debt Collector' sits sandwiched between the seemingly incompatible sugary sweet vocals of 'Badhead' and the quirky robotic mayhem of 'Far Out'. Elsewhere, the pure pop of 'End Of A Century' is followed by the punk rock blast of 'Bank Holiday'. This kaleidoscopic range of styles should have clattered together in one unholy mess, but somehow Blur cleverly pulled it off, with the weird musical variety adding to their achievement, rather than cluttering it up.

Thematically, *Parklife* introduced many oddball characters and weird scenarios that had been fermenting in Damon's head for months. Whereas some bands looked to drugs and tour misbehaviour in a desperate attempt to shock, Blur looked inward at the sexually and socially deviant lives of the British population. 'Tracy Jacks' was a golf playing civil servant transvestite whilst the barrow boy chant of 'Parklife' saw Phil Daniels of *Quadrophenia* fame filling the shoes of a potty park-keeper, wiling away his hours watching pigeons shag and laughing at flabby suited men avoiding the red faced joggers on the grass. A series of superb couplets told tales of grandma's dentures, barbecues, pizzas and Snickers bars on 'Bank Holiday', perhaps the sequel to 'Sunday Sunday'. Damon's anti-Americanism reared its head again for 'Magic America', despising the shopping malls and cable TV culture. He even featured the Shipping Forecast, in the sad and dreamy trip around Britain's shores for what is widely seen as one of Blur's greatest songs, 'This Is A Low'. This penultimate track was a dark and introspective near-finale, bulging with emotion. The two instrumental tracks – 'Debt Collector' and 'Lot 105' – along with 'Clover Over Dover' (noted in the sleeve as 'Theme From An Imaginary Film') gave the album a cinematic quality as well. Like *Modern Life*, this album reflected something of Blur's past, but unlike its predecessor it was far more wide reaching in scope, exploiting the themes suggested at previously with much more depth. Damon warned people of this when he said to *NME*: "This album is in a lot of ways a massive departure from the last one. If people are scared of that then there's not much I can do about it."

Damon was not holding these people up as outcasts or weirdos, there was a genuine affection – he told *Puncture* he empathised with them: "I've always liked the idea that everybody is capable of deviant behaviour, however private. I've never been spiteful or angry about the characters – their malevolence is just comical. They're all doing peculiar things in small ways, not making a big fuss about it."

Damon later revealed that the rivalry with Suede and his belief that they had stolen some of his ideas had been a major motivation for him during the writing of this album; even so, Suede's focus tended to be more romanticised, more ambient drama, whereas Blur's was a very real, very gritty London of false teeth and fly-overs. The London focus was very clear, as he told *NME*: "I use London for a metaphor for almost every situation I'm in. I can't help it. I never think of London as just one person, there's so many different elements to it. It's not one girlfriend, it's twenty." Damon also denied in *NME* that this was another record in danger of getting lost in fascist rhetoric, saying all his characters were actually fed up and trying to escape England: "The English are so mean-spirited, and I am ashamed, but that's us isn't it? I suppose our songs are just telling each other how crap we are. All my songs criticise this country." The third person narrative style enabled Damon to recount all the lurid stories of his cast with superb detail. Back in the autumn of 1991, Damon had once been asked, "What do you stand for?" to which he answered, "So we don't have to keep lying down." It is sometimes hard to believe that this was the same lyricist as on *Parklife*.

The huge analysis that focuses on any album of such magnitude throws up many comparisons, and it is worth summarising these, since much of what the media said was very accurate. The central theory was that Blur were the next in line of a long heritage of English pop, going back to the beat groups of the sixties, in particular The Small Faces and The Kinks, then through bands like Buzzcocks, The Jam and Madness, on to electro pop such as Gary Numan. Great British albums such as The Kinks's *The Village Green Preservation Society* were cited as similar examples of narrative records which contained revealing vignettes of English life and insights behind the net curtains. At the time of *Parklife,* such lyrical tale telling was still largely unfashionable, so it was a brave reference point for Blur to go for (it was not entirely new however, as Blur had admitted many of these influences way back on *Leisure).* There was also a 'quaint' nature to some tracks, like 'Trouble In The Message Centre' that again fitted in with this British heritage. There were lyrical similarities too, with Ray Davies of The Kinks being particularly referred to, as well as more unusual analogies for 'Tracy Jacks', a sexual misfit possibly descended from Pink Floyd's 'Arnold Layne'. Damon's vocal delivery especially tied him to The Small Faces, and Graham's guitar linked back to other craftsmen such as Johnny Marr. Blur readily admitted their influences, and openly revered many of the bands they were now being compared to. The point to remember is that the result was always greater, or rather *different* to the sum of its parts. Nothing wasted, only reproduced.

★ ★ ★

The alternative title of *British Pop 1965-82* was often bestowed on *Parklife* by the unending comparisons and analogies to The Small Faces, The Kinks, The Jam, Madness, Steve Harley, The Who, Magazine *et al.* It was indeed a very referential record, as Stuart Maconie of Radio 1 put it, "an instant record collection in miniature." He was right to observe that this made *Parklife* an album of endless listening, one you could keep coming back to time and time again. In most cases many of these comparisons are valid, but it is interesting to look perhaps further back than that. As well as Steve Marriott and Ray Davies, it is also feasible to look at the music hall heritage which directly inspired tracks like 'The Debt Collector' and 'Lot 105', and indirectly influenced much of Blur's very essence. Various British bands had played around with music hall and Vaudeville, with The Beatles's track 'Being For The Benefit Of Mr Kite' from the *Sgt. Pepper* album being perhaps one of the better known examples. Herman's Hermits enjoyed success with music hall pastiches (Trevor Peacock's 'Mrs Brown, You've Got A Lovely Daughter') as well as actual music hall ('I'm Henry The Eighth I Am'). Their frontman Peter Noone was a pretty-faced drama student whose theatrical style and good looks reaped rich rewards for the band. Also, many of the bands which Blur were now being compared to were steeped in a music hall tradition, for example The Small Faces's track 'Lazy Sunday'. What is interesting is just how far back Damon's fascination with English music can be traced, and the influence this had on the band's sound, their live show, his lyrics and performance.

Music hall as an entertainment tradition was largely fading by the late 1940s, having enjoyed a heyday in the late Victorian era through to the 1920s. The 1950s and 1960s saw it increasingly being replaced by variety shows, with the likes of Danny Kaye and other American acts dominating venues like The Palladium. Many of the original British stars of music hall, such as the great Marie Lloyd, had a performance style peculiar to this British tradition, namely 'audience address' whereby the performer directly sang to the crowd, rather than at it. This was most obvious on the song 'The Boy I Love Is Up In The Gallery' from the turn of the century, but was also visible on her more famous numbers such as 'My Old Man Says Follow The Van'. Damon himself brought a dramatic quality to Blur shows, and that theatricality is also prevalent in his songwriting. In the case of *Parklife,* it is not impossible to imagine Damon singing 'To The End' to an actual member of the stalls. He himself said to *The Face,* "There is a lot of acting in me. The characters I create exist for me, and I have to be them for the three minutes I am singing it." On *Parklife,* there are direct music hall spin-offs as mentioned above, but there are also more subtle examples, such as 'Parklife' which employs a humour and ultra-reality that was a core element of this period of music.

There has been a long tradition of music hall and musical writers working in the pop vein, and really Damon was just inverting that age-old trend. Just as Lionel Bart had followed the legendary *Oliver* with pop songs for Tommy Steele, so now Damon was following very modern pop songs such as 'Bank Holiday' with throw-backs such as 'Debt Collector'. Damon has made it clear that during this period of his career he saw himself very much in this vein: "I am part of a tradition. I am part of a music hall-clown-entertainer tradition that's been in this country since the turn of the century. It's a theatrical tradition which if you come from this country you lean into. It's like pantomime, we've all been to those at Christmas, so it's in our blood. I used to love going to pantomime and always feel the need to entertain." Fast-forward to The Good, The Bad And The Queen and he still clearly draws heavily on this tradition; despite his many personae, there are still very rich veins of creative themes that have been constants in his entire career.

Another link with Blur and this more theatrical British tradition, which pre-dates the beat groups of the sixties, is the radical theatre of Joan Littlewood, who worked at The Theatre Royal Stratford East. Obviously, Damon's mom working there whilst pregnant with him is the most direct connection. Also, one of Littlewood's greatest productions was *Oh, What A Lovely War*, which was one of the key musicals Damon participated in at Stanway Comprehensive. It goes deeper than that. Littlewood, along with their partner Gerry Raffles, pretty much single-handedly changed the face of British music theatre in the late 1950s with her unique productions, and fought off the influx of American actors, placing it in the hands of home-grown innovators. There is a parallel in what Littlewood achieved here with *Parklife's* achievements – the fourth Blur album heralded a new era of British music, when the crown of pop was snatched away from visiting American bands. Similarly, Littlewood took alternative theatre which pre-dated the fringe circuit and invaded the West End mainstream. Forty years later and Blur were leaving the pages of *NME* to appear on the covers of nationwide tabloids, at huge venues and on arena tours, with the year's most critically acclaimed album under their belts.

One of the hardiest followers of the Littlewood school of thought was East 15, where Damon attended drama school in his late teens. Damon always refers back to this acting background and clearly enjoyed applying these skills on stage with Blur. Simply Red would have gone to RADA, Damon went to East 15, the angry young man's drama school. It was Tom Courtenay taking on Gielgud. Blur outselling Wet Wet Wet. Both were new waves in their own right.

The other key link here is with Weill and Brecht, who are obviously not British, but easily pre-date the sixties groups. Damon's fascination with, and admiration for, these two writers has already been mentioned. Having participated in *Die Drei Groschen Oper* with its hit song 'Mack The Knife' at East 15, Damon was aware at an early stage of the oddities and almost atonal appeal of some of Weill's music. Similarly he was also knowledgeable about Brecht's radical playwriting. Bits of both can be seen in his work. Most obvious is the influence of Weill, whose odd chromaticisms and nuances are mirrored in the way Damon takes the popular form and twists it, especially on songs like 'Debt Collector', which has remarkable similarities to the stylistic brashness of *Die Drei Groschen Oper*. Whilst Damon is nowhere near as political as Brecht in his Blur-era lyrics, the fresh subject matter and unique characters were similar features.

Pushing the connection still further, there could even be seen to be a vague similarity between Damon's open attitude to his reverential use of pop's past and Brecht's infamous 'Theatre of Alienation'. This was best seen during the work of The Berliner Ensemble (again something that Damon had worked with in his teens), where the cast abandoned all traditional attempts to suspend audience belief – they walked on stage without a curtain, did not hide the lights or have complex scenery, and even introduced themselves as actors who were about to perform a play. Now, obviously Blur don't do this live, but this attitude of creating a pastiche that is greater than the sum of its parts is more than apparent on *Parklife*. Indeed, Damon's honest admissions about plundering the past were first expressed in interviews for *Modern Life*. They are both saying, "we know you know, but look and listen, it is still something new and special."

One final parallel is with Damon and Kurt Weill's writing

prowess. Weill is still seen today as a classical composer in his own right, and yet he also went on to write popular songs ('September Song' which has been covered by Lou Reed, and 'Mack The Knife'), folk opera ('Down In The Valley') and Broadway musicals ('Knickerbocker Holiday' and 'One Touch Of Venus'). Similarly, Damon has started off writing linear pop of the day ('There's No Other Way'), but has also written film themes ('Decadence' and a track for *Trainspotting* entitled 'Closet Romantic'; Blur also contributed 'Sing' to the soundtrack), and has had his work arranged for orchestra. Even the Steven Berkoff connection is also relevant – Berkoff comes very much from the school of Weill and Brecht, and is famed for his highly physical performances – something Damon was also renowned for in Blur's early days.

In summary, the multitude of more recent popular influences on Blur, circa *Parklife*, are justifiably highlighted. However, with Damon's background, it is too myopic to simply look at these more recent reference points. The above suggestions are certainly worth exploring, if only to understand the breadth of his work better. Damon himself had once said "I can't agree we are a sixties band – I think we are a very nineties band, the only nineties band around. If you're going to analyse a set of individuals and their music, you've got to look further than what you see on the record. Journalists always try to look further without knowing enough." He had himself given hints about where to look, as he suggested in the infamous "Empire Under Siege" article: "We have such a rich musical heritage, and it doesn't just start with rock 'n' roll, it goes back to the post-war period of Joan Littlewood and Lionel Bart, and before that to Music Hall."

Whatever your view of *Parklife* is, it was undeniably a classic album. In a pop world where CDs and (later) selective downloading have enabled listeners to flit effortlessly from track to track, here was an album that demanded playing all the way through, time and time again. Amongst all the protracted discussions and theories that surrounded the year's most celebrated album, just one sentence in the *NME* summed it all up perfectly: "It is easy to forget that albums can be this fabulous."

CHAPTER 8

JUBILEE

The sheer musical quality of *Parklife* translated into a colossal commercial impact. Much to the band's amazement, it outsold Pink Floyd's chart topping *The Division Bell* by 3-to-1 and entered the charts straight at No.1. *Parklife* went on to stay in the Top 20 for 90 weeks and sell over 1.8 million copies. It captured the very zeitgeist of the moment like no other album of the 1990s, and the run of achievements seemed endless. *Parklife* was nominated for the prestigious Mercury Music Award from a list of 130 acts, along with excellent records by The Prodigy, Therapy?, Paul Weller and Pulp. Blur were pre-match favourites at 2-1 to take the award that Suede had won the year before, but they were all beaten to the post by M People's soulless pop, apparently seizing the crown from Pulp's *His 'n' Hers* by just one vote. *Select* hailed Blur as 'The Best British Band Since The Smiths' claiming that *Parklife* was the guitar pop album by which all other records of the next decade would be judged. Damon even achieved his life-long ambition of appearing on the BBC Radio 4 chat show *Loose Ends* with the late Ned Sherrin. With mass coverage in the music press, the tabloids, the teen mags and the broadsheets, Blur had now successfully straddled the often impossible gap between critical acclaim and mass commercial success.

The extent to which Blur had crossed over into the mainstream only became fully apparent during the tour to promote *Parklife*. Starting in May 1994, the sixteen dates took in relatively small venues considering that Blur were now arguably the biggest band in the country, with Nottingham's Rock City as the opener. As the tour progressed, the success of *Parklife* increased, so that by the last date Blur were being greeted as conquering heroes. Damon in particular was being treated like some kind of pop messiah. At one show in Wolverhampton he crowd surfed and lost his shoe, then clambered back on stage and said, "I need my shoe back, I'm not Jesus you know" at which point the crowd began chanting "Je-sus, Je-sus". This routine became a regular feature of Blur gigs, and on this tour alone Damon lost six pairs of shoes. The popular appeal of *Parklife* was reinforced by the sing-along nature of most of these Blur gigs – the audience participation was immense, especially on the title track.

Blur were assisted on these dates by Cara Tivey on keyboards who filled out the musical textures of the set when Damon was too preoccupied with being Jesus. He was highly theatrical now, drawing on his drama background to play the roles of his characters on stage, colourfully animating the songs one minute, then plunging head first into a sea of hands the next. His oft-maligned Mockney accent was getting sharper and sharper, and he hammed it up, drawing in the swooning girls and admiring lads.

Alongside Damon's greater stage dramatics, Dave's drumming was noticeably more precise as well. Having experienced terrible drinking problems on tour in the past, he had now gone tee-total. During the band's problem days, he often spent day and night drunk, as he told *NME*: "Mentally I got quite ill, I started to get very paranoid, I was always a miserable drunk and when I got pissed it started to affect me mentally." One morning after a huge night with Siouxsie And The Banshees at the aforementioned stadium gig in Portugal, Dave decided that enough was enough, and stopped there and then. He had recently got married and felt it was no longer acceptable to survive purely on a liquid diet. Since then, Dave has been taunted habitually by the band for his sobriety. He said to *Melody Maker*, "I miss things like going down the pub. Do I miss the oblivion? Well, I can't say I do because I could never remember anything. The reason I stopped had a lot to do with waking up with a hangover everyday for three years."

Graham meanwhile seemed to vacillate between disinterested and bored on stage. Being the shyest member of Blur, this demeanour was borne of studiously playing his ever-more complex guitar lines, mastering his effects and being too scared to look up. Alex, on the other hand was not so shy. With his ever-present fag hanging out of the corner of his mouth and his lanky body curling round the bass, he was suave and smouldering.

Backstage, the band were plagued by the press and groupies, but still managed to enjoy themselves. Lager was the drink of choice – this was Essex man on tour, playing mainstream songs about middle and working class people, eulogising in interviews about their manifesto and christening themselves, in Damon's words, "mythical lager eaters". Blur were quick to deny any suggestion of drug use however, at least Damon was, as he told *Melody Maker*, "A lot of people I know take too many drugs. It messes with their emotions and in their quietest darkest hours makes them very unhappy. It certainly has nothing to do with creativity."

With *Parklife* sales showing no sign of slowing down, the Blur steamroller continued. At the Glastonbury Festival, the nation's current favourites found themselves only on the second stage (and not even headlining that), as the show had been booked before the release of their era-defining third album. They played alongside Radiohead, Inspiral Carpets and before headliners Spiritualized. Damon took to the stage in druid's robes whilst Graham, for some reason, performed in full combat gear, complete with regulation helmet. Blur were in esteemed company, with Peter Gabriel, Bjork, Rage Against The Machine, Orbital, Paul Weller and Elvis Costello also playing the festival, but as with Reading the previous year, they took the honours.

The story was not so rosy in Europe for their extensive tour that took in most of the Continent and included many summer festivals. *Parklife* was the most British album for years, and despite Europe being an open market place the cultural divides still clearly existed. The sheer complete Englishness of people like Tracy Jacks and Damon's comic park-keeper were largely lost on continental audiences, and much of the media still had Blur down as another Jesus Jones. Shows were well attended and reasonably well received, but there was nowhere near the impact seen back at home. The only other down side to this series of live dates was when Alex went home after the Shepherd's Bush gig and found he had been burgled. In typically nonchalant fashion, he said he didn't mind because he never gave money to beggars!

★ ★ ★

Having reduced the pop masses to its knees with 'Girls & Boys' it was typically perverse of Blur to release 'To The End' as their second single from the album. The lush string soaked ballad could have easily been a James Bond theme, or a John Barry masterpiece. With the Anglo-French lyrical dalliance and the rich campness throughout, this was a turning point for Damon that elevated his writing in the eyes of contemporaries and the record buying public alike. It reached No.16 in the charts in June, but more importantly attracted a whole new audience to the band. Whereas 'Girls & Boys' had scooped up thousands of new younger pop fans, this elegant ballad won over countless older listeners, a fact confirmed by the variety of age groups visible at Blur gigs after this single. Blur also found time to appear at the *NME* film festival entitled 'Punk Before And Beyond', where *Star Shaped* was shown.

Blur returned to the pop stakes in early September with 'Parklife', the third single from the album and the best song ever about pigeons. Phil Daniels' cameo performance was perfect for the nutty central character, and made Damon's live version seem rather tame. This appearance mirrored Stanley Unwin's barmy showing on The Small Faces 'Ogden's Nut Gone Flake'. Daniels was in many ways a theatrical parallel to Blur. He had starred as Jimmy, the ill-fated Mod in the legendary *Quadrophenia*, a film based around a soundtrack by The Who and made at the height of the late 1970s Mod revival. Jimmy entered Mod mythology by driving his scooter over the white cliffs of Dover, an act mirrored in Blur's 'Clover Over Dover'. Daniels had also graced several Mike Leigh films including *Meantime*, which Damon and Graham had been brought up on. Further more, Daniels had always expressed a distaste for Hollywood and the American culture, and whilst many of his contemporaries moved across the water to sunnier and more glamourous climes, he stayed firmly put in England.

'Parklife' was, of course, a totally ridiculous single, and a considerable commercial success, reaching No.10. Along with 'Girls & Boys', Blur had now released the finest brace of pop songs in 1994. In keeping with Damon and the band's ever-prolific writing, there were two new instrumental tracks included in the package, 'Supa Shoppa' and 'Beard' as well as a much sought after French version of 'To The End'. This had been recorded with Francoise Hardy, a famed Parisian singer who had worked with The Beatles but whose career had been prematurely cut short due to chronic stage fright.

This release preceded Blur's two biggest ever headline gigs in Britain, at the Aston Villa Leisure Centre on October 5 and the cavernous Alexandra Palace two days later. Their only other planned date in the autumn was a headline slot at Glasgow's 'T In The Park', along with Manic Street Preachers and D:Ream. Preparation came in the form of a warm-up date at Cambridge Corn Exchange – a sizeable gig for many bands but now merely a small quickie for Blur. The Aston Villa gig sold out in hours, and Radio 1 broadcast the performance live as part of their 'Octoberfest' season of shows which also featured Suede and Sinead O'Connor. The Alexandra Palace gig had been announced back in early August, the same week that *Parklife* achieved gold album sales of over 100,000. Blur had worried about their ability to sell enough tickets – after all, the hangar-like venue had not heard a guitar in anger since the Stone Roses had played there in 1989. Yet within three days of the show being announced they'd had enough enquiries to fill Alexandra Palace *five* times.

1994 was a year of superlatives for Blur and Damon, and their Midas touch seemed endemic. If any single moment encapsulated everything about their achievement, all that they stood for and all that they had fought against, it was this triumphant Ally Pally gig. On the impressive bill were an infant Supergrass (one of Damon's favourite bands), Corduroy and the voyeuristic Pulp, one of the few bands who shared Damon's liking for behind-the-net-curtains Britain, and perhaps the only act capable of supporting Blur with any credibility at this show. For a mere £2.40 extra, fans could buy Blur Rover tickets, which included transport back to Trafalgar Square after the gig. On the night, proceedings began early at 6.45pm, but Supergrass already showed signs of the talent that would send them supernova in the spring of 1995. Corduroy were largely forgettable, but Pulp certainly weren't – newly crowned sex god Jarvis Cocker held sway with his limp wristed foppery and unique 'epileptic coat hanger in a suit' style of dancing. Once Pulp had completed their warmly received set, there was an intermission, where ladies sold ice creams and handed out bingo tickets, which declared the top prize was "A Night Out With Blur." Shortly after, a bingo caller came on and started reading out the numbers, and gradually every single person in the hall began crossing off all the numbers. When the last number was called out, 7,000 people had a full house and Blur walked on stage to a Palace full of winners.

The stage set was a monument to Blur's peculiar domestic fascinations with huge red lampshades swamping the stage (Blur lost money on this gig because of the operation costs). Launching off with 'Tracy Jacks' followed by a soaring rendition of 'Popscene' the standard was set early on for what became an incredible event. Everything clicked – the stage set, the brass sections, the band's musical performance, and especially the Phil Daniels rendition of 'Parklife' which sent the audience nuclear. Even the raw egg that hit Damon or the lack of new material other than 'Mr Robinson's Quango' seemed not to matter. Towards the end of the set, Damon hushed the crowd and thanked them for the way they had treated Blur in 1994, and it was delivered with heartfelt and genuine gratitude. All the arrogant and overtly ambitious claims that he had spewed out in interview after interview over the years now made perfect sense. Fortunately, for those not able to get in, the band released a long form video of the gig in February 1995 entitled 'Show Time', which committed to celluloid one of the pop year's finest moments. The artwork was typical Blur, with an old-school painted clown pronouncing "Re-live the thrill of it all – Family entertainment up the Ally Pally".

★ ★ ★

The band's success was not universal however – the tour of the USA was only lukewarmly received, reinforcing the gulf between what Blur represented and what the American audience wanted to hear. Damon as a frontman was largely unknown stateside. Such was the absolute failure of *Modern Life Is Rubbish* in America that most people thought *Park Life* was in fact the follow-up to *Leisure*. There was pressure on Blur to succeed stateside – after all, they had pretty much conquered the home market now, so it was the next logical step. Blur themselves did not see it this way, and chose to visit only nine cities including Los Angeles, Boston, Chicago, and San Francisco, supported by Pulp on all dates. All of the travelling was done by plane, and everything was done to avoid a repeat of the debacle of their last major US tour. The impact of *Parklife* was therefore inevitably limited but that was as much to do with the music and subject matter as the size of the tour. Suffice to say, the dates sold out well in advance, albeit in venues of between 1000- 1500 capacity. Those that did attend were fanatical, and the band were highly amused to see small collections of Mods on Lambrettas outside each gig.

Blur rounded off the year yet with the release in November of the fourth single from *Parklife,* the jaunty pop of 'End Of A Century'. The record was perhaps most notable for the duo of appalling B-sides written by Alex and Graham. Graham's 'Red Necks' was a laughable comic Country & Western track which accompanied the single, whilst other formats carried Alex's fantastically titled 'Alex's Song'. This suggested that the excellent 'Far Out' that he had written for *Parklife* might well be a one-off, and confirmed Damon's claim that "Alex only writes a song every two years and they're all about planets." The inferior musical package mattered little – by now the momentum surrounding Blur almost guaranteed them hits, so the single reached No.19. They had notched up yet another hit, and it made their travels around an unconvinced Europe at this time a little more comfortable. Inevitably, the inferior B-sides also focused more attention on Damon as the core writer.

There was no let up for Blur right until Christmas. Damon fronted *Top of the Pops* and then they appeared on *Later With Jools Holland*, alongside Stevie Winwood and Ruby Turner. However, the best event of this Yuletide period was definitely the secret gig at Colchester Sixth Form College on December 16. Considering they had just been on a world tour taking in Japan, Scandinavia, Europe and America, Colchester hardly seemed to be the next logical port of call. Nigel Hildreth wanted to raise funds for an orphanage in India, so he called Damon's father Keith and asked if his former pupil would mind making a personal appearance. Much to his amazement, Damon said that rather than just turn up and sign autographs, he would much rather play a gig at the college, which had now relocated to a site on North Hill in the town centre, just up from the Army Recruitment centre. Furthermore, Damon said he wanted Hildreth's class to arrange six Blur songs and accompany them on stage with their own 17-piece school orchestra.

Hildreth takes up the story: "We had a major security problem on our hands now, because Blur were massive and our gym is hardly the size of Alexandra Palace. So we finalised details and gave the students the sheet music, and then on the morning of the gig, I was just talking to the class about some homework and I said, 'Oh, by the way, Blur are coming in tonight to play a gig in the gym ...'

Damon had said the charity side appealed to him, but also the fact that it was so intimate – they seemed uncomfortable with the big arenas they were now playing. Needless to say, there were outsiders absolutely frantic to get in, but it was a strictly students only-performance, that was the whole point. All the engineers and record company people were fantastic, and during the day they all gave their time for free – Blur seem to have an excellent crew and group of friends around them. I was in London for a boring meeting that afternoon, and I was late getting to the train station to get back to Colchester, so I just dived on the first carriage as it pulled away and there was this big cry of 'Heh!! Mr Hildreth, over here!!' I looked up and Blur were sitting there. I went over and had a chat but when the conductor came I had to go to the second class compartment."

Hildreth and Damon worked on the musical arrangements right up to the last minute, and they also talked about the school days they had shared. Damon made it quite clear he was grateful to Hildreth's open attitude, and told *Kaleidoscope* "He gave me and Graham a real confidence about doing lots of things, neither of us are incredibly proficient, he gave us that confidence to busk it really." He also privately thanked him for shouting at him all those times his mind had wandered!

The new school site was built after a disgruntled ex-teacher reportedly burnt the old building down, in an act that could have easily slotted into Blur's suburban dystopia. Local papers had enjoyed a hate/hate relationship with Blur ever since Damon's early criticisms of the town such as "There's an unwritten law in Colchester that says you can talk about it but never achieve it." They had returned the insult with negative coverage, which now backfired on them as they were all banned from the show, although the gig still made the front page of the *Colchester Evening Gazette* – fame at last. When the 5pm showtime arrived, Damon walked on to a stage covered in tinsel and fairy lights and said, "Hello, thanks for coming, nice to be back" and launched into 'End Of A Century', at which point the 400 strong audience went into mass hysteria for the next sixty minutes. Amongst the songs arranged by the students were 'Parklife', 'Tracy Jacks', 'To The End', 'End Of A Century', 'Debt Collector' (Simon Exton, the student who had re-arranged 'Parklife' later submitted the piece for his 'A' level music course). It was a classic night, and for a while there was some discussion of releasing tracks from the show with the orchestra, but the recording quality was not high enough. To cap it all, they raised £3000 for the charity fund.

After the gig, they all piled into the nearest pub and later Damon and Hildreth went to Colchester Arts Centre, which had been the scene of one of Damon's first ever gigs all those years ago. Perhaps the best part of the night was when Alex missed his bass cue for 'Girls & Boys' whereupon Damon immediately stopped the song: "No! no! no! You've missed it. Now, if you'd been taught by Mr Hildreth you wouldn't have done that. You wouldn't have dared!"

Simon Exton's 'A' Level re-arrangement of 'Parklife'

CHAPTER 9

LONDON LOVES

By the time of Blur's pre-Christmas secret gig, Britain was fully gripped by the phenomenon called Britpop. In 1994, there was an inspired renaissance of British music that saw a whole collection of new native bands breakthrough. Previously, against a backdrop of American slacker-driven grunge culture, British music had been largely ignored and in fact derided during the early 1990s, ever since the demise of Madchester. Alongside this American rock domination, the commercial charts were swamped with one hit wonders, cover versions, novelty songs and old timers.

Many factors combined to create Britpop. Undoubtedly the arrival of Suede was a key catalyst in 1992, with their highly stylised, romantic London dramas, and Brett's peculiar camp Englishness. Pat Gilbert, Clash biographer and revered journalist, was a fan of Britpop and he believes Suede were essential to its inception: "Britpop's genesis has its roots in Suede, who were the first post-indie band who refused to be mulling and wantonly middle class, they didn't want to recreate three-minute perfect pop songs in the line of the Velvets and the Byrds and they came along with a bit of swagger. Suede were definitely the first time in years that English bands had reclaimed some sense of occasion about what they were doing, and people started looking back at British bands rather than all that American stuff. Suede started all that."

Nevertheless, *Modern Life* was Blur's first quintessentially English album and many of their British ideas pre-date Suede, including crucially the 'our culture is under siege' theory. What Suede had was the commercial exposure and success that gave their ideas recognition. In April of 1993, *Select* magazine ran a feature not so subtly titled "Yanks Go Home" which featured a whole list of English style bands. With Suede on the cover, there were also features on Pulp, St Etienne, Denim and The Auteurs. Notably, Blur didn't even get a mention, even though advance copies of the first of their English trilogy albums were already in circulation in the industry. The humourous piece with a prophetic undertone ran thus: "Who do you think you are kidding Mr Cobain? Enough is enough! We don't want plaid. We want crimpolene, glamour, wit and irony. If 1992 was the American year, then it's time to bring on the home guard." Maybe grunge encapsulated a cultural low, that coincided with the economic depression, and perhaps with the recession fading there was a new positivity springing up which brought the resurgence of more optimistic British bands.

The home guard grew during 1993 with *Modern Life* being complemented by Suede's eponymously titled, No.1 award-winning debut album. The rejuvenation of the festivals that had been helped by memorable performances by the likes of Nirvana and Pearl Jam was now taken over with stunning live shows by Blur and Suede of course, but also by The Boo Radleys and veteran British pioneers New Order. Nirvana's *Nevermind* follow-up *In Utero*, silenced some of the doubters for a while, but with designer grunge now prancing along the catwalks and grunge-by-numbers advertising American jeans, the voices of dissent grew.

1994 was when it all exploded. Gilbert believes that Britpop was jump-started by the energetic emergence of New Wave of New Wave at the tail end of 1993: "The NWONW was important in the sense that it kick started an interest in really live energetic bands. Crucially, some of its reference points were very English, the Grange Hill 1978 school boy look, Adidas trainers and tops, short spiky hair, The Clash and The Sex Pistols. Perhaps it was more important sartorially than musically, in helping to define what Britpop was going to be."

Once Blur's *Parklife* had pushed the speed-fuelled NWONW aside, the flood gates of Britpop opened, and the untimely death of Kurt Cobain did indeed act as a tragic heralding of the end of an era. Throughout 1994, streams of new bands came through, and with the mainstream media picking up on Britpop, the resurgence of British music was quite astounding: in the next splendid eighteen months, Pulp finally broke their fourteen-year duck and produced a sexually subversive, comical seedy masterpiece in their first major label album *His 'n' Hers*; Elastica broke away from their suffocating early NWONW status to release a volley of classic pop singles, stating the case for female writers, as did the slightly more lightweight Sleeper; The Auteurs more sombre style had somewhat underachieved; Oxford's Radiohead filled the void with a queer debut album which was soon followed by *The Bends* and their latterday global-conquering status. At the opposite end to the saintly patience of Pulp came Supergrass, who only formed in early 1994, and within eighteen months had smashed into the album charts at No.1 with their excellent debut album *I Should Coco*. The ranks were also swelled by the likes of Shed Seven, Portishead, The Bluetones, Marion, Powder, Dodgy, and the album chart topping Boo Radleys. There was also the ultimate derivative Britpop band Menswear, who appeared on *Top of the Pops* before their first single was even released. Ironically, Suede had experienced a bad year in 1994 with the loss of guitarist and key songwriter Bernard Butler – fortunately, with the arrival of Richard Oakes as a replacement and the excellent and under-rated second album *Dog Man Star*, Suede temporarily returned from the brink. Blur at Alexandra Palace, Suede's debut album, Supergrass on *Top of the Pops* and Jarvis on Pop Quiz were all great Britpop moments. The Mod phenomenon also underwent something of a revival, with Modfather Paul Weller enjoying renewed success after a dubious start to his solo career. Blur's own Mod leanings on the second album were no longer dominant but many still tagged them as part of the new movement. However you looked at it, this was a great new era for British music, and now grunge bands in the UK couldn't get arrested.

The Britpop phenomenon caused/coincided with a resurgence in various other areas of the British music industry. For example, at the time the late, lamented *Top of the Pops* had a new producer, Ric Blaxill, who single-handedly rejuvenated what had become a joke programme in the early 1990s. Blur, Elastica, and Pulp all presented the show and scores of Britpop style bands appeared. Blaxill's first gig was Steve Harley at Crystal Palace in 1973 and that passion for new British music was instrumental in the famous show's renaissance – after all, *Top of the Pops* presented these bands to a nationwide audience: "My basic philosophy [was] that the programme [was] called *Top of the Pops* and that [was] what it should represent, genuinely good music. Fortunately, the BBC gave me a large degree of editorial freedom to go with the bands that I wanted. I [thought] it should feature the obvious stars, but there [were] also bands who maybe hadn't got a huge record deal, maybe hadn't got an album, maybe not even a single, who could be seen and heard. The way the programme was run before meant that each week only about six or seven record companies would be at the meeting; I [would] sometimes have maybe 25 or 30 people competing for 9 slots, because all manner of bands knew that the door [was] open for them. Blur's contributions [were] always excellent, they knew how it all worked and they were a very bright band, they played up to it. Their spirit and attitude [was] very open, bands like that [were] superb for the programme."

Record sales rocketed in the UK by 14% on the previous year, so that total sales reached an all-time high of £1.5 billion. Also, live shows suddenly became something to see again, and 14-year-olds began switching off their Nintendos and forming bands once again. Pat Gilbert is in no doubt that Britpop made a significant contribution to British musical history: "In twenty years time, people will look back at 1994 and the two years after it as one of the great eras of British pop, the same as they do with the 1960s. I think we were living through an enormous maelstrom of great new music." This was best shown at the so-called Britstock in Leeds for the Heineken Music Festival in July 1995 – whereas the previous year might have been filled with introspective American guitar bands, now the entire bill consisted of supposedly Britpop acts such as Pulp, Powder, Menswear, The Bluetones and Marion.

Certain older bands became fashionable influences again. The majority of the great British bands draw on the unique character of British life. Just as The Sex Pistols laughed at the tabloids, The Jam detailed small town precincts and The Smiths mythologised the normality of life, now Damon and the new generation were hailing the good and bad of their home country. Many of the Britpop groups had grown up in Britain without the first hand clutter of punk, so this was barely involved, although some bands drew on it for live shows. Far more substantially, many of the 1960s beat groups that were cited as references for *Modern Life* and *Parklife* now enjoyed a renewed popularity.

Vocally if not lyrically, Damon's so-called Mockney accent mirrored the Cockney Rebel Steve Harley and who else but Jarvis Cocker could sing about "wood chip" in a Sheffield accent? Cynics successfully argued that many of Britpop's contingent sounded too much like their influences, a kind of 'spot the reference', slicing up history and re-selling the same package. Defenders pointed to acts who were re-inventing the past with their own dash of originality, taking a pastiche and working it with enough intelligence to create something fresh and new.

So 1994 was the year of Britpop's arrival, with Blur's *Parklife* as the album of that year beyond question. However, if you accept that Britpop as a musical umbrella existed, then you also have to acknowledge its enormous diversity. The peculiar English musical reference points of Blur and Supergrass were hardly acceptable influences for Radiohead. Pulp and Blur talked of a behind-the-net curtains Britain, but Johnny-come-lately Oasis didn't, neither did Marion. Elastica sounded as much like Menswear as Nirvana did.

Also, the vital thing to remember is that none of these bands really considered themselves to be part of a movement. There were some groups who enjoyed success on the coat-tails of the bigger bands, but that is the case for any musical movement. Suede distanced themselves from Britpop hastily, as did Marion. Oasis refused to appear on the BBC2 documentary entitled *Britpop Now* although Damon presented it and Pulp, Elastica and Menswear appeared. Britpop remained a banner of convenience to label a rich new seam of British talent.

Britpop *was* a media fiction and, crucially, an industry compatible one, as Gilbert explains: "At the same time that Britpop had parallels with punk in terms of removing the old guard, whilst punk was a revolutionary force, Britpop was a very reactionary force. It fitted in to the industry, it was very tied up with commercialism and selling records. Britpop didn't threaten anyone, it benefitted everyone, and it didn't pose any threat to society – it was not drug oriented, it wasn't socially subversive, it was a phenomenon because it wasn't a threat." This is very true, as shown by the huge coverage the key bands enjoyed in the national tabloids and the subsequent cross-over into the mainstream. Britpop was huge news and Damon Albarn was arguably, like it or not, the movement's best-known face.

* * *

As publicly elected leaders of the pack, Blur were unavoidably involved with many of the aspects of Britpop. One of these was the emergence of the so-called 'New Lad', borne to rebel against a tide of political correctness. Perhaps the most visible and successful backlash against this trend was the launch of the hugely successful magazine *Loaded*, whose motto was "For men who should know better" and whose pages were filled with footy, beer, birds and bands. *Front*, *Nuts* and *Zoo* followed suit and enjoyed buoyant sales for the best part of a decade. 'Fantasy Football' made a similarly amazing breakthrough, despite John Major railing against the "yob culture". Blur were not unaffected by all this – Damon had himself spoken out against PC and many of his interviews in 1994 were about football and beer drinking. Alex was involved in a drunken brawl at a Menswear gig after he shouted, 'I shagged your sister" to the drummer from the band Panic. Damon even contributed an article for his beloved Chelsea FC programme. He was also not averse to strictly un-PC language: "As far as bisexuality goes, I've had a little taste of that fruit, or I've been tasted, you might say. But when you get down to it, you can't beat a good pair of tits."

This laddishness was also apparent with various appearances at celebrity football matches, and perennial visits to The Good Mixer in Camden Town, official home to many of the drinking bands (including the ultimate lads' band of the day, Oasis). Damon said to *Select*: "It's necessary to have a comic fill to the whole politically correct revolution. That's what the New Lad is ... it's a way of expressing the more visceral side of being a human being in this age." Graham was less convinced, and found it embarrassing to see that "Parklife" as a yob chant had now come to represent much of this new attitude.

Unfortunately, the more toxic side of being a 'New Lad' caused Damon much ill health at this highly successful time, a problem which was severe enough for him to require professional medical help. Damon claimed never to have felt depressed before, even during the band's worst times, but here he was, standing astride British pop's throne and he was waking up unhappy. Clearly, Blur's enormous work load around *Parklife* didn't help matters and the drinking and occasional cocaine use were joined by the arrival of sporadic insomnia. With the public eye suddenly focussed on him, it was a real culture shock: "I had to grow up in public in 1994, because I was still a teenager at the age of 26." He was now regularly crying, unsatisfied, depressed and angry, and the occasional incidence of depression in his family history unnerved him even more. He became slightly hypochondriac, worrying about shoulder pains and soon deciding he might have heart disease. By the time he was performing 'To The End' on *Top of the Pops*, he was desperately unhappy. He attended a Harley Street doctor who told him that his lifestyle and environment had affected his nervous system and caused his health problems. He was given some prescription tablets and sent away, being told it could be up to a year before he was fully recovered. With admirable discipline, he stopped taking the drugs after two days and instead decided to change his lifestyle. Stimulants – even coffee – were stopped and the drinking was cut back, and he started to use a gym occasionally. On the subject of cocaine, Damon told *The Face*, "I don't think that was the problem, but I stopped and I'd be very reluctant to do it again. Although I loved it, it was idiotic." He also said of his renaissance from this difficult phase: "When Kurt Cobain killed himself, I thought I was having a nervous breakdown, which I wasn't at all. I felt very disturbed by his death and it did haunt me for a while. But in 1994 I realised that I can do this, and that you can be fairly level headed about it and not go mad." His six months of neurosis had been dealt with typically pragmatic realism from a man who should have been a star celebrity, but seemed capable of hanging on to his old self with engaging ease. He had undergone a transition from a sane person to what he called "a sane pop person" with fewer scars than most.

★ ★ ★

So in the end, Blur made it to the close of their most successful year to date with relatively few problems. Despite a last minute flurry from Oasis with their debut album *Definitely Maybe*, Blur's fourth album was equally historically significant. Both had resurrected British music and renewed interest in young and old native bands alike. Handsomely supported by Britpop's cast, Blur had turned American mastery into British retaliation. There were a litany of victories along the way. *Parklife* made a clean sweep of just about all the major end of year music polls. They took the prestigious Q 'Album of the Year' Award whilst *Smash Hits* Awards by the bag full confirmed the lasting cross-over had been made into the massive teen market. Even when they lost the Mercury Award, their record sales shot up by 125% in the next two weeks. *Parklife* hit platinum sales within its first week of release and did not fall out of the Top 20 from then until the New Year. Part of the longevity of this success was Blur's astute single releases, with each new record drawing different people into the experience. 'Girls & Boys' was adult pop, 'To The End' won over many of the 30-something public that had made Mick Hucknall a multi-millionaire, 'Parklife' was a comical appeal to the younger generation and 'To The End' covered all the bases.

The band's status as celebrities rocketed. They attended film premiere's and Alex snogged super models, (he denies anything more serious with Helena Christiensen). Damon scooped virtually all the 'Sexiest Man of the Year' awards, despite Justine saying, "He has one of the lowest sex drives of any man I have ever met. He's not that into sex." They were asked to record a theme tune for the 1996 European Championships by the FA, along with Oasis. *Spitting Image* did a Blur piss-take with the troubled Prince Charles called "Charles Life" and Martin Amis asked for a copy of their album after having read that it was a sonic version of his acclaimed novel, *London Fields*.

Biffo, a close friend of the band, has seen their success arrive and noted how they have maintained their normality: "Damon [saw] Blur as his brainchild and so he [was] always wiling to talk about it, but he [did] not like the intrusion into his private life. As the lead singer whose girlfriend [was] also famous this [had] caused some trouble with idle gossip. Graham is still a very shy man, and he hates the attention that his fame has brought. When we go out we find places we know he will not be recognised, and he really dislikes any public exposure of his private life. Alex is still Alex, the same as he was when they first started. Being so intellectual, he finds that people are wary of that and he will play up to it, teasing them. Dave is quieter now, he is not into the partying so much, he loves his flying and is still very much into computers. It amazes me how they have been able to keep that four brothers mentality going, and don't seem to have picked up any of the trappings of big pop stars."

Even Blur's problems during this fantastic period were turned with some panache to their advantage. Some saw the *Parklife* album artwork as glamourising the sport of greyhound racing. Betting slips were now constantly thrown on stage at Blur gigs, and one Japanese version of *Parklife* barked when you opened the case and the dog's eyes on the cover lit up when you pressed them. Many people were not impressed – one letter to a weekly paper raged "Don't buy anything by Blur – they sanction the killing of defenceless animals." Blur were a little taken aback by the extent of the criticism, and subsequently paid for a retired greyhound to be put in kennels for a year. More publicly, they paid for a joint poster campaign with The Canine Defence League which showed a dog with the legend "Not Just For Christmas" alongside the band's album cover. It was a clever manoeuvre which negated much of the anger.

In the media, it was a year-long campaign that eventually bordered on over-exposure. Hundreds of articles saw Damon's headline grabbing skills blossom as the country's new mercurial pop genius. He transferred to teen magazines as easily as he did to *GQ* and *Modern Review* (where Damon wrote a piece about the yob culture, comically the same week that Alex was being featured in *The Daily Star* as a celebrity drunk), and they appeared on *Later With Jools Holland* as comfortably as they did on European tea time television. One particular funny incident saw them play *Top of the Pops* brilliantly, then head off to Stringfellows only to be refused admittance because they had some Tesco carrier bags with them. Peter Stringfellow had previously brandished them drunken louts and said they weren't welcome in his club: "I found them to be the most obnoxious little shits I have had in my club for a long while."

The biggest achievements of all were at The Brit Awards ceremony at Alexandra Palace, the scene of Blur's greatest triumph. Blur scooped a record breaking four awards for 'Best Album', 'Video', 'Single' and 'Best Band'. For the last acceptance speech, Damon said that Oasis should have received the award with them jointly. With his previous *Top of the Pops* recommendation ("This is

Oasis and they are wonderful"), maybe this was the start of a long and happy friendship?

Parklife had crystallised everything that Blur were about, and on a commercial scale EMI were astonished at its success and the depth of Blur's comeback from the lows of 1992. The band were also understandably delighted with the year's work – no-one had realised just how massively their album was going to succeed. Damon said to *NME* with typical modesty that, "I don't think there's another band that have qualified what they are about in the world as much as we have. We have come to a point where we've met our market full on. I know it will change, but right now, it's all ours. When we started I really wanted to be part of something, but we are out on our own now. Untouchable."

CHAPTER 10

EVERYTHING'S GOING JACKANORY

Blurmania continued into 1995 whilst the band were already writing and demo-ing new material for the next album. Damon appeared on *The White Room* to sing a version of 'Waterloo Sunset' with Ray Davies, after The Kinks frontman had been on a European TV show with them and liked their material. Damon didn't care that the impromptu 'Parklife' they also sang was rather painful, and later told *NME:* "This is one of the most exciting things I've done. He is as much an influence as anyone else for me. He's fundamentally a part of what I do. What he did is just in my blood, it's a part of my upbringing." Of Davies' most famous song Damon said, "Without a shadow of a doubt, it is the most perfect song I could ever wish to write."

Damon's childhood interest in Two Tone meant he was delighted to work with Terry Hall at the start of the year along with the enigmatic Tricky, on some material for the latter's new project Durban Poison. The cosmopolitan Tricky had also been a rude boy in his youth, so there was much common, ground (although Damon's contribution, 'I'll Pass Right Through You', was eventually removed from the record at his own request). Damon also appeared on an Amnesty International video called "Use Your Freedom" alongside Gary Lineker and Andy Peters which coincided with the 34th anniversary of the organisation.

Blur won several *NME* Brat awards and shared the limelight uncomfortably with Oasis, and then played a short but blistering three-song set at The Forum for the corresponding live show. Damon also made a special guest appearance with The Pretenders at an acoustic show in London, joining Chrissie Hynde on piano for a version of Ray Davies 'I Go To Sleep', and even edited the *NME* for a week. Absolute fame and fortune were finally guaranteed with a cartoon series on Blur in the *News Of The World* Sunday magazine, whose readership was over 11 million. Although a little factually incorrect, the captions were hilarious: "Four lads from Essex, unheard of a year ago, have blown pop apart to become Britain's hottest band. Blur have catapulted to instant stardom." For Damon and his band, 1995 had begun as 1994 ended – how would it progress?

★ ★ ★

The new campaign started brilliantly with Britpop's finest hour, Blur's 27,000 seat show at Mile End stadium in London's East End on Saturday June 17. First, an amazingly shambolic warm up date at Camden's Dublin Castle was played, arguably the smallest London venue on the circuit. Understandably, due to the size of the gig, and the fact it was Blur's first UK show since selling out 7,000 tickets at the Ally Pally, the 200 or so tickets were in ridiculous demand and secrecy was paramount. Despite having been regular giggers at the trendy Camden Falcon, Blur had never actually played the minute Dublin Castle, and found that the small size and bad PA meant the show had to revolve around the more savage punky numbers, although two new numbers were also aired, namely 'Globe Alone' and 'Stereotypes'. Regardless of the technical difficulties, it was an extraordinary event, one of Britain's biggest bands playing one of the country's smallest venues.

It was all a far cry from the massive shows they were now used to playing, and for that reason the band loved it. Several celebrities were in attendance, including Elastica, Pulp and Menswear (who claimed listening to Blur had made them form a band in the first place – they later recorded a spoof western track called '26 Years' especially for Graham's birthday).

The day of the Mile End gig finally arrived and so did the summer rain. It was a grey, windy and overcast East End that greeted the thousands of Blur fans, but this did nothing to dampen the spirits. Outside the venue, fears were expressed about a large gathering of skinheads and Hells Angels who were congregating ominously, but nothing unsavoury transpired. Inside the stadium, the cast of pop celebrities was endless, and even Prince Edward was rumoured to be in attendance. The excellent Shanakies opened the show (featuring Eddie Deedigan from Damon's school days) and made life difficult for a drab Cardiacs, whose set paled in comparison to the hard guitar driven music of the openers. After that, Dodgy confirmed their place amongst the country's finest bands, after years of being outsiders, then the newly fashionable Sparks played their quirky electro pop to mixed responses. Neither they nor the Cardiacs seemed entirely appropriate for the day. There were no such reservations when The Boo Radleys took to the stage – in the past they had played their fair share of awful live shows, but now the songs that gave them a No.1 album with *Wake Up Boo* were greeted wildly, and whetted the crowd's appetite for the show to come.

Red flares signalled the start of the second half of the show, but the double decker bus which Blur were rumoured to be driving on stage in never appeared. Instead, Damon entered in a blonde wig and a fake pot belly for the opening 'Tracy Jacks', set against the backdrop of giant hamburgers, neon lights and video screens. Only three new tracks were aired, the two from the Dublin Castle show and a third one called 'Country House', but despite the scarcity of new material, no-one minded. This was Blur's moment, the peak of their career perhaps, and nothing could take that away from them. When Phil Daniels emerged from a box marked 'Daniels' to perform yet another 'last ever' rendition of 'Parklife', the cheers were almost painfully loud. The encore of 'Daisy Daisy, Give Me Your Answer Do' and then 'This Is A Low' capped what was a generation defining performance.

As if to confirm their ability to perform on this level, Blur supported REM at the massive Milton Keynes Bowl in late July. Blur flew in by helicopter, and despite initial reservations about these style of shows, they performed well and seemed comfortable with the huge surroundings. Doubts that their quirky English soundscapes would translate to a stage that often demanded bland sloganeering proved groundless, although the jingo-istic chants of "Enger-land" that worryingly followed Blur everywhere were again present. This was very much REM's gig, and hardly America's finest being challenged by Britain's champions, (as some said Damon wanted it to be), but nevertheless it confirmed the arena-filling potential that had first been seen at Mile End.

One criticism of Blur at this time was that they were manipulating the working-class for their own gain, by focussing and mimicking their lifestyles. The subject of class had plagued Blur almost since their inception. Many writers derided them as middle-class softies toying with working-class imagery. The band's further education (even though they attended comprehensive *not* private schools) and particularly Damon's fascination with literature were seen as a sign that any sense of working-class in Blur is purely fake. Damon claimed to have never read a rock biography and instead hailed many literary greats. He thanked Herman Hesse, Lobsang Rampas and D. H. Lawrence on the sleeve notes for *Leisure*. He paraphrased Beckett in 'Repetition'. Even their T-shirts, often the reserve of 'fuck you' statements, were emblazoned with book covers of classics like 'The Thin Man'. Despite performing poorly in his 'A' levels, Damon was quickly picked up as a pop intellectual and his own comments reinforced this view: "Herman Hesse was the first writer who actually had any effect on me. He was always trying to define a spirituality but at the same he stayed clear of any sex or dogma. He was one of the first urban pagans." For *Modern Life Is Rubbish* Damon cited Douglas Coupland's *Generation X* as his key inspiration and, as mentioned, he went on to revere Martin Amis' *London Fields* novel for *Parklife*.

Despite this intellectualism, they played gigs in the East End, they drew on Music Hall as an influence and Damon openly exaggerated his accent for dramatic affect. For many, this was like The Rolling Stones, middle-class boys who convinced the world they were East End yobs, when arguably all they were really doing was feigning a working-class persona. To some, Damon would never be a real lad, real working-class, a real 1960s beat musician nor a real East-ender.

However, this angle was rather tiresome. Damon had readily admitted he was fascinated by working-class lives, but claimed that his work was much wider than that – he felt that the broader focus of *Parklife* was often missed: "Not all the characters are bloody working-class, the majority of that record concerns itself with the worst things I hate about middle-class people. The only real references to working-class culture are the cover of the album, the greyhounds, but too much has been made of that image." At the

Mile End show he said, "I'd better make sure I haven't got a Cockney accent 'cos I'm not allowed." He later dismissed the issue as tedious: "There was a time when any pop star who even admitted to enjoying books was dismissed as a middle-class twat. They've virtually given up calling me that because I have actually admitted "Yes, I am a middle-class twat!"

★ ★ ★

Blur had been working on their new album since late 1994, and by the New Year they had thirty songs in demo form. This created problems in itself, as they had to constantly switch from writing the new work to promoting the still-active *Parklife*. In keeping with their ceaseless work ethic, this third album in three years was completed ahead of schedule, recording at a consistent rate of three songs per week. Alex explained: "There's no mystery why we've got better, we just work hard. Very few bands work as hard as we do, and if you work very hard you will get better. I don't think it's about being clever. Academic cleverness doesn't really come into pop music." Stephen Street agreed, as he told *Mojo*: "They are incredibly prolific. All the great acts have gone through a period of intense creativity, like Bowie in the early RCA years and The Smiths who produced a load of great singles as well as albums." One major benefit of this prolific nature is that Blur's B-sides always offered interesting diversions from the lead track – 'Peach' (from the 'For Tomorrow' single) is just one of many examples of a flip side track that was easily strong enough to released as a single in its own right.

Deciding which tracks finally made it on to the fourth album was difficult – deciding the first single was a lot easier. The response to 'Country House' at Mile End had been overwhelming, so it immediately usurped 'Stereotypes' as the first recorded taste of the new album. It was a jaunty pop song with superb musicality and a dark side that made it a stand-out, addictive Blur single. The multi-layered nature of the song contrasted the pop sensibility and the darker lyrical sub-text. The scene was set in a country mansion Damon had visited in Suffolk as a child, and concerned an escapee from the rat race who survives on Prozac and panic attacks – twelve months ago this could easily have been Damon. Its obvious mass appeal also made it a perfect contender to follow up the huge success that had been *Parklife*.

Unfortunately, the considerable musical merits of the new single were lost amongst the furore that erupted when Oasis's single 'Roll With It' was released simultaneously on August 14, creating what was dubbed 'The Battle of Britain'. With a seemingly endless supply of classic pop singles and a smash debut album, Oasis had won popular approval at a startling rate. Add to that their boozy, drugged excess and the Gallagher brothers volatile relationship and Britain was captivated. Glastonbury headline slots and three No.1 singles were accomplished with swaggering Mancunian ease and arrogance. When Oasis released their first single 'Supersonic', Blur were preparing to release their all-conquering *Parklife* album – now the Mancunian band were a very serious threat to Blur's British music supremacy.

Their relationship with Blur had started off well, with Damon championing their cause several times, but things had soon started to turn sour. In The Good Mixer one night, Liam spotted Graham and harangued him so much he was thrown out – the ceaseless berating later continued in The Underworld Club. At an autumn 1994 radio interview in San Francisco, both bands were booked at a conniving radio station at the same time, and the only greetings that were exchanged were "Wanker" and "Geezer". Liam had initially said "Blur are a top band", but at the Brat Awards photo sessions he refused to be snapped alongside Damon. Although Noel gladly took part, Liam was later incensed when Graham sneaked a kiss on his cheek, and from that moment on the two parties were at each other's throats. Noel retracted his earlier praise of Blur, saying he had been out of his head on drugs at the time. So when it was announced that both bands were to release their new singles from new albums on the same day, the battle commenced.

The battle, like Britpop itself, was gleefully fuelled by the media. The bands had to take a large portion of blame, because they didn't have to take part, they could have changed release dates. Opposing sides claim the others caused the fight, and the truth will probably never be known. Damon later said he had called the clash after Liam was abusive to him at a celebration party for Oasis' No.1 single 'Some Might Say'. So the rough Northerners with a belt full of

No.1 singles but less musical acclaim lined up opposite the art school Londoners with a No.1 album and a cupboard full of awards, but no No.1 single. Some said it was the biggest battle since the days of The Beatles and The Rolling Stones, but these two legends had in fact staggered their releases for mutual benefit – despite the huge volume of singles both bands put out they did not clash. The Clash and The Sex Pistols, and The Stone Roses and The Happy Mondays were always plagued by rumours of rivalry, but nothing from those periods eclipsed this.

Blur seemed more equipped for battle than Oasis. They had brilliant fake estate agents boards pronouncing 'For Sale: Country House. Enquire Within" erected outside London record shops. When Damon appeared on Chris Evans' Radio 1 morning show, he sang Status Quo's 'Rockin' All Over The World' over the lead line of Oasis's track, and christened them Oasis Quo. Even in the single's lyrics, Damon made a sly reference to Oasis's forthcoming album title *(What's The Story) Morning Glory?* Also, Blur's formatting was more astute, with live versions of Mile End tracks being available on alternative CDs, causing many people to buy two singles, whereas Oasis could only offer £1 off. Damon was also anxious to remind the public who had been around the longest, as he told *Melody Maker* "As far as I can see, Oasis have everything to gain and nothing to lose. Everything for them is just a bonus now, they're a household name now and I don't think they were before."

Blur's video was far more entertaining than Oasis's rather dry black and white performance footage. Damien Hirst, the acclaimed Turner Prize winning artist, directed what was a bizarre Benny Hill-on-acid-style promo, complete with busty Page Three girls, surreal board game and general cavorting and titillation. Hirst had attended Goldsmiths with Alex and Graham and had even considered managing Blur after seeing them perform at a college exhibition where he was showing his latest piece of art, a cupboard full of medicine. He had not really noticed their success until bumping into them at the celebrity haunt The Groucho Club one night and realising he went to school with them. The sexual overtones and tabloid nature of this video perfectly fitted the nature of the week's mayhem and received considerably more air play than Oasis's offering.

Oasis meanwhile were playing the 'We're so hard we'll be No.1' card. They had opened the stakes by premiering their single at Glastonbury to 100,000 people, but after that they were less direct. Less flashy videos, less subtle media manipulation and decidedly less subtle soundbites – Noel said to one paper, "Blur are a bunch of middle-class wankers trying to play hardball with a bunch of working-class heroes." For the whole week they were touring Japan as well, which put them at a distinct disadvantage. Still, they had a massive database of 130,000 fans and had already achieved the No.1 spot, unlike Blur.

Both bands were shocked by the media hysteria that took hold the week of release. Despite continued atrocities in Bosnia, VJ Day and Mike Tyson's release from prison, all the tabloids were involved with *The Daily Sport* producing the best headline of "Blur Job". All the major television stations also joined in, with even the *Six O'Clock News* running a feature. Magazines as far away as Brazil were phoning up to get the latest, and bookies reported brisk business on the outcome.

It rapidly became a wider issue than just the music. According to some, this was North vs South, middle-class vs working-class, rock vs pop, intelligence vs brawn. It was also EMI vs Parlophone, Food vs Creation, even one press agent against another. Tabloids battled for scoops with 0891 phone-ins, and the resulting haste produced much misinformation, including one hilariously erroneous story about mods against rockers.

All week it was neck and neck, with contrasting reports from media sources and record shops claiming first one band then the other were in front. Blur hastily retreated from the Pandora's box they had opened – Damon was on holiday with his parents in Mauritius. Dave had been okay at first but as the week progressed he couldn't sleep, so he flew to France with his wife. Graham went AWOL for the week. He hated the whole ludicrous affair, and even thought about buying 300 copies of each single to sabotage the contest. He later told *NME*, "I went into a state of shock and I don't think I got out of it. It's a circle of freaks and I don't want to be involved in it." Only Alex seemed more than happy to stay at home and watch the spectacle. Despite withdrawing from the frenzy, Blur were by now desperate to win. Damon told *The Face*, "If

I come back on Sunday and we're not No.1 someone is going to suffer some sort of grievous bodily harm. We haven't had a No.1, and they wouldn't have if we hadn't got the ball rolling in the first place. We exhumed the corpse of pop music."

Damon needn't have worried – when the charts were announced on Sunday evening, 'Country House' hit No.1, with Oasis straight in at No.2. Records sales had hit their highest peak for ten years, and of the 1.8 million singles sold, nearly 500,000 were from these two bands. Blur outsold Oasis's 220,000 by 22%, some 270,000. The Battle Of Britain had taken over so much that Britain's biggest selling pop band, Take That, was easily dethroned, and Madonna's new single went virtually unnoticed. Blur's triumph was reinforced by also hitting No.1 in Ireland, Belgium and Portugal.

Obviously Blur were delighted. Dave misleadingly said, "I never had the slightest doubt that we were gonna get to No.1" and Damon said, "These are great times, anything's possible. Do Blur deserve it? Of course we do." The truth is there was great relief in the Blur camp. *Parklife* had been such a huge success that it needed something on this scale to upstage its memory. It needed this media overkill and fictitious battle to supersede the previous album and prepare for the next long player. Graham was relieved but still unhappy, he hated the tackiness of the video and left the band's own celebration party early (he didn't even attend the EMI party for his group). Blur were graceful in victory, with Alex wearing an Oasis T-shirt for their triumphant *Top of the Pops* appearance, of which he told *NME*, "It was a magnanimous gesture. I think that they are a great band and that this is the defining moment of Britpop. It's not Blur vs Oasis, it's Blur and Oasis vs the world." For this performance, Dave had other issues on his mind, namely Prince's claim that he was a 'slave' to Warner Brothers (after all, he was only worth $100 million). Dave painted his first name on his cheek in mockery and said: "I was considering writing 'wanka' on my face but it wouldn't fit. I have changed my name to the Drummer Formally Known As Dave. I did it because Karen at the record company told me to. Me and Prince have got a lot in common – EMI won't release my solo album either."

The media scam that the battle had become was highlighted by the lack of animosity between rival fans and the fact that many people bought both singles. Whether it was a scam or not is irrelevant – everyone won, the bands, the press, the record shops, the record companies, it was a very positive event, however superficial. And in a year dominated by the pop anti-christs of Robson & Jerome, few would argue.

Noel Gallagher was devastated he hadn't achieved his long time ambition of beating his hero Paul Weller's record of four No.1 singles. The Oasis camp claimed they had experienced bar code problems, leaving thousands of sales unregistered – this smelt of sour grapes, but Oasis would not be down for long. With Blur now reigning apparently unchallenged at the top of the charts, many observers felt they could now go on to even greater success by winning the album war, whilst Oasis' more one dimensional guitar pop would suffer badly from having lost. They could not have been more wrong.

* * *

"The best record you can make is recorded on Monday, cut on Tuesday, pressed on Wednesday, packaged on Thursday, distributed on Friday and in the shops on Saturday." So said John Lennon, and it was this ultimate punk ethic that was used for the War Child charity album, *Help,* released in early September. Blur joined the likes of Paul McCartney, Oasis, Paul Weller, Radiohead and Suede to contribute to the album for the Bosnian appeal to raise funds for medical supplies, food and social help for the children of the conflict. Blur's contribution was recorded during tour dates in Milan, and was originally titled 'I Hope You Find Your Suburbs' but later changed to 'Eine Kleine Lift Muzak'. The album sold massively but because of ludicrous rules concerning compilation records, it was refused a position in the main album chart.

At this point, Blur were busy preparing for the release of the new album. They played the Feile festival in Cork, coming on after The Beautiful South and M People, an impressive indication of their ever-growing status. The Oasis war of words also accelerated in advance of their two respective album releases. Liam claimed that he thought Justine actually fancied a bit of rough with him, and that he was setting out to get her, although Justine seemed to disagree.

Damon at a Residential Orchestra course, Wicken House, Essex, 1982.
Photo courtesy of Nigel Hildreth

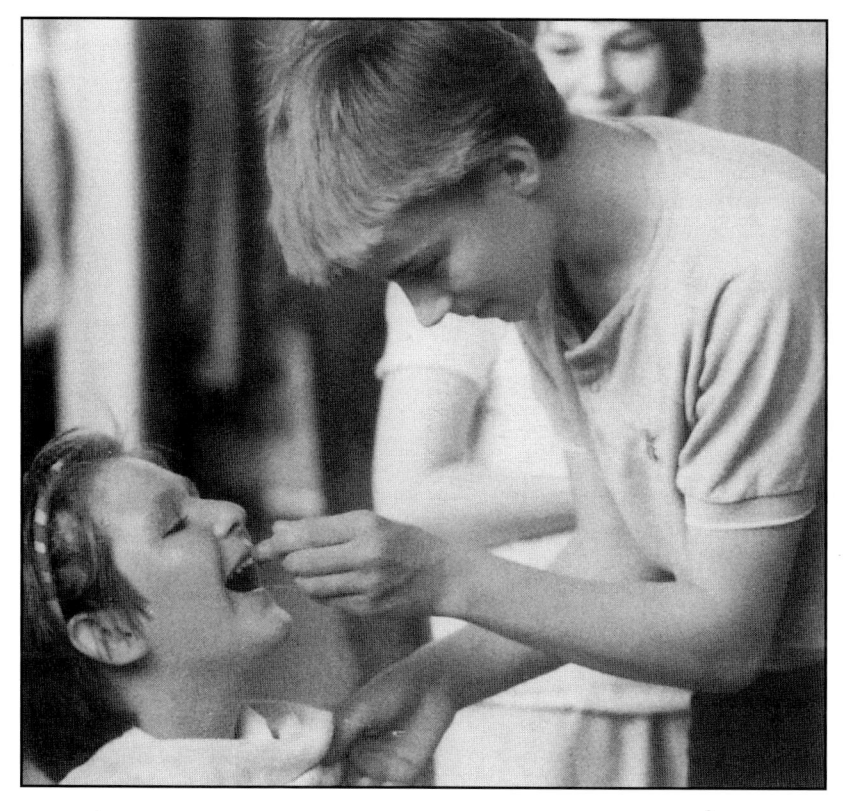

Damon helping with make-up for *Joseph & His Amazing Technicolour Dreamcoat*.
Photo courtesy of Nigel Hildreth

Damon as 'Bobby The Boyfriend'

Photo courtesy of Nigel Hildreth

More performances during his earlier years when drama was his first obsession.

Photo courtesy of Nigel Hildreth

The secret gig at Colchester Sixth Form College, December 1994.
Photo courtesy of Andy Roshay

The founding four outside the Dublin Castle in Camden, May, 1995.

Photo courtesy of Retna

Blur *sans* Coxon, backstage at Brixton Academy, 2003.

Photo courtesy of Sarahphotogirl/Retna

During Anti-Iraq war protests in London, November, 2003.

Photo courtesy of John Horsley/Retna

Backstage with De La Soul during *Demon Days*, the Apollo Theatre, April, 2006.

Photo courtesy of Rahav Segev/Retna

Backstage with Jaimie Hewlett at the 'Designer of the Year' Awards, 2006.
Photo courtesy of Pete Mariner/Retna

Artwork for the launch of *Monkey* and Manchester International Festival, 2007.
Photo courtesy of Fiera Fyles/Retna

The Good, The Bad And The Queen, live at The Tower of London, July, 2007.

Photograph courtesy of Pete Mariner/Retna

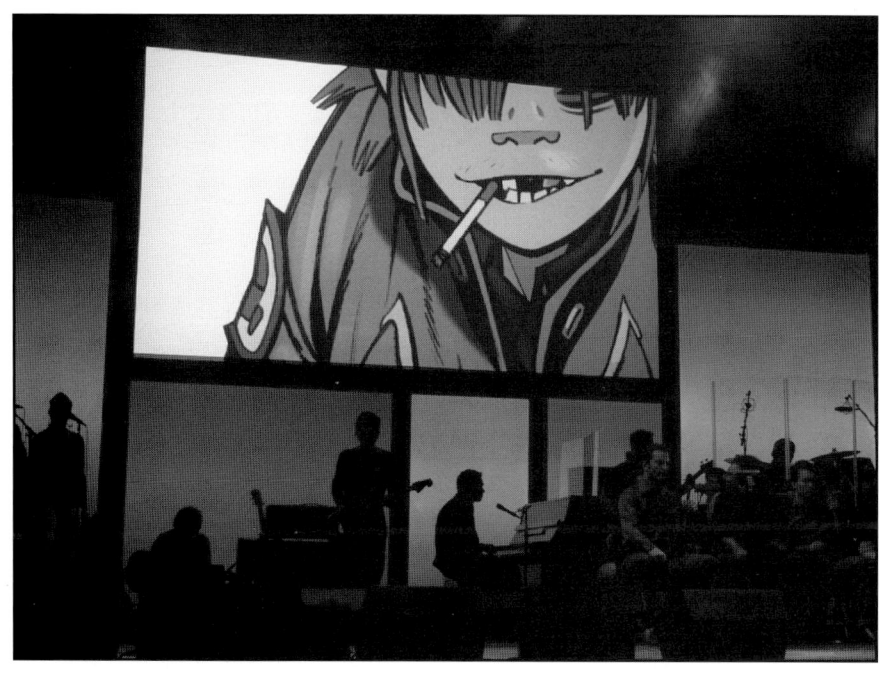

The Gorillaz live on stage, forever shrouded in mystery.

Photograph courtesy of Retna

Damon Albarn, music hall, piano, full circle, March 2007.

Photo courtesy of Karin Albinsson

Unfortunately, the whole rivalry reached a pitiful nadir when Noel told *The Observer* magazine that he hoped "Alex and Damon caught AIDS and died." Outrage and anger ensued, and Andy Ross of Food Records said, "This is supposed to be the clever one talking." Eventually Noel was forced to write an apology, in which he said "Although not being a fan of their music, I wish both Damon and Alex a long and healthy life." Some said that on top of the singles defeat, this comment would maybe kill Oasis, in the same way The Happy Mondays homophobic comments in their heyday had hastened their own demise. For Damon, the situation was out of hand, as he told *Melody Maker*, "When the whole thing started with them, it was quite fun. Prior to the whole thing we got on quite well, there was the sense that things were going great for both bands. Now the whole war of words has just left me sad, it just got so ugly." The media would not let go, however, and continued to bait both bands, even though the personal venom between them had already dissipated. Ric Blaxill of *Top of the Pops* gave a telling insight into the Oasis/Blur war when they both appeared on his show in early 1996: "One of the finest recent performances on the show was Blur's 'Stereotypes', just before Oasis went onstage for their two numbers. For the whole song Liam was dancing along in the crowd, he was really enjoying himself. Afterwards in the bar he and Damon were chatting away merrily, they certainly weren't going at each others' throats. Both bands seemed to get on very well."

CHAPTER 11
BEST DAYS

The pressure to follow up a key album like *Parklife* would have stifled and even snuffed out some bands – The Stone Roses being the prime 1990s example – but Blur were completing the writing of their new set whilst *Parklife* was still riding high in the charts. Once again, Stephen Street was in the producer's chair. Proudly, yet with typical immodesty, Damon said this of Street and his work: "In him, you have The Smiths and Blur and as far as I am concerned that's the 1980s and 1990s taken care of." Street himself was not surprised the record was done so quickly again, but in *Melody Maker* modestly played down his part in the process: "They give you so much good material in the first place, you'd have to be a complete moron to bugger up the production on a Blur album."

With the release of Blur's fourth album, *The Great Escape*, which completed the trilogy of records on this theme, it seemed that the world would now be at their feet. Eventually the proposed title of *Sex Life* had to make way for *The Great Escape,* as the band could not think of a better title with the word 'life' in it. Structurally and musically it was another superb record, despite the popular misconception that it was only a modest commercial success and despite Damon's later public distaste and disregard for it.

Released on September 11, 1995, *The Great Escape* was a highly detailed, multi-faceted album which took a more cosmopolitan angle on the odd, suburban dystopia of the previous two records. Unlike the dog track stylings of *Parklife's* artwork, the band were now cast as young City types on the make, plotting their fortunes with an eye on the exit to a quieter life. Musically, the record was Graham's masterpiece and Street loudly declared him to be on a par with Johnny Marr. Apart from using five guitars on the record, Graham also played baritone saxophone, soprano sax, banjo, acoustic guitar and contributed many backing vocals. He swayed from the insistent, XTC-esque stabs that opened 'Stereotypes' to the punk pop of 'Charmless Man' or the aggressive 'Globe Alone', and the string backing for the elegant 'The Universal'. Even on 'Country House', which was superficially a straight-forward pop song (albeit one tainted by the Blur vs Oasis battle), Graham's dexterous textures gave the track great depth and colour. Perhaps most fascinating was his ability to do so with minimalist simplicity, making what he missed out as important as what he put in. Alex's bass was impressive too – his odd, lazy rhythms were highly visible on 'Fade Away', 'Country House' and perhaps best on 'It Could Be You'. Alex also championed the beautiful 'The Universal' which had been around at the time of *Parklife*, in a poor reggae/calypso form, but now reappeared as a lush, sad ode. Dave proved to be a living metronome again, with faster rolls, more dynamics and more variation than on previous Blur records. This was vital since the sonic variety and sheer detail of the record demanded a rigid and absolutely perfect rhythm section.

The Great Escape was chock full of odd sounds, taking it way beyond the range of traditional pop. 'Ernold Same' featured Mayor of London Ken Livingstone – then merely a Member of Parliament – droning on about the rat race, with noises from the Goldhawk Road and the local swimming baths doubling up as a train station. Odd whirling organs flew all across the record, with special note on 'Stereotypes' and 'Mr Robinson's Quango'. 'Fade Away' was eerie and melancholic with downbeat trombones creating the weariness of a dying marriage. 'He Thought Of Cars', although rather cluttered, is a sad and desperate tale filled with painful guitars and quirky organs. 'Top Man' has comically deep backing vocals mixed with happy whistling, whilst 'Best Days' has contrasting android backing vocals. On 'Yuko And Hiro' the Casio-tones and muzak instruments take over completely, with this electronic lament full of fizzy space sounds. Generally, this was a more programmed album than any previous work by Blur, and the musical textures far surpassed even the broad palette of *Parklife*.

The influences were still there. The Specials were clearly important to 'Fade Away' and Damon readily admitted that 'Top

Man' was a direct result of his recent writing work with Terry Hall. Madness were still visible in the piano use, and The Style Council's 'Life At A Top People's Health Farm' mirrored 'Country House'. The sonic experimentation reminded the listener more of Sparks, Wire, Brian Eno, Kraftwerk and the aforementioned XTC rather than The Kinks or The Small Faces; it was all far more electronic than Davies, Weller, Marriott *et al* could ever be. Generally, this was a far less derivative record than its predecessor, with the Blur sound now being something established in its own right, without the need to refer elsewhere.

The 'Stereotypes' and 'Country House' tracks were misleading in that they were typical Blur-by-numbers – 'Country House' was, thankfully, the only concession to the knees-up mentality that had featured so heavily on *Parklife*. Elsewhere they were producing music that had hardly been hinted at before, even so late as *Parklife*. Blur's minute attention to detail throughout the record layered tune upon tune and these multi-dimensions demanded the most from Damon (and Graham's) long-established composition skills. Somehow, they managed to keep the complex mass of ideas simple and direct.

Lyrically, many tracks pursued Damon's characteristic third person voyeurism. Most of the lyrics were written on the roof top balcony of the house in west London he shared with Justine, and with the pressure of *Parklife*, he found this task harder than any other on the album project. The new characters were similarly disenchanted types, but more sexually active and deviant than on *Parklife*. 'Mr Robinson's Quango' was a tragi-comedy about a council worker who dressed in stockings and suspenders under his suit, inspired by a graffiti confession Damon once read on a train station toilet door. 'Stereotypes' hailed the pleasures of wife-swapping and 'Entertain Me' (originally titled 'Bored Wives') details a bored middle-aged man looking for relief by flagellation. 'Yuko And Hiro' tells of an over-worked Japanese employee struggling to control his life and dreaming about the girlfriend he never sees (a thinly veiled autobiographical song as Damon and Justine only saw each other for three weeks in 1995; they even split up temporarily over the Christmas period). There's little doubt that 'Country House' was about Dave Balfe, the ex-Food Records partner who had since sold Food to EMI. Elsewhere there was talk of pointless marriages, friendless spongers, Prozac addicted executives, the futility of the Lottery, boy racers, and even a character called Dan Abnormal. This was an anagram of Damon Albarn which Justine had thought of to poke fun at her boyfriend, and he used it in a vaguely self-mocking wander around the dull shopping arcades of life. There was also a focus outside of just Britain – from the country houses of rural England to the factories of Japan, this was Blur looking further afield. Even so, the characters were still desperate to make their own great escape, from the boredom, the mundanity and the dissatisfaction of life.

Damon was still singing in his Thames Estuary vowels, but on 'The Universal' he showed that his voice was now genuinely capable of sublime ballads, singing from his boots with an Anthony Newley air. Elsewhere, his accent was occasionally a little strained but, in the context of the subject matter, oddly fitting.

It was a complex, sumptuously layered, and sonically complicated album, frequently eclectic, quirky, odd, queer, harsh and strange. It was also Blur's most accomplished album so far, including *Parklife*. Damon himself told *Mojo*: "We've always seen ourselves as putting on white coats and going into the lab," when he spoke of the attitude to recording the album. And it showed. He also spoke of their motivations to work harder when he told *NME*, "The pressures were strange. I've never had that thing about fame and making money. I just wanted to make something that I thought was good because I knew the attention this album would get."

Admittedly, *The Great Escape* is far less immediate than *Parklife*. Indeed, many people found it too hard listening, too labyrinthine, too complicated. However, that was its beauty. Where *Parklife* had opted for easier targets, the cheap laughs of the sing-alongs, pub stomps, pure pop and softer instrumentation, *The Great Escape* was musically far more ambitious. It reached for weirder sounds and textures and repeatedly sacrificed the obvious for the unusual. It was not crammed with hit singles granted, but that should never be the sole criteria for a classic album. In the context of following up *Parklife*, Blur should defy any of their peers to better *The Great Escape*. Stephen Street told *Music Week*, 'It is a step on from *Parklife*, but it won't alienate anybody who got into Blur with it. It's a bit darker but I think that's the only way for us to go.' Johnny Cigarettes in *NME* was more direct: 'We can only demand a masterpiece, and they've damn near delivered it.' Now all that remained was to see if the public agreed.

★ ★ ★

Initially, the response to the release was superb – the album went straight in at No.1 in the charts in the UK, and also in Iceland and Hong Kong, whilst across Europe it achieved Top 5 spots in most territories. By the end of October, less than two months after release, it had already passed one million sales worldwide. Reviews in the UK were generally very strong and platinum status was earned by the third week of October. When Blur announced a seaside tour of unusual venues, followed by their biggest ever arena tour, all tickets were sold out in hours.

With typical Blur panache, they performed two promotional events in the two weeks after the album release that just reinforced the void between the linear style of so many of their contemporaries and their own colourful approach. Firstly, on September 15, they played on top of the roof of the HMV shop in Oxford Street in London. Accompanied by a four-man brass section, Blur played for twenty minutes whilst huge crowds gathered below, mimicking the last time this had happened for Echo & The Bunnymen in the mid-1980s. At one point Damon dangled the microphone down to the crowd to sing along, then he later risked death by skipping along the edge of the roof, whilst his record company bosses went into apoplexy below. Five tracks from the new album were played, then the spectacle finished off with 'Parklife'.

The second clever event was to play a live daytime Radio 1 show at BBC Broadcasting House, prestigious treatment not even afforded to The Smiths or The Stone Roses. To a hall filled largely with journalists, Blur played a blistering set from the album, then once off-air launched into a punk rock set that ruffled a few of the mainstream feathers in attendance. Both these events were typical of the style with which Blur promoted themselves during this period – the live radio, the unexpected secret shows, the forthcoming seaside dates, the 'Country House For Sale' boards, even their band logo and adverts (a map of the East End for their Mile End show) had a style and creativity that others lacked.

The success continued when the second single from the album, 'The Universal' was released in November to coincide with the various live dates – it was considered to be a genuine contender for Christmas No.1, especially with the two new songs 'Ultranol' and 'In Me' included. The festive top spot eventually went to Michael Jackson's 'Earth Song', with Mike Flowers Pops cover of Oasis's 'Wonderwall' a close second, and 'The Universal' reaching No.5. Blur's superb ballad was accompanied by a sinister *Clockwork Orange* video that went some way to banishing the growing embarrassment felt at the cleavage-heavy 'Country House' promo, which was now seen as a mistake. The reservations would eventually run much deeper. History, those around the band and even Damon himself, would not be kind to *The Great Escape*. Damon would even later use the album as an example of how *not* to do it and even his other half would be damning about it, seeing it as a signal to all concerned with the scene that things had to change. "In a musical sense, it seemed like all the good intentions had gone awry, very quickly." Justine Frischmann told *The Observer* when asked about the period some seven years later. "I thought [it] was a really, truly awful album – so cheesy, like a parody of *Parklife*, but without the balls or the intellect."

For now, however, all seemed well. Blur continued their British fascination by playing a small tour of eight run-down coastal venues that hadn't been used on this level since the bingo heydays of the 1950s. The gigs included in this supposedly low-key (less than 1000) series of shows included Pier 39 in Cleethorpes, Eastbourne Floral Hall and Great Yarmouth Ocean Rooms. The idea was to offer an intimate and highly unusual show for the fans whilst providing Blur with an excellent warm-up for their forthcoming nationwide arena tour. Starting in Cleethorpes, the tour made its way around the coastline, cramming creaking old venues to bulging point with great success. The frequently poor sound systems didn't seem to affect the celebratory atmosphere at these shows, and the horn section and additional keyboard player augmented Blur's sound still further.

However, the problem came when the band were nearing Bournemouth. Oasis had originally been booked to play the same night, and there was great excitement at the prospect of another great battle. Unfortunately, some took this a little too literally and there were soon rumours of marauding Oasis fans planing to ruck with Blur supporters, whose ranks were apparently going to be swelled by scores of Wolverhampton thugs down for the fight. The situation could have been very nasty, and Oasis and Blur's offices swapped worried phone calls in search of a solution, their concern fuelled by the police's refusal to put extra officers on duty. Eventually Oasis were forced to change their date and were furious at Blur's intransigence. Blur were disappointed for slightly more trivial reasons. They had planned to shine their logo Batman-like on the walls of Oasis's venue, and even hoped to have a huge inflatable 'No.1' floating in the sky above. At least the whole 'Blur vs Oasis' thing never got *childish,* eh? With the 20/20 power of hindsight, even Alex James admits that pop rivalry will never again reach such heights of silliness: "It's hard to imagine the whole country getting galvanised by two bands calling each other wankers," he told *Red* magazine in 2007. "I often wonder if that was pop music's last great hurrah."

During this winter schedule, Blur signed copies of their official *Blurbook* photo collection at Books etc in Charing Cross Road on November 14. Over 2000 kids queued for up to nine hours, but only about 750 books were signed as Blur had to rush across town for another appearance on *Later With Jools Holland.* The period was so busy that a proposed long-form video entitled *B Roads* had to be postponed from its original December 1995 release date until spring 1996, by which time it would include all of their world tour. The tour footage will be complemented by interviews with road protesters, a one-off Blur show for Eastbourne pensioners, 'kinky' housewives and international storyteller Taffy Thomas.

By the time these cleverly selected seaside dates were complete, Blur's planned arena tour had swelled to fourteen dates. Two additional Wembley Arena dates meant that by Christmas Blur would have played to over 180,000 on this leg of the tour alone. At one stage the media were suggesting that Blur should play Wembley Stadium, although the band made a statement distancing themselves from this spiral of bigger and bigger concerts, with Damon saying: "Wembley Stadium is for wankers! That's my last word."

Damon felt that Blur were ideal for the arena stages as he told *NME*: "We made the step up at Mile End, that was the best gig we've ever done. These shows will be like that, except they're indoors so it won't rain. We feel quite comfortable in those venues, they seem quite intimate to us." The stage set itself was an amusement arcade right from one of the seaside venues they had just played, complete with flashing lights, silver disco balls, and neon decorations. During 'The Universal', a giant Prozac tablet was lowered from the ceiling and opened to shower the audience with thousands of fake tiny pills. To coincide with the resurgence of easy listening, Blur were supported by an unnamed MOR orchestra (whose members changed each night) who played fantastic cover versions of songs by Pulp, Oasis and Supergrass amongst others. With the fuller stage personnel, the renditions of mostly *Parklife* and *Great Escape* material were impressively accurate. Damon took to the bigger stage with consummate ease, using all his acting abilities to provide pure theatre to match the musical excellence. The best night was reserved for Wembley Arena's last show, when they were joined on stage by Ken Livingstone for 'Ernold Same' and Phil Daniels for (yet another) last-ever performance of 'Parklife', where both he and Damon dressed up in full pantomime regalia for that added Christmas feel.

The mellower band was now living more healthy lives on tour and this showed in their vibrant performances. A vegetarian Damon was into jogging, and all of them except Alex were taught Tae Kwon Do before each gig. Alex saved his energy for the bottle of champagne he sipped on stage at each show. Also, the band rule of 'no drinks thirty minutes before a show' was now firmly established. Blur also seemed much more mature personally, as Damon told *Melody Maker:* "It's that sense of everything being normal and levelling out that's changed us. I used to spend so much time thinking the whole world revolved around me, that I was destined for great things, but not anymore." He publicly declared that he regretted things he had said about Suede and felt they were under-rated and mistreated by the press. Even his normally arrogant statements were now injected with a dash of humour. "By 1999 we will be the most important band in the world ... and also the moon.

And maybe Mars." Despite this far more laid back approach, the new Blur couldn't always be on their best behaviour – one top London hotel banned them after riotous, drunken behaviour left one guest fuming. "Nobody in the place knew who they were and they were just scruffy and noisy."

This arena tour confirmed that Blur were now mega-stars in the UK, capable of filling the nation's biggest sheds and playing a two-hour set full of classics. The presence of both the teenage front rows to the thirty- and forty-somethings at the back – and the spread of reviews for each show – confirmed the absolute cross-over the band had made between teen/alternative/mainstream media. Even John 'Mr Spock' Redwood, one time Tory leader candidate, wrote about Blur in *The Guardian* and TV comic Harry Enfield ridiculed them in his "Oi! Albarn!" Hula Hoops advert. This was indeed sheer mass appeal.

★ ★ ★

The foreign dates for *The Great Escape* were lengthy and comprehensive. Starting with a few gigs in America, they moved on through Europe to Japan, then back to Britain for the Christmas shows, then Brazil for a one-off festival and finally back to America and Europe, finishing at Amsterdam's Paridiso Club on March 22, 1996. This policy paid rich dividends in Europe, with *The Great Escape* being better received than any previous Blur album. Although people had as much difficulty relating to Blur's peculiar Englishness on the Continent as they did in America, they seemed more willing to try. In fact, sales were so high in southern Europe that each gig was sold out in advance to an average crowd of 9000 people.

The historically difficult American dates were marred right at the start when Damon was threatened at gun point. He and Alex were in a car heading for The Black Cat club in Washington DC when the singer gave the beady eye to a passing car. This was something he had always done – *Melody Maker* used to run a feature called 'Each Week Damon From Blur Causes The Rest Of The Band To Have Seven Shades Of Shit Beaten Out Of Them.' Unfortunately in American, the stakes were a touch higher than in Camden – the car's occupants were fully tooled up. One man pulled his gun out, pointed it at Damon's temple and said 'Pow, pow', then the car screeched away. When Damon took to the stage later that night, four songs into the set he introduced 'Top Man' and said: "This next song is about blokes who go out getting pissed and being naughty. Until four hours ago this seemed like a hard song, but now it seems soft."

The posters for this small tour announced 'Be prepared for a shower of Evian' in the wake of Damon's previous Stateside troubles. Attendances were high, although the venues were small, and the crowds clearly knew the material well. The internet was covered in gig reviews throughout this tour and the response was ecstatic, including one site which listed "Twenty Reasons Why Blur Are The Best Band Ever" which featured 'they don't have a song about walls, and they all have two eyebrows' amongst the prime examples. Blur were now on Virgin Records (like SBK a division of multi-national EMI) and although success was still limited, the band/record company relationship was much stronger. Unfortunately, throughout the lengthy album tour, the band suffered a series of setbacks with their health, which for a change were not excess related. Graham began to suffer from repetitive strain injury on his hands, a condition which had allegedly forced Elastica's bassist Annie Holland to quit her band completely. Dave contracted gastro-enteritis before the band's Belfast King's Hall show and briefly had to go to hospital. At that evening's gig, Damon stepped on a piece of broken glass and lacerated his foot, causing him to attend the MTV award ceremony with a walking stick. Despite all these difficulties, no gigs were cancelled and Blur's momentum continued ever forward.

★ ★ ★

At this point, it's worth mentioning Blur's continued failure to crack the huge American market, and the growing sense around this supposedly triumphant time, that the band were on a downward slide. Their difficulties in the USA are well documented from the time they first set foot on that disastrous 44 date tour to the above mentioned gun incident. It seemed that Blur's habit of success in the UK simply could not be replicated across the Atlantic. History is not in their favour. Although The Beatles obviously took the States by storm, since then there have been several huge UK bands who have completely failed to translate their success. Obvious exceptions include Whitesnake, Pink Floyd, Def Leppard, freakish, short-lived triumphs by the likes of Wang Chung, Right Said Fred and Jesus Jones, and latterday triumphs by The Prodigy and, of course, Radiohead. However, several big bands from T Rex, Slade, The Jam, Madness, later the likes of Suede and Blur and more recently The Darkness have all failed in a territory that represents 40% of the world's market, making it a costly nut not to crack. What these bands have in common is a distinct fascination with their English culture and environment, and whilst America seems happy to export tales of Seattle, Broadway, Detroit, New York and so on to us – and we happily involve ourselves in it – the reverse is rarely true. Mention Primrose Hill or Camden and suddenly all interest dries up. Blur fitted into this litany of great British bands who struggled in America, and in many senses were doomed to fail unless their central themes changed. For example, David Bowie had won a small Stateside following for his gender bending, space age early material, but he did not really cross over into the mainstream until his 1975 album *Young Americans* album. Like Marie Lloyd's Music Hall shows, in America playing to the gallery can really pay dividends.

Another problem is that British bands often do not tour long enough – The Cranberries had to tour for twelve months before eventually cracking the market on a massive scale – and they are Irish. Bush, a British band who have enjoyed great Stateside success actually based themselves over there for the same reason. For *The Great Escape*, Blur toured three times, but each series of dates was only a month long. Other British bands openly mock the country when they arrive – Suede infamously derided the States on their debut tour there and were sent packing pretty quickly, complete with a change of name. Brett's sexual dalliances and gender bending was just not acceptable to America, and his apparent distaste for the US made this worse. Damon frequently and aggressively said America owed Blur a chance, and coupled this with vicious public criticism of their culture: "I just feel physically unwell when I'm in America. I can't help that I have this Americaphobia, I just find it difficult to adapt to the scale." Many Americans see this as tiresome whinging. With talk like that there's no way Blur would *ever* make it in the States ...?

Then there's the language barrier. Slade's colloquialised titles such as 'Mama Weer All Crazee Now' were hardly understood by people outside of the Black Country, let alone 5000 miles away. One of the more simple factors that contributed to the utter failure of *Modern Life* was the title. The word 'rubbish' is unused in American culture, and this simple semantic clash was perhaps indicative of Blur's problems. *Modern Life Is Trash* would not have been the same. Blur were not alone. Whilst Britpop bands flew the flag at home, the majority of their parochial pop was ignored in America. Only Elastica and Oasis enjoyed any sizeable success, both through heavy touring, with the latter finally reaching the *Billboard* Top 5 in early 1996 with their second album. Meanwhile, Blur's chart topping *The Great Escape* barely dented the *Billboard* Top 200 and left after only one week. *Modern Life* was so unsuccessful (a paltry 33,000 sales) that even most Blur fans over there hadn't heard of it. *Leisure* sold more than *Parklife*, but neither topped 100,000. Damon's statement that 'The only thing we have in common with Oasis is that we are both doing shit in America' turned out to be painfully incorrect. For the time being at least.

Oasis had American tastes on their side. Quirky English pop tunes do not fit easily into the MOR rock radio programming which dictates much of what succeeds there.

The Burnage boys straightforward rockaboogie is easier meat to digest. One source at Virgin Records claims that a memo was circulated to all independent radio pluggers early in 1996 to completely forget Blur and concentrate on Oasis, even going so far as to suggest that this was because Blur might not be around much longer. Even grunge was acceptable as guitar-based rock, whereas a song like Blur's 'Intermission' was unlikely to get them any attention. Older Brits such as Rod Stewart, Phil Collins and Eric Clapton have enjoyed success largely because their more recent music 'sounds American'. The best selling CD in the USA in 1994 was Ace of Base, so a parky singing about pigeons shagging had hardly got much chance.

There were, however, some positive signs on the second

American leg of the *Great Escape* dates in January and February 1996. Although record sales were still very low, the attendances at live shows was disproportionately high, with venues of 2000-3000 selling out well in advance. Also, some of their gigs were broadcast live on radio in various states. Damon was more realistic this time around when he told *Melody Maker*: "America feels good this time around, but only time will tell if it's a fad or something that's gonna make sense to people there." He was also not about to give in either, saying, "We don't like chickening out of something. It's a challenge." He also said, "It vaguely annoys me when people say we've never done anything in America – we went four months touring there with *Leisure*. We've gone there every year, we sell out 3000 venues across the country and songs like 'Girls & Boys' go Top 50.' Also, in April 1996, they played at the opening of the New York Virgin Megastore, the world's biggest record shop, and Damon was quick to point out that their venues were the same size as those played by Radiohead, a band who were already being hailed as a US success story, even before *OK Computer*.

However, it remained an uphill struggle for Blur. Mike Shea, publisher of *Alternative Press*, the most respected alternative magazine in America was quite clear about Blur's failure to translate in his home country by 1996: "'Girls & Boys' did well in the clubs but was seen over here as a novelty song, and people just never got the whole English 1960s/Kinks background. Blur's style doesn't work over here – the catchy, cute, accessible music and English themes just aren't universally accepted. Even though Blur were here first, it appears that Oasis cracked America. In the midst of all The Beatles re-issues, the mainstream rock 'n' roll fans in the US bought into Oasis, their sulking, pouting rock [was] infinitely more palatable to Americans. People [took] Oasis as the only Brit band, but that's it, they didn't want anymore. If you turned on any alternative commercial radio in 1996 you [would] hear Oasis forty times a week minimum and you'd be lucky to get Blur ten times.'

This sense of frustration in America added to a growing, nagging feeling that all was not well in the Blur camp. Some observers ridiculed their continued failure in America and this stigma was now suffocating. This was compounded by Oasis's success there and at home. Since the 'Battle Of Britain' and Noel's AIDS comment,

Oasis had ironically leapt ahead. Exactly the opposite of what everybody expected ... had happened. Their second album, *(What's The Story) Morning Glory?*, was tepidly received by the critics but paradoxically loved by the public. It sold 350,000 in its first week alone, the biggest sales since Michael Jackson's *Bad* and was the No.1 album in Britain for months. After a slow start in America, *(What's The Story) Morning Glory?* reached the Top 5 in the *Billboard* album charts, making the Gallagher brothers the pop world's most mouthy millionaires in the process. A trio of Brit awards and two nights at Earl's Court for the country's biggest ever indoor gigs confirmed that Oasis were now the biggest band in the country, despite all their personnel problems. It was an astonishing triumph.

Blur meanwhile were plagued by press rumours of a split, with many fingers pointing at Alex's growing distance from the other members of the band. He still loved the pop star life, the Groucho Club, the champagne and the fame, and there were media intimations of alleged escalating drug use. Alex himself bragged that he drank for six days solidly then had one day off to clean up. Graham told *NME* that he resented this: "I hate a lot of the things that Alex stands for. I don't want people to think it's what this band is about. All that Groucho Club bollocks and him going on about birds and boozing all the time, I hate that." He also admitted he had come to blows with Alex over this. He told one magazine the factors he thought might split the band would be "death, or if we made another *Parklife*. I don't think we could carry on if one of us left ... unless it was Alex." Damon was now so famous that in many people's eyes he *was* Blur and, inevitably, this rankled. Graham tired of the way people always assumed Damon's views were his when he told *NME*: "If he goes on about football and Page Three girls that means we all get associated with it. I hate football and hate Page Three girls, but people always want to hear Damon's opinion." With Graham unfairly tagged as 'the unofficial strangest man in pop', his frame of mind was always open to intrusive media speculation, and his drinking habits were often cited. When one journalist approached him during a quiet pint and said, "Aren't you Graham out of Blur?" he answered, "Only when I'm working." There were suggestions that Damon and Alex were also not getting on, and that Alex felt the singer and guitarist were siding against him. For his part, Damon said he was tired of the excesses of some of his friends, telling Q magazine: "There's a blizzard of cocaine and I hate it." Some even suggested that Dave was tiring of the lifestyle, and being well into his calmer 30's was finding it increasingly difficult to leave home for each tour.

Other people worried about the dilemma that Blur's massive success had created – with huge status in the UK and great success in Europe, if America continued to close its doors, what aspirations would Blur be left with? Would they risk self-parody consolidating their successful territories or alternatively release increasingly obscure music and plummet in popularity? Also, *The Great Escape* had sold well initially in the UK, but its chart life had not nearly matched *Parklife* and in a world where constant commercial improvement is vital, questions were being asked. Despite exceptional reviews in the vast majority of the press, including becoming only the second band to win two Q 'Album Of The Year' awards, the general feeling was that *The Great Escape* had slowed down Blur's success somewhat. This fuelled the split theories still more.

The spring of 1996 was full of such rumours, none of them remotely substantiated. Matters were not helped, however, with several grumpy television appearances, such as on Chris Evans' *TFI Friday* where Damon seemed bitter about their lack of success at The Brits and made derisory side remarks about Alex. For some European television shows, Dave, Alex and Graham were replaced by cardboard cut-outs, and much was made of the various reasons for these absences. It was actually all perfectly clear - Alex had booked time off and the TV show he missed was a last minute booking (he was replaced by their bass roadie, also called Alex). Dave was having his wisdom teeth removed and Graham had family commitments. Needless to say, this emerged in the press as Blur on the verge of falling apart. No way, Graham told *Melody Maker*. "I don't think there has ever been a time when we felt like giving up. Even during the dark years, we had this feeling it would all come right in the end." He also doubted that they would stand alone musically, as he told *NME*: "We can make good music together but God knows what might happen if we tried to make music individually, it'd be shit."

CHAPTER 12

"DAMON'S GONE TO ICELAND"

It was then – rather inconveniently for some but with immaculate timing for others – that someone killed Britpop. The finger of suspicion was pointed at Damon Albarn; even if he wasn't entirely guilty, he seemed more then happy to take the blame. The issue didn't appear to be a commercial one. By March 1996, *The Great Escape* had already overtaken *Parklife's* worldwide sales figures of 1.8 million, and by the start of April, the fourth album had passed the two million mark. This time around, Blur had cleaned up in Europe, an equivalent sized territory to the USA. Previously, where they'd been asked to play on European festival bills, now they were being asked to headline them. The latest single from the album, 'Stereotypes', had eased into the UK Top 10. *The Great Escape*, despite all assumptions otherwise, had far outstripped the sales of *Parklife*. But this was about something else, something different from just sales – that was last year's thing. This was a question of credibility and future prospects. The long game.

The final single from the album was 'This Charmless Man'. In the accompanying video, the band are an omnipresent annoyance to a gangsterish figure, the charmless man of the title. Damon manages to do that puppy-eyed look to the top right of the screen he'd perfected in so many of the band's previous promos throughout the *whole* video, only seemingly able to engage the viewer with full eye contact on the very last shot. It was almost as if the singer was embarrassed about something. The single reached No.5 in the British charts in May, but it was time for a rethink. Changes were needed and 'This Charmless Man' was the first of several nails in the Britpop coffin. The changes that occurred would virtually amount to an airbrushing of history, with Damon Albarn being the artist-in-chief. Never mind modern life ... it would be *The Great Escape* and anything connected with it that would be deemed rubbish.

Blur's fanbase and the nature of their appeal was a cause for concern. A favoured Alex James joke of the time was: "What's forty yards long, has no pubes and goes *Aaaaaaaah!?* The front row of a Blur concert." Alex – always happy to give Damon a run for his money in the pop crumpet stakes – had nailed the issue in his own inimitable way. The teen issue was especially galling to Graham, as Damon revealed in an interview with *Esquire*. "He'd got to the point where he could no longer go drinking at his local, The Good Mixer in Camden, in case people accused him of being in a little kids' band. Which is fair enough really, because that was the way we were going." As any student of pop knows only too well – and Damon is a keen student – the transition from teen favourite to long term proposition is the trickiest there is, but Damon seemed to think this could still work to the band's advantage. "They haven't been to gigs before," he told Q when asked about the band's following of screaming female teens. "But they've seen something that isn't cynical ... so in that respect I know it will pay off in the future. Going to see a band is more of a throwaway thing [to older audiences]. They've lost that magic of going to their first gig, which a 14-year-old hasn't." Drummer Dave Rowntree was baffled, however, about their apparent teen appeal, telling *Select* magazine: "As far as I was concerned, we were playing left-field, weird artpop, posturing and making a nuisance of ourselves. And yet here were thousands of teenage girls treating us like Take That. It was like going shopping for apples and coming back with a motorbike. It's very nice to have a motorbike, but it's singularly inappropriate."

Then there was the company the band was perceived to be keeping. Six months beforehand, Damon had been happy to front the BBC show *Britpop Now*, introducing the 'cream' of the movement to a TV audience: Pulp, Supergrass and Elastica. And Menswear. Although an easy target, Menswear are an irresistible one in terms of highlighting what had gone wrong and why the smart money would soon feel queasy about propping up the Britpop pound. By wearing the right suits and kipping on the right floors – including Graham Coxon's – Menswear had been formed, signed and had appeared on *Top of The Pops* in the same amount of time most bands take to decide what to call themselves. Their stop-go brand of two chord post-punk – Menswear's single 'Daydreamer' is Britpop's single most blatant homage to UK new wave pioneers Wire – had aroused suspicion almost as quickly as it had triggered derision. The lowest common denominator is always going to drag the average down and the steady line of bands using Camden Town as their spiritual home and the Cockernee patter as their chosen language was quickly devaluing the currency.

Britpop infighting wasn't helping either. Suede vs Blur. Blur vs Oasis. Oasis vs anyone looking at them in a slightly funny way. It was time someone showed some mettle, took Britpop down to the woods and ended it's short life. In an article in *The Big Issue*, Damon started by announcing that Britpop was dead: "Britpop as an idea is no longer valid, it's no longer challenging." Elsewhere he told *NME*, "It's all over now. We killed Britpop, we chopped it up and put it under the patio long ago. And any band which is still Britpop in a year's time is in serious trouble." Bad news for Menswear; and not great for the future prospects of Sleeper, Echobelly and Powder either.

Damon was so keen to distance himself from the movement that he appeared almost desperate: "I didn't call it Britpop and I never will," he again said to the *NME*. "We didn't invent anything – we just made British sounding music sell a lot of records." It was time to step off the Britpop treadmill, which Albarn did in two highly unusual ways; he made a film and he buggered off to Iceland.

Face, directed by Antonia Bird was possibly not the best film to be in when you are trying to escape accusations of faux Cockneyisms. It was an East End gangster revenge picture starring Robert Carlyle and perennial London landmark Ray Winstone. Clearly crafted as populist yet political, *Face* tells of an ex-union leader who turns to armed theft, selling out any remaining ideals with a gang who turn on each other when their heist goes wrong. The dimmest of their number is played by Damon Albarn. With a soundtrack of songs culled from The Clash, Paul Weller and Billy Bragg, any unease that may have been generated by its subject matter and potential harm to Damon's wider plans were offset by favourable reviews for the film and the singer's performance. *Time Out* called the movie "muscular, raw and aggressive" with "a knockout cast."

"I went to drama school so at some point I always felt I would act," Damon pointed out to *The Guardian* with that familiar, matter-of-fact confidence. "I had to, really, my mum was very upset when I left drama school. I found it very difficult the first week [on the set]; then I just sort of allowed myself to relax and it was enjoyable after that. It's a very different thing performing onstage compared to acting on screen." Good fortune had once again shined on Damon Albarn and the own goal of 'doing a Sting' – the heinous crime of being a pop star giving a bad performance in a lousy film – was artfully avoided. Despite the good notices, Albarn decided to quit whilst he was ahead in the film acting stakes, telling *Muse.com* that "The idea of turning up every day and having to speak someone else's lines is not for me." If nothing else though, the experience of *Face* and of acting on film really taught him something. "It taught me that I didn't want to do it."

His movie career may have been short-lived, but Damon's relationship with Iceland would prove to be a longer term proposition. With London still in full 1990s swing, Damon and Justine Frischmann – in their honourary positions as Britpop's most glamorous couple – were fair game for the capital's paparazzi. Alex James summed up Albarn's dilemma thus: "It was five years of trying to get into the papers ... and five years trying to stay out of them." Damon was not happy, as he made plain on *WTN* radio in America. "There are a lot of people who thrive on the sort of media attention I was getting. But I've realised I'm just not one of them." The other person on the receiving end of the media assault had slightly more mixed views. "For a while I found myself being Posh Spice," Frischmann told *The Observer* in 2002. "It was really exciting for a while. It was like a mad, surreal experience."

Damon decided he needed to get away from it all, somewhere no one would find him: Iceland. However, such was the power of his indie mojo, the decision to make business and property investments in and around Reykjavik led to the Icelandic capital becoming culturally as well as physically ... cool. The Kaffibarrin, the Reykjavik bar Damon co-owns with Icelandic film director Baltasar Kormäkur has become a magnet for indie tourists. "The Icelandic tourist board is trying to make out like it's responsible for Iceland becoming cool," Kormakur told *The Guardian* in 2001, "and it's bullshit. If people come here, it's nothing to do with guys in suits sitting in an office. It's the work of Björk, of Damon ... maybe even me." For Damon, the attraction to the country had been instant, "I'd love to live there," he told *Rolling Stone*, "but I don't think Justine would like that. I feel very much like two people sometimes. Half of me is into living somewhere like Iceland and having kids, and being really simple, and the other half likes the wildness of life in a rock band." There would be another reason Justine might not have liked it. As Damon's visits to the country increased, one TV comedy show ran a sketch about a population explosion of babies ... all called Damon.

But Damon's Icelandic discovery was no pop star fancy to be dropped on a whim – his connections with the country would remain a constant, recording with local acts like Ghostigital, taking Blur to play there – the band would perform in September 1996 at the Laugardalsholl venue in Reykjavik – and campaigning on environmental issues, including a high profile protest about the building of a hydro-electric plant in Iceland's Eastern Highlands. In 2006, he would describe himself to Icelandic TV viewers as "a frequent visitor ... a sort of migratory bird." "I've got a house there, so I have to go out there to make sure the central heating hasn't packed up. It's really a fantastic place. It's partly the escape but it also happens to be one of the most civilised places on the planet, which is important when you consider how uncivilised the world we live in is. And as for pressure, I'm still in the spotlight, it just doesn't *feel* like I am and that's the way I like it."

Refreshed, Damon returned to Britain to begin work on new material, positive that change was vital if he and Blur were to progress. An acute irony was beginning to evolve with regards to the famous Anglophile's next musical step. "Nothing in Britain was interesting anymore," he told *Rolling Stone*. "We'd always been fans of bands like the Pixies, Beastie Boys and Pavement. [Their music] had more life and intelligence to it than Britpop, and we just began to relate more to those people."

Just to drive the point home about how Britpop was having difficulty relating to people, in August of 1996, Oasis played to a combined audience of 250,000 people at Knebworth in Hertfordshire, a very, *very* big house in the country. A quarter of a million people applied for tickets, many of those who managed to get them complained of poor sound, expensive food and drink, endless queues and grotesque VIP areas.

Even Oasis realised that things had gotten *too* big. There was a need for change. Not just in Britpop, but everywhere. After their Dublin show in June, Graham Coxon had stopped drinking, making Blur fifty per cent tee-total as Rowntree had already sworn off the booze. In Coxon's case, the new leaf would be a temporary one, but it came as a great relief to Damon. "[Drinking] totally wrecked our ability to get on with each other," Albarn told *Rolling Stone*. "When he was drunk, he'd be likely to tell a journalist to fuck off, or I'd hear reports of him being unconscious at four in the morning somewhere in London. That was upsetting because he's my closest male friend."

Change in musical direction ... change in lifestyles ... how much change could be handled? Quite a lot, it would appear. Brixton boy made good, Prime Minister John Major, had seen his powerbase within the Conservative party ebb then flow away that year and was seriously under threat from his own party, as well as New Labour's rock 'n' roll friendly opposition leader, Tony Blair, the Edinburgh-born alumni of Fettes College and Oxford University. Blair was openly courting rock stars and the weekly music press as part of his pre-election campaign, but victory was far from a foregone conclusion. The landslide was a distance away yet.

It's easy to forget that Tony Blair would become the *post*-Britpop PM. Mention the word Britpop and it conjures up a rally of images: Liam Gallagher and Patsy Kensit in a Union Jack bed, Blur up to their eyes in cleavage in the 'Country House' video, Brett Anderson wiggling his arse ... and, of course, Tony Blair. The bright young things of British pop, hand in hand with a Labour government, led by the first Prime Minister who knew how to handle a Stratocaster. Perfect. But memory can be a convenient deceiver. Britpop has gone down in history as if it was invented by Tony Blair and his right-hand man Alastair Campbell, to make them and the party look good. In fact, Britpop was a fast growing flower of the *Conservative* years. And the first post-Britpop single of Damon Albarn's career – the first post-Britpop single full stop – was released when John Major was still Prime Minister in January 1997. New Year ... New

Blur ... New Damon.

With its simple, downward sliding guitar riff, 'Beetlebum' was a love song — albeit an apparently one-sided one — to a lover who does nothing and just gets 'numb'. It has been widely interpreted as being a song about heroin and the alleged use of the drug by Justine Frischmann. With its doleful verse, and the promise of a brighter future in its sunny chorus, the single was a deserved No.1. In the video, virtually the first thing that Damon does is look directly into the camera lens — straight down the bottle, as cameramen call it — no problem with looking us in the eye this time, unlike 'Charmless Man' less than a year ago.

Far greater change was afoot. The Stephen Street-produced album that followed — *Blur* — was a genuine departure from its predecessor. It even looked different. The city slickers pictured on *The Great Escape* had been replaced by photos of a 'proper' band, sitting down to concentrate fully on getting what they wanted from their instruments. If 'Beetlebum' was a dragon-chasing downer of a song, then what followed was a tune turned into a full-on PCP rush — and in the process single-handedly reinvented Blur in just 122 seconds. 'Song 2' was as American as Blur's previous output had been British. Although usually credited as a homage to Californian alt rockers Pavement, it's actually far closer to the "quiet bit/loud bit/really loud bit" model patented by The Pixies and cherished by Nirvana. It's the second track on the album, it's two minutes and two seconds long and, just as the country was readying itself for a General Election, it made No.2 in the charts.

The repercussions of this monumental song were manifold and *global*. Remarkably, the song took on a life of its own in America — finally giving Blur the US success they seemed to crave. It made No.6 in the *Billboard* Modern Rock chart. By undermining the very Englishness that had given them their initial blast of success, they had achieved their desire for American profile via a song that took half an hour to create, had meaningless, onomatopoeic lyrics and was only put on the album as an afterthought. "We're not idiots," Damon warned Q in 1997. "Deep down we knew that Blur records weren't tangible to Americans generally. But once you take out the commuter belt and the oompah elements, we stand a pretty good chance." The 'Woo-Hoo' song entered US culture at countless sports venues, as an indie 'We Are The Champions' ... scored a touchdown/hit a home run/won an ice hockey match? Woo Hoo! 'Song 2' was also used to advertise beer and Pentium Intel, though an approach by the US military to have the new Stealth bomber unveiled to cries of "wellafeeleavymedal!" were rejected by the band. Compared to the Stealth offer, the Intel approach seemed the lesser of two evils. "You have to remember that it came in the aftermath of the US military asking us if they could use it, so Pentium seemed harmless after we'd turned them down. Everyone has their own way of justifying getting involved in advertising, but ours was that everything uses the Pentium chip. Pathetic, I know..."

Back with the album tracks, and a barrier of brushes, a stand-up bass, Jew's harp, wibbling guitar lines and odd creaking noises are erected in between the band and the listener to put them off the scent of 'Country Sad Ballad Man' – it doesn't work because it's the perfect comedown after the sectionable insanity of 'Song 2'. It's apparent that someone programmed the running order of the new album very carefully. To prove the point, 'M.O.R' is next. Clearly a touchstone to keep existing fans on message, it's a straight-forward rocker with a Bowie glint in its eye. Interestingly, when it was released as a single, 'M.O.R' only managed No.15 – perhaps the audience didn't need to be thrown a bone from the band's previous stylings to keep them interested after all. Singalong glam protest song 'On Your Own' is next, all electronica and guitar tics; Albarn sounds remarkably like Steve Harley of Cockney Rebel as he sings of The Ganges, psycho killers and gorillas. The fairground organ opening of 'Theme From Retro' gets you ready for a potential knees-up scenario, but instead delivers a tonal poem, the kind of 'soundtrack to a lost film' piece that The Specials used to do so effectively. 'You're So Great' is back on Bowie territory, with vinyl crackle sound effects, acoustic strums, slide guitar and very little else. The organ is whipped out again for 'Death Of A Party', the album's explicit *Britpop Is Dead* track as Albarn charts not only the demise of the good times, but also of the teenager – lyrically offering to hang himself in a distinctly Morrissey-esque fashion just in case anyone thinks he's faking. 'Chinese Bombs' is an 84-second palate cleansing punk rock moment – it really is all in the *scheduling* of these tracks – before its time to loosen up again, get the wah-wah pedal, the megaphone vocal effect and the 'Hey Joe' Hendrix riff out for 'I'm Just A Killer For Your Love.' 'Look Inside America' starts a touch like *Parklife's* 'End of a Century' with it's string-laden tale of life on the road. Damon makes his peace with the country that he had seemingly disparaged in the past: America, in his view, is now alright – if you look hard enough that is. 'Strange News From Another Planet' is stripped down acoustica save for some blips and beeps – Planet David Bowie is again the world that's being visited with 'Space Oddity' the obvious reference point. You almost expect that ascending Rolf Harris Stylophone solo to pop up at any time. 'Movin' On' is another scheduled back reference – it's the kind of XTC dischord and two-finger synth playing that'd be familiar to anyone who'd bought *The Great Escape*. Final track 'Essex Dogs' – there must have been some rows about using that title; could it be *more Parklife?* – but it's another mood piece, a tonal poem with Albarn painting low-life word pictures with a cinematic air. Coxon grinds away on his feedback heavy guitar as Rowntree and James lock into a dubby groove. It wouldn't be out of place used as montage music to Antonia Bird's film *Face*. Plus it's eight minutes long. Take that, pop kids. That enough to shake you off our tails?

So, just as New Labour were taking over the reigns at 10 Downing Street after the May 1997 general election, then New Blur had taken over as the post-Britpop leaders of a more grown-up musical direction. Mission impossible had become mission accomplished. 'Song 2' was the obvious nucleus of the chain reaction but the album as a whole was complicit. The musical and cultural umbilical cord to all things 1995 had been decisively cut. But Damon's satisfaction at the time might seem cynical to some. "Our audiences have got a lot more adult again, not so distressingly teenage," he reasoned to Q magazine. "It didn't preoccupy us because we picked them up accidentally." If you were unfortunate enough to be female and aged between 13 and 19 when 'Boys & Girls' was released, you might even consider Damon's pleasure to be offensive. Either way, the deed had been done and the scene had been put to bed and smothered with a pillow. Britpop was a done deal, moved out, just as Tony Blair was moving in.

So, who – or what – killed Britpop? Was it the end of Conservative rule in Britain. With nothing to rebel against, what have you got? Perhaps that sliding guitar motif of 'Beetlebum' and loose-limbed psychedelic fun of the *Blur* album did it. Oasis live at Knebworth, perhaps? Was it the heroin, or the *whoo hoo*? Perhaps it was something simpler. As straightforward as a glass of champagne. In July 1997, Noel Gallagher, with his then-wife Meg Matthews, accepted an invitation to 10 Downing Street by the new Prime Minister Tony Blair. Damon had been invited but refused, claiming that he had become a communist, but urged comrades Noel and Tony to "enjoy the schmooze". The event was just weeks before the release of *Be Here Now*, the album that marked the end of Oasis's run of true credibility and perhaps indicated where the "blizzard of cocaine" that Albarn had mentioned the previous year had drifted to. Although it sold 350,000 copies on the first day of its release, the album's contents – a sonic mugging of excess and din – means there's little mileage to be had in comparing Blur and Oasis from here on in. They part company at the point of the album's release. Everything had changed.

There had been concerns about Gallagher behaviour before the event, as revealed in the diaries of Number 10 spinmeister Alastair Campbell published some ten years later. "TB [Tony Blair] was worried that Noel Gallagher was coming to the reception tomorrow. He said he had no idea he had been invited," wrote Campbell. "TB felt he was bound to do something crazy. I spoke to [Creation Records boss] Alan McGee and said can we be assured he would behave. Alan said he would make sure he did. He said if we had invited Liam, it might have been different," recalls Campbell. Blair's press man remembers the Prime Minister's children being "pretty gobsmacked" when Noel Gallagher walked in and that the guitarist thought that that 10 Downing Street was – and I quote – "tops". "[He] said he couldn't believe that there was an ironing board in there," reported Campbell. Meg Matthews was offered a tour by Cherie Blair. "She and I had one of those girly chats about how grotty the place was and what she wanted to change," Matthews later told *Grazia* magazine. "It amazed me that they seemed like such a normal family. One of the little boys' beds was unmade, there was a bottle of ketchup on the kitchen counter and in the master bedroom, Tony's guitar was leaning against the wall next to an Oasis CD." How convenient.

Back at the party, it's claimed that Blair cracked a gag to Gallagher about the different ways the two of them managed to stay awake till the morning on election night. Snaps are taken – and for all-time an image is preserved of Gallagher, his eyes crinkly with pleasure, smiling at Blair. The wild rocker from south Manchester apparently tamed by the wannabe guitarist from Westminster. Gallagher would later report that the second the picture was taken, Blair made himself scarce. It appeared that when it came to Blair vs Oasis, Noel came off second best. Nearly a decade after that party, Gallagher has had time to reflect on his support for Blair and the effect that party has had on how the Oasis man is perceived. "Tony Blair came along and it was like: 'Ah, he's gonna outsmart all of these public schoolboy cunts.' But we all got carried away in '97" he told *The Guardian* in 2006. "Once the veneer wore off – even taking the Iraq debacle out of the equation – we've all just given a massive shrug. I think the Labour party's crowning achievement is the death of politics. There's nothing left to vote for." It's to Noel's credit that he can look back and reassess his role in the musical and political landscape so candidly.

... And his reward for bigging up Blair on the run up to the election? It's there in Gallagher's hand: a glass of champagne. The second the camera flash ebbed away from that picture of Gallagher and Blair – and Tony Blair had got what he wanted – Britpop died.

CHAPTER 13

SUZI

What do you do with a set of fractious individuals, prone to occasional mood swings, drinking bouts and acute musical differences that have been to the edge of disarray and only just avoided going over it? It's obvious really. Put them on a world tour for the best part of a year. The road was Damon Albarn's home for most of 1997. After a low key start in the UK, it was on to America, Germany, Scandinavia, Spain and Italy before some island hopping: Thorsaven in the Faroe Islands, Damon's beloved Iceland and even Greenland. The singer described the country as mesmerising, in *Select* magazine: "Greenland was pretty insane. There were only 1200 people there but considering there's only about 45,000 in the whole country and it's the size of Australia, that's quite a good turnout. They had bleary eyes. It was like, 'Leave your rifles and harpoons outside.'" Leaving the islanders behind, they returned to America, toured the Far East, went south to Australia before returning home for a British arena tour. Although Damon had gone to great lengths to shed Blur's following of any hint of teeny squeal, he would prove indignant at any suggestions that this had been achieved at the expense of the band's popularity. The core fact is that, despite its harder edge, the new album was a commercial peak. Backstage at the Cardiff International Arena he told music journalist Peter Kane: "I know it's perceived [as less successful], but it's unfair because we're still playing the biggest stadiums in the country; 10,000 last night in Manchester, for instance. I don't see that as any great alienation. I've said it *ad infinitum* but, just to ram the point home yet again, *Blur* is our biggest selling album to date."

Meanwhile, Justine Frischmann – who'd managed to tour America with Elastica *seven* times in the space of the previous 18 months – had returned home to London. The title of a key Elastica track says it all: 'Never Here'. Justine's work rate and success totally belied the image of her as second fiddle to Damon: *Blur Indoors* if you will. The relationship broke down. "It was very difficult," she would explain to *The Observer* about the complex reasons behind the pair ultimately splitting up. "It's actually very taboo to stop and say, 'OK, I'm in a band and I'm really successful and my boyfriend's a pop star and he's really handsome and lots of girls fancy him, but I don't want to be with him.' I was just thinking: 'This just isn't the life I want.' There's something very unromantic about being with someone that hundreds of thousands of teenage girls fancy. There really is."

According to Frischmann, one of the first questions that Damon asked her when their relationship started was if she wanted children. She revealed to Q magazine just what a deal-breaker the issue was: "Damon said, 'You've given me a run for my money, you've proved you're as good as I am, you've had a hit in America – now settle down and let's have kids.'" Albarn confirmed that the matter of a family became huge to him. "I started to resent Justine massively. I kept thinking, 'Why the fuck don't you want a child with me? What's the matter with you?'"

While Damon was on tour, Frischmann invited an old, platonic friend to stay at the Notting Hill home she shared with Albarn – Loz Hardy, former singer with Kingmaker, someone she describes as being the closest she's ever had to a brother. The move caused a ripple of appalled excitement among the young fans who spent their lives camped outside Damon and Justine's house. There was worse to come, and if anything was likely to press Albarn's buttons, this would be it: Justine rekindled her friendship with Brett Anderson. She began to appear at Suede gigs and the two even went away (as friends) for the weekend to Dublin. "We' re just really cool friends," Anderson told *Select* when the issue became a talking point on the London scene. "I hate the thought of investing all this time in someone and they just disappear and all that time just slips down the drain. They remain in your memory ... you should stay friends with them because there's obviously a bond there." There were also rumours of another bond. In the alarmingly candid official Suede biography, *Love and Passion,* drummer Simon Gilbert recalls a backstage incident during this time. "I remember walking into the dressing room and Justine was there," he told author David Barnett. "And there they were, doing a bit of smack together." Since the 1990s – and in the wake of 'Beetlebum' and its tale of someone who gets nothing done and just gets numb – Frischmann had been repeatedly pressed on the subject of heroin. "I had a dabble," she confirmed to Q in the year 2000, but has since gone further, using the word "junkie" to describe the 1996-98 period. "It's impossible to get anything finished as a junkie," she would later tell *NME* with admirable honesty. "You have lots of great ideas but you don't have the capacity to actually finish them off." By 2002, she was in a more philosophical mood for *The Observer:* "I think the problem with hard drugs is that they get you when you're most vulnerable. They hadn't really been a problem until we were at rock bottom and we were all very unclear about who we were, what the fuck we were doing with our lives. You get home and you don't really feel like it's home. At that point, doing hard drugs is very dangerous."

"It was horrible," Damon recalled to *The Face* when asked about the period. "It was absolutely hell. I felt ... quite alone. Had a few of those misery-defining moments there. I was still holding on as strongly as I could. When you're in love with somebody ... you're in love with them, aren't you? It was just a very, very protracted and painful separation."

Another separation was on the cards too – this would be a painful one as well. Damon decided that another umbilical cord needed to be cut that connected Old Blur with New Blur – this time with producer Stephen Street. After a peerless run of albums, and a recording relationship going back to 'She's So High' in 1990, they parted ways. "Yes, it was difficult," Damon confirmed to writer Danny Eccleston. "He'll be forever part of what we are and, ironically, he gave us the tools we needed to go it alone. I had to do it." "It wasn't my choice," Street later diplomatically confirmed to *Sound On Sound*. "I just think they wanted to stretch out a bit more and, having made five albums with me, the best way to do that was to work with someone different who would approach the project in a different way. I understand that perfectly and certainly wasn't offended. I did five albums with the band and I must admit I thought each one would be the last because they were bound to want to try something new."

Meanwhile, the singer was about to be on the receiving end of more change himself ... from Justine Frischmann. Elastica were inert, wasting money on studio time that seemingly went nowhere and had picked up a reputation as a drug band. With her life and band seemingly in similar states of suspended animation and sensing a need for change, she separated from Albarn. "We were together for eight years," Damon told *NY Rock*. "Eight years [is] a long time, a very long time. Especially if the relationship is as public as our relationship was. I went through a phase where I thought I've got to justify my feelings, everything I invested in that relationship. As a musician, usually music is your way out."

Domestically, the way out was a move away from the home he'd shared with Justine to the even more boho Westbourne Grove, sharing a flat with friend and comic artist Jamie Hewlett. Hewlett had known Damon since 1990, after he'd interviewed Blur for *Deadline* magazine, home of his most revered creation, Tank Girl. Blur would even pop up in the strip itself from time to time and the rise and fall of the publication – it finished in 1995 – seemed to mirror the fortunes of Blur and Britpop. "Arsey" and "wanker" were the words Hewlett used to describe Damon at the time of the *Deadline* piece, although the two had mutual friends. "They told me he was a cunt," Hewlett sagely informed *Q*. "And they told him I was a cunt." Both heading for thirty, they created their very own *Men Behaving Badly* world at the flat – albeit one surrounded by designers, galleries and groovy restaurants. "Damon's place ... whoooo!" was Alex James's warning to journalist Sylvia Patterson, when asked about the singer's new living arrangements. "Large house, The Danger Zone, bachelor pad mayhem." "We're both recovering romantics," was how Damon fantastically described his friendship with Hewlett. "It's been really great having loads of parties and have a laugh. I'm sure it has its own mythology already. We've had a lot of people round."

In fact, everyone from Radiohead to the Spice Girls, Kate Moss to All Saints were attendees at the flat – Damon was, according to one tabloid rumour, squiring a member of both aforementioned girl bands – and there was a celebrity waiting list to get through the doors. Damon recalls answerphone messages from David Bowie and Pete Townshend – both left on the same afternoon – asking when the next shindig was. Tales of escalating excess spread across London – often involving cocaine, it was claimed: "I did have some amazing parties in that place," Damon told *Esquire* when the accusation was put to him. "Parties where I managed to get Pavement and the Spice Girls hanging out with each other. They were good parties, but that is a gross exaggeration about the cocaine ... Jamie and I always thought we'd make that place legendary for nine months and then bale out." True to their plan, the Westbourne Grove wildness ended – and the last blacked out limo was turned away – for one simple reason ... during this spell of partying, Damon had met someone who would change his life.

Suzi Winstanley was already one half of a partnership. An artistic partnership that had already existed for more than ten years whereby she and collaborator Olly Williams literally worked *together*. They first met at Central St Martins College of Art in 1987 and had decided to operate as a single unit. Their signature wildlife pieces, created by painting together – 'hand over hand' – had taken them around the world in some of the most inhospitable conditions, coming face to face with some of the planet's most fearsome animals. "Our work is still a collaborative, mutual response to the wild," Olly described to *The Times*. "But we're starting to be intrigued by the people who live on the peripheries of the wild, and who hold the survival of the wild in their hands. They are the ones who subsist in the bush and are at one with it. We're intrigued by the fact that there are men who feed their families by hunting with eagles or living off the forest." The artistic pairing had faced tigers, orangutans and tarantulas; they'd smeared a painting with fish guts and blood in South Africa to encourage a shark to bite it and become part of the canvas - this would be good preparation for when Suzi first got together with Damon and had a glimpse into his very different world. 'It was funny when I first met him,' she recalled to *The Times Magazine*. "We were in my flat in east London, and we had to go west, and I said, 'Oh, it's really quick from here. Just jump on the Central Line.' He said, 'No, I don't think we should go on the Tube.' I had literally just met him, and I said, 'What are you talking about? It's twenty minutes. It's the quickest way.' Anyway, we went down to the Tube, and there were all these people shouting, all these girls running around, and I suddenly thought, 'I don't like this.'" At first, the relationship was kept very low key, with Damon dropping hints that he had met someone new, but that they were "not famous." That's the way things would remain. No more Posh and Becks for Damon Albarn.

Plans were being laid for the new Blur album and a new producer would be needed. The choice was William Orbit, who'd provided an alternative version of 'Movin' On' for the *Bustin' + Dronin'* project, essentially a stopgap set of remixes that was originally meant for the Japanese market only, but eventually received a low profile release in the UK. Orbit was the man of the moment, having just pushed Madonna to the top of the charts with the ambient mood piece 'Frozen'. The album he also shaped for her – *Ray Of Light* – would provide her with the kind of edgy vibe she hadn't commanded for years. Madonna was effectively an indie artist by now, releasing records through her own Maverick label – the Orbit collaboration worked and won her a clutch of Grammy awards. Edge, success and mainstream awards – not an easy trick to pull off. Through the summer of 1998, in studios in London and Iceland, Orbit pushed, prodded and cajoled Blur towards the next stage of their career. "It was such a personal thing going on, we needed to have someone who didn't really know us ... William was a bit of a psychiatrist through all of this." "There were certain days when I'd get home and I couldn't even get upstairs," Orbit recalled to *The Face*. "I'd be suffering from sheer emotional exhaustion from trying to carve out a musical consensus, from trying to harness all this talent." Graham Coxon believed that Orbit totally changed the band and their approach. "Working with William was like having a make-over on *Richard and Judy*," said the guitarist in an interview with Q. "A complete surprise. It was like feeding your personality into a computer and saying: 'Here's your sound, Mr Coxon.'"

The result of all that harnessing of talent was the new album *13*, recorded at 13, Mayfair Studios and Sarm West in London and Studio Syrland in Reykjavik. And if *Blur* was the 'Britpop Is Dead' album, then *13* is unashamedly the 'Justine' album, a fact that Frischmann was made all too clear about prior to its release. "I bumped into Damon," Justine told music journalist and author John Harris, "and he said ... '*Brace yourself*.'" Damon Albarn – an artist so often criticised for hiding behind characters and stories in his songs,

Damon Albarn

was about to bear his soul. Big time.

From the start of *13,* 'Tender' – with its shaky, delta blues stylings – tells of a lover that Damon loves too much; a ghost who lives only for the night. Sharing vocals with Coxon and the London Community Gospel Choir, Albarn's singing slides from delicate falsetto to determined growl as he urges himself on through the pain she's causing – he can get through it, to a new life on the other side. An unlikely lead single – albeit slightly shorter than the seven minutes forty seconds here – it reached No.2 in the charts. In true style, 'Bugman' is scheduled next to wipe things clear; like a grungier version of early Roxy Music, with a false white noise ending and a wig-out finale, it's there to wipe away the melancholy of the previous track. 'Coffee & TV' – famed for its walking milk carton video – has Coxon on verse and Albarn on chorus, lyrically recalling the two things the guitarist used to help him quit drinking. It oozes charm and wit and it's amazing it only made No.11 in the charts. Blur's manager Chris Morrison caused a controversy at the time, claiming the band had been denied a Top 10 placing for the single because of a cock-up on the sales logging front. Albarn is back in charge for 'Swamp Song' – another blues, this time in the style of Elvis fronting The Fall – as he pleads for hedonistic pleasure. Perhaps it's a nod to the flat-sharing wild times with Jamie Hewlett. With its aloof classical structures, '1992' is an aloof slice of electronica with Coxon using every effects pedal he has at his disposal to disrupt the calm. 'B.L.U.R.E.M.I' – you can tell by the look of the title – is the Blur punk rock moment before 'Battle' weighs in for a stay of almost eight minutes. From its synth pulse opening, it's clear we're back on the domestic front; a life summed up in the oft-repeated one word title as chaotic as the jam that the band provides as background and the prog rock finale. Pastoral soothings are then used in 'Mellow Song' to find a way through the previous jumble; it's as if Damon is lying on his bed staring at the ceiling, wondering what's to become of him in the new life that's around the corner, as the echoing notes tumble from Coxon's guitar in a reminder of that other great art rock four piece, The Passions, on their tale of similarly doomed romance, 'I'm In Love With A German Film Star'. 'Trailer Park' is back to The Fall vs Presley – *Mark Elvis Smith* if you like – as Albarn laments losing his woman; not to another man, but to the Rolling Stones. Its fade out is rather reminiscent of 'Is Vic There?' by Department S. 'Caramel' also had a familiar ring, reminding the listener of 'Driver's Seat' by Sniff 'N' The Tears. You're left satisfied after four minutes – it then continues for nearly another four. The cool beats and piano cascades of 'Trimm Trab' has Damon sleeping alone – the reason why is explained in the next track. There's no sadder piece of writing about the lonely ache of a relationship than 'No Distance Left To Run'. Like the failing love affair it documents, there's very little to it; Damon's voice, Coxon's guitar, James's walking bassline, Rowntree's brushes and a single finger picking out an electric piano lament. It's also a measure of brevity at just over three and a half minutes. Perhaps that was why it was chosen as a single. Hardly a radio friendly strummerlong, it still managed a No.14 chart placing. 'Optigan 1' shuffles us off into the sunset and *13* is done. Hindsight gives it a place among the best work – if not *the* best – of their career. At the time, there was admiration as well as puzzlement. Q magazine's take was that *13* was, "a dense, fascinating, idiosyncratic and accomplished art rock album." *Rolling Stone* had it down as, "their sloppiest, most playful set yet." *NME* was impressed and frustrated in equal measure. "Blur's most inconsistent and infuriating statement thus far. Infuriating, because divested of four solid-gone clunkers *13* could pass muster as the best of Blur."

13 is not unusual in that it documents the break up of a relationship – are their many albums that don't reflect that in some way? What made the whole experience stand out was Damon's willingness ... *eagerness* almost ... to use his pain to good effect. "This record, hopefully, takes the positive and the negative side of that whole relationship and turns it ultimately into something," was how he explained things to *The Face*. "It was a very big thing for both of us. Hopefully one day we'll be able to look back on it and go, 'Well? Cheers, love.'" Not everyone was quite so impressed. "[When] the press started rolling in, it was a bit of a surprise how that campaign was handled," Justine told *Q*. "Talking about it an awful lot. Almost selling it on 'the poor boy's had his heart broken.' The only thing that broke Damon's heart was not getting his own way." "You know the press in England," was Damon's justification to *NY Rock*. "There were already enough rumours flying around. I thought it best to take the bull by the horns, you know, to get out there and tell them. You could say I came out with raised arms and was hoping they wouldn't shoot."

With the new album released, 1999 was another harsh year of touring for the band. Most of Europe, America (north and south) and the Fuji Rock Festival in Japan were all visited – so was John Peels' birthday bash in Suffolk. But it was the Reading Festival in August that got tongues wagging again. During a set dominated by songs from *13,* Albarn told the crowd that the band were going to take a break – there'd be two more UK gigs before the end of the year – a B-sides show in Camden and a London Wembley Arena show where they'd play all their singles back to back. Then what? A spokesman for the band compared the statement to U2's reinvention in 1989, where Bono had told his audience they were going away to "dream it all up again". "There seems to be such a different feeling in the way we make music now," Albarn told Q. "It's hard to imagine going back. It has to get more free-form from now on."

As the sunset coda of 'Optigan 1' suggested, better times were just around the corner. The party may have been over at the bachelor pad with Jamie Hewlett, but Suzi Winstanley's international artistic lifestyle would open up new vistas for Damon Albarn. The world was there to be explored ... properly explored, not just as a travelogue from a tour bus window ... and like any good adventure, it would need a soundtrack.

CHAPTER 14

EVENTS TAKE A CINEMATIC TURN

By March 1999 – within a year of beginning his relationship with Suzi Winstanley – it was revealed that the couple were expecting a baby. Damon's long held and explicitly stated ambition to be a dad was going to be realised. With this news came the decision to come off the road. In an interview with music website *Muse.com*, Damon explained the reasoning behind what appeared to be such a drastic decision for a tour hungry performer to take. "Once I knew I was going to have a baby, I did everything I could to speed up the process of decommissioning, so to speak. Today, the subject of parenthood is the only one that truly engages me, it's given me a sense of purpose. And what that means is that you know when to say no, really. I don't really believe in not working. But I believe in working and for the quality of life when you're working to be good." The pair had moved into a house in Notting Hill. They managed four days of privacy before *The Sun* newspaper printed a picture of their new "very big house (but not in the country)." Partner Suzi Winstanley was appalled by the press intrusion into the pair's life: "It's all very well for him, because he courted that in the past, although he's not interested in it now. But it's got nothing to do with me, that's his life before he met me. So I just keep my head down." The couple managed to keep their baby out of the public eye for the best part of nine months, until Damon and Missy were papped on a west London street. The pictures were splashed in *The Sun* under the headline "Doting Damon". "It's changed the way I apply myself," he told *Radio 1* on being asked how being a dad had changed his attitude to music. "You can't be so liberal with your time spent working, so you have to be a lot more constructive. So it's made me more constructive."

As is often the case with new parents, it was time to take stock.

It appeared that the time could indeed be right to fulfill a few more constructive ambitions, for Damon to start stretching himself further, to prove there was more to him than even the *Blur* and *13* albums had suggested. As for Blur the band, events would unfold that would mean they would never be the same unit again. That spring, drummer Dave Rowntree had sounded a warning note in an interview with *Q* about the nature of the interpersonal relationships within Blur. "We're together for the music. We wouldn't be great friends if we weren't in a band and it would be stupid to pretend otherwise. Because we all get on each others' nerves. You're bound to after ten years."

As the 1990s were heading for the Noughties, British pop meant a very different thing to the spin it was given five years earlier at the height of the Britpop wars. With the big guns of the Spice Girls and Take That out of commission, lesser mortals had taken their place, throwing all the right shapes but missing the pure pop target by a mile. "I'm no longer interested in touring the world and being a pop tart but I love pop music," was Damon's view to *Metro* as he stepped back from the limelight. "Pop's very fickle, but there are always good songs – although there seems to be a lot of cover versions around at the moment. Bands such as [floppy-haired boy band] A1 should be banned. They won a Brit, which sends out the wrong message, but it's an industry thing to sell more records." As ever though, Damon's competitive streak was never far from the surface: "Blur won four in 1995 which is more than anyone else has [at that time] in a single night. People forget that."

Collaborations would provide a stepping stone to areas outside his apparent comfort zone. He was no stranger to working with other singular pop talents. As well as his keyboard playing and apparent co-songwriting input to Elastica's debut album under his Dan Abnormal persona, there was a co-writing credit with former Specials' singer Terry Hall on his 1995 'Rainbows' EP. Albarn's loyalty to Hall would continue, with contributions to Hall's *Laugh* album in 1997 and *The Hour of Two Lights* in 2003. Albarn's first solo piece, 'Closet Romantic', had graced the must-have soundtrack of 1996, *Trainspotting*. Increasingly, he seemed to be more comfortable in the company of others. From the sections marked 'sublime' and ridiculous', he'd also recorded a version of 'Waterloo Sunset' with his hero Ray Davies and contributed to a 1997 Gary Numan tribute album alongside Matt Sharp of US alt-rock band Weezer. The album was called *Random*. Working with other pop musicians? All well and good. Most singers can manage that. Next up, holding your own against Britain's foremost living classical composer? Try *that* Mr Noel Gallagher ...

With his repetitive cycles and rhythms, Michael Nyman has always been the one classical artist that rock musicians found it easiest to 'get'. Despite his bookish appearance and owlish glasses, Nyman has always been approachable to worlds outside the classical. His first recorded piece – *Decay Music* in 1976 – even has a cool title like a rock album and he initially performed under the guise of 'The Campiello Band' and later, 'The Michael Nyman Band'. He's recorded over 100 albums, of which the best known are his soundtracks, initially with Peter Greenaway for his breakout film *The Draughtman's Contract* in 1982 and later with Jane Campion for her film *The Piano*, ten years later. The soundtrack album for the latter film sold three million copies worldwide, figures that put most rock acts in the shade.

Nyman and Albarn had already experienced a brief coming together, as part of a Noel Coward tribute album brought together by Neil Tennant of the Pet Shop Boys. The unlikely pairing's contribution to 20th *Century Blues* was a virtually unidentifiable version of 'London Pride' which reportedly nearly didn't make the final cut of the album. In the end a tweaked version did appear, alongside the likes of Sting, Texas and Suede. But collaborating with Nyman for Albarn's first full soundtrack – for the 1999 'period cannibal' film *Ravenous* – would be a slightly more daunting proposition than a one-off tribute track. *Ravenous,* set in Sierra Nevada in the 1840s stars Robert Carlyle and Guy Pearce. It's a schizophrenic piece – *Face* director Antonia Bird was brought in late to the production after original director Milcho Manchevski departed – and the film didn't exactly set the box office alight, perhaps because of confused marketing; it was far too splattery to be a black comedy but had too many sly gags to be an out-and-out horror flick. The *LA Weekly* review just about nails the problem: "Although the hinges connecting the film's elements – slapstick, political satire, thriller, gross-out shots – sometimes squeak loudly, they hold the movie together nicely." Director Bird has been generous about Albarn's involvement. "It's about collaboration. I think that that is what making films is about, it's about creative collaboration. That film should be about [Robert Carlyle], me, Guy and Damon Albarn." What interests us though is the soundtrack. "It was collaborating with Michael Nyman on the soundtrack to *Ravenous* which gave me a confidence I didn't have before," said Damon, relishing the experience of not being the cleverest person in the room for once. "I realised that I would rather be able to call myself a composer than a pop star."

The generous Nyman has since given Albarn the lion's share of the credit for the twang and drone *Ravenous* soundtrack, while insisting that it wasn't a collaboration in the truest sense, telling *Soundtrack.net* that, "Damon Albarn composed 60% of the tracks, and I did the rest. He had gotten a hold of the film before I did, and as it was his first, he was very excited by the prospect and chose the scenes he liked and wrote music. I, on the other hand, being a bit more tired and not so excited and involved, just sat back, and the cues that he didn't do, I did. It wasn't a collaboration in any sense whatsoever except for the fact that you see the composer credits as being 'Damon Albarn and Michael Nyman.' My stuff was totally self-contained." Although the pair didn't sit down and actually write pieces together, they did put together a team of people – an orchestrator, programmer, music editor and so forth – to turn the music into a soundtrack that would work as an accompaniment to the film as a commercially available OST (Original Soundtrack). Nyman has since described Damon's ideas as "instinctive, fresh and quite stimulating" but that they also needed work. Damon was very open about who was the more experienced composer in the relationship, telling *Muse.com,* "I learned a lot from Michael. I basically had a month in which to learn a lot of stuff. He gave me a realistic view of it, which is very important. I did a lot more of the music on *Ravenous* really that Michael did, but he was always there more as a teacher. I think he would agree."

"I was actually very shocked at how courageous, independent and imaginative Damon was," is how Nyman summed up the experience to *Esquire.* "He has a very good musical instinct. He's fearless and he's got supreme confidence so he'll get on all right in the world of composing." "I was rather disappointed," says Nyman generously, "because the one thing I wanted to gain from that opportunity was to add something to his music, and have him add something to mine. But by the time I came on board, his music was so good and self-contained that the only thing I could do was to point him in the direction of an orchestrator!"

Damon had clearly caught the soundtrack bug from the prolific Nyman: "He was the man who taught me, 'never waste a note ...' I've got that pinned up in the next room actually," Damon told music365.com of his work with Nyman. "I work everyday and I've got so many things going on. It's not nine-to-five, but I work every single day making music in whatever form, and I've really just started to understand what it means to *not* waste a note." Ever the workhorse, Damon put his fame into good use, travelling to the Cannes film festival to help promote the film.

Clearly fired up, Damon was quick to get another OST under his belt, though this experience wasn't to prove quite as rewarding as his work on *Ravenous*. In the throes of moving house and with a baby due at any time, Damon threw himself into writing his first solo OST for *Ordinary Decent Criminal,* a crime drama based in Dublin starring Kevin Spacey. The film, inspired by events in the life of Irish gangland figure Martin Cahill who was shot and killed by the IRA in 1995, suffered greatly on release because of its similarity to John Boorman's movie *The General*. What does mark it out as different from Boorman's piece is its soundtrack which seems – on the surface at least – to be at odds with the subject matter. "My girlfriend has family in Cuba," he told music365.com, "and if I'd had the time and money, I'd have done the soundtrack out there. I wanted to give the film that Catholic Latin quality which I thought was a great thing to couple up with Dublin, which seems a much warmer place than anywhere in the British Isles, there's a very Spanish feel there. I thought it was a nicer thing to play with than getting an Irish band and going that route."

Damon's perfectionism and his willingness for the Latino-themed soundtrack to succeed was captured by the cameras of ITV arts programme *The South Bank Show,* loudly taking one musician to task for not playing the piece the Albarn way. "It's great working with other musicians, it's just really terrifying when they just don't understand what it is you're trying to get," was his explanation of such an approach to *Muse.com*. "Then you really wish you were with people you've worked with for years. It kind of balances out. It's the same with the band. I have the same kinds of arguments with them, really, when they're not doing what I want them to do. Except we've known each other a lot longer. They're less likely to listen to me." The compilers of the *Ordinary Decent Criminal* OST also didn't quite see things Damon's way either, adding tracks by the likes of Bis, Shack and Bryan Ferry to the album that don't actually appear in the final cut of the film. "What I really wanted to do was take all the original music I'd composed for the film, spend another month on it and make it into a cohesive score. I don't see any point in putting a record out to a film unless you do that. Something like *Get Carter* or *Taxi Driver* – all those wonderful scores have become popular as records and keep selling. With those albums you can go into a world for however long it is that record lasts."

Despite this unease, Damon again put his back into promoting the film, making regular trips to Dublin just as Suzi gave birth to baby Missy (named after rapper Missy Elliot). Damon embraced his new role of father as wholeheartedly as every other opportunity that had come his way in life so far. "You're just witnessing a life force, aren't you?" he said to *Esquire*. "She looks like an Eskimo. She looks more like Björk than either me or Suzi. Not that either of us look like Bjork ... it's a slightly bizarre thing for men really, especially if they want to be involved in the whole process; all I could do was be a comforter. It's great, though."

In a post-Britpop world, British musicians had replaced movie stars as the main focus of attention for the media and therefore, by default, the public (possibly because Britain didn't have enough genuine movie stars to go around?). So unsurprisingly, Damon and Suzi were quickly swamped with offers from celebrity magazines for the exclusive rights to pictures of them with baby Missy in their 'beautiful new home.' These offers were all firmly turned down. Not only did they not need the money – 'Song 2' alone is understood to have generated £2 million of revenue by 1999 – but Damon had been appalled to see Noel and Liam Gallagher in the pages of the celebrity glossies. "The Gallaghers have totally fucked themselves over by doing celebrity magazines. It seems to me that as soon as you appear in one, it's over, really. Idiots! It's the most stupid thing Liam and Noel have ever done. I feel really sorry for them. They just haven't handled their fame and money very well, have they?"

The rest of Blur meanwhile, were handling their fame and money in their own singular and very different ways. The most visible success had belonged, rather bizarrely, to Alex James. He'd scored a No.1 with Fat Les the previous summer with the glorified footy chant 'Vindaloo', accompanied by artist and 'Country House' director Damien Hirst and comedian, 'Country House' video star and professional rock 'n' roll sidekick, Keith Allen. There was worse to come with the follow-up single 'Naughty Christmas (Goblin in the Office)'. "Obviously the records are shit," James admitted to US journalist Rob Tannenbaum with admirable honesty and remarkable accuracy. "But you wouldn't get Radiohead making a Christmas record, would you? If I want to make stupid records with a bunch of idiots from The Groucho then fuck off, I will." On a higher level, he'd also become involved in the BEAGLE project to launch a 27 kilo Mars probe that would land on the planet's surface, unfold and commence drilling into the surface. All the while accompanied by a specially composed Blur tune. Both James and Rowntree were involved in BEAGLE, raising cash and the project's profile. In May 2003, BEAGLE hitchhiked a ride from a European Space Agency rocket bound for Mars, but sadly never made it. As well as his BEAGLE interests, Dave Rowntree had advanced his training and abilities as a commercial pilot – a bug he would infect Alex with – and taught himself computer animation. Graham Coxon was winning friends and admirers with his solo work, a sonic cross between Nick Drake and Iron Maiden. He was also about to become a dad – to baby Pepper – with girlfriend Anna. Blur were still a band, but were splintering with each passing day.

With plenty to occupy them but no touring commitments, Blur was effectively on hold. "Blur exists if everyone wants to make music together," Damon stated. "That's not something you can predict. I certainly don't keep tabs on everyone's life like maybe I would've done when we started out ten years ago. We all need our own identities."

In terms of defining his identity, Damon Albarn began to look further afield. In 2000, he flew to the African nation of Mali as ambassador for Oxfam, to see first hand the work that the charity were doing in the area. Under the heading 'On The Line', the project's aim was to highlight countries and communities on the Meridian line and encourage exchanges with the West. Initially uncomfortable about mixing the roles of musician and charity ambassador, Damon decided to stick with making connections via music, and came armed with a humble melodica – a cross between a harmonica and a mini keyboard that's been used to good effect by everyone from reggae artist Augustus Pablo to Ian Curtis of Joy Division. "I just listened and talked and occasionally joined in with my melodica," he told *BBC Online*. "I played it on the last few albums I've made and it's just become my instrument of choice. In the context of Mali music, it worked really well. It's a very simple instrument and it sonically fits in, for some reason." Damon returned to London with forty hours of material but was in no rush to release the results; this was something that clearly had to be treated with care and respect. "You can become very insular in a band when you're only playing with the same people," Albarn explained to *Mojo* magazine. "It's not healthy. You have to see how wide the world is. You certainly get a feeling of how wide it is when you're in Mali." Tapes went back and forth from London to Africa with key musicians given carte blanche to add instruments and sounds as they saw fit. The final recordings, featuring over a dozen Malian musicians including kora players Afel Bocoum and Toumani Diabate were eventually released two years later under the title *Mali Music* on the Honest Jon's label, inspired by a West London record shop with a vibe similar to the classic Rough Trade set up. Pop stars dabbling in World Music has a high crash rate – it runs on a scale similar to that of pop stars trying their hand at acting – but again fortune was on Damon's side and he produced a simple, unpatronising set that was well received, though clearly didn't break the tills in terms of sales, a shame as the proceeds went to Oxfam. World Music's image was traditionally seen as a turn-off to record buyers.

To maintain the international vibe, Damon turned his hand to another soundtrack, working with Einar Örn Benediktsson of the Sugarcubes on the music for Icelandic film *101 Reykjavik*, directed by his Kaffibarrin colleague Baltasar Kormakur. The film soundtrack – finally released in 2001 – was also never going to be a massive seller, but it all bolstered Damon's growing solo/non-Blur reputation. One album that was genetically programmed to be a huge winner was Blur's first *Best Of ...* collection. Focus groups were used to work out what the running order should be, when it should be released and even what people's perceptions of the band were. Alex James: "I've never seen anything so brutal, but it was very illuminating. Apparently, when these people think of Blur, the first thing they think of is Damon's eyes. Among other things, it came across that we were a fully integrated band. People didn't perceive us as different personalities. They perceived us as straight-down-the-line musicians." Perhaps to counter the apparent lack of band personality beyond Damon's eyes, the entire group were pictured on the sleeve of *Best of Blur* – designed by Julian Opie – in the simplest possible terms: black lines with paint chart colours. Each member boiled down to their most basic visual element: Graham's glasses, Alex's fringe, Damon's little boy lost look and Dave's gingerness. It's a terrific piece of branding that now seems so obvious it's become a cliché. *Guardian* art critic Jonathan Jones disagreed and voted the portraits as one of the ten worst pieces ever when the pictures were first acquired by the National Portrait Gallery. "Blur themselves are embarrassing subject matter," Jones wrote. "They're the quintessence of Britpop and what was supposedly hot in our culture in the 1990s. Now they're just deeply unfashionable." The reviewers were kinder to the band than Mr Jones was. "*The Best of Blur* serves as a document for an astonishingly consistent career," *Pitchfork* said. "As with any retrospective, the track listing isn't going to please anyone ... Still, it's hard to argue with the material that made it to this record." *Mojo* had it down as "essential" and *Q* pointed out that there was plenty more where this came from: "Blur have had many more than eighteen hits; certainly there are sufficient omissions to form the bulk of a second disc."

Damon claims he agreed to deliver the compilation – plus the customary bonus track – in return for a one-single deal for a new musical project he was toying with. "I thought that was a pretty good offer," he told London's *Time Out* magazine. The additional track was the atypical 'Music Is My Radar.' "We weren't getting along very well at the time, but the song we produced was completely bonkers. It ends with me repeating this phrase, *'Tony Allen got me dancing'*, as I was listening to a lot of Nigerian music at the time." Allen, by now in his 60s, was the master Afrobeat percussionist who had driven the infectious rhythms for legendary African musician Fela Kuti. He was a revered figure in World Music.

Now, if someone could tap into the potential international beats and appeal of World Music, but mould it into a package that wouldn't repel the casual buyer ... then the industry really would go ape.

CHAPTER 15

CARTOON BEGINNINGS & NEW ENDINGS

There are, of course, precedents for cartoon characters being used to front up pop music. The Beatles have done it. The Jackson Five and The Osmonds had a go. Never underestimate the contribution made by Josie And The Pussycats. But one example remains the template – and that involved monkeys too. Or should we say Monkees ...

When Mike Nesmith, Davy Jones, Peter Tork and Micky Dolenz – TV's premier manufactured answer to The Beatles – started to rebel against their taskmasters, who made them international stars with the zany series that bore the made-up band's name, there was one straw that broke The Monkees' back. And its name was 'Sugar Sugar'. The Monkees, led by rebel-in-chief Nesmith, were becoming increasingly disenchanted with the material they were being asked to record and decided to make a stand against the latest song put before them. A simple tale of love for a "candy girl" who's got our unfortunate two dimensional hero "wantin' you", 'Sugar Sugar' was a bubblegum confection too far and the band refused to have anything to do with it. Don Kirshner, the creator of The Monkees and the series, hit upon an ingenious solution. If The Monkees wouldn't do as they were told, then he'd make a band that would – a cartoon band called The Archies who took 'Sugar Sugar' to No.1 in America and Britain in 1969. The song stayed on the UK charts for six months. The real musicians, the true voice of 'Sugar Sugar' – session singer Ron Dante – remained hidden. No one needed to see them or even know their names. That would be distracting.

Damon Albarn had stepped back from the fame of Britpop, escaped to Iceland when the pressures of Posh 'n' Becks-ness became too much and hidden behind the relative anonymity of soundtracks and World Music; now was the time to remove his name and face from a project all together. Using the leverage afforded him by the need for a Blur *Best Of* ..., he did indeed cut a deal initially for that mooted one-off single. Former flatmate and Tank Girl creator Jamie Hewlett was in on the act too. Damon would write the songs, Jamie would design the band and the world they inhabited and a floating coterie of musicians, singers and collaborators would be parachuted in as required. The pair were born a few weeks apart in 1968, the year of the monkey. Hence the initial banner for the project: "Gorilla". This was soon funked up to ... Gorillaz.

"Jamie and I spent our twenties being successful in many ways, but the residue of that success had left us questioning what we were doing and the nature of the world we lived in," Albarn explained to *CDNow*. "One of the things that really got to us was the nature of celebrity and the cynicism of popular culture. That was really the genesis of Gorillaz, besides the fact that he's a cartoonist, and I'm a musician, so the logical thing to do was to create an animated band."

The band in question was a virtual four piece: a slightly vacant, pin-up boy lead singer, 2D; Murdoc, a Lemmy-esque bass player; a bulky beatmaster in the shape of Russel and hyper cute pre-teen rock chick, Noodles. Anonymous it may have been – bland it definitely wasn't. "It demands that people use their imagination more than pop music generally allows for these days," was one of countless explanations Damon gave to the obvious initial question about the 'band' ... Why? He told *Metro*, "If you can believe in figures such as Eminem and Marilyn Manson, why not get your head around something which takes that to its logical conclusion?"

The demarcation between the two men and the way they worked – collaborative yet separate – seemed odd to outsiders. "Jamie and I work together in a very kind of isolated parallel with each other," Damon told *The Bulb*. "We're very good friends but we don't invade each other's space at all. We've basically got a given where everything I do he likes and everything he does I like. It doesn't matter what that is. It's only very occasionally that he would come up with some visuals and I'd go: 'That's shit,' or I'd provide some music and he'd say the same."

Hewlett was adamant that none of the Gorillaz were based on

anyone involved in the band, "Everyone thinks 2D is Damon," he told Q. Despite this he gave the magazine a very specific breakdown of the band. "2D is the classic stupid pretty boy singer, he's the fall guy, the stooge. Everybody takes the piss out of him." Noodles was originally called Paula, with greasy hair, bad teeth and was a "bit of a slut." "She's the mysterious one," says Hewlett. "All she ever says is Noodles." Murdoc, according to the comic artist, was modelled on a young Keith Richards, "a heavy metal bass player who wants to be the singer but isn't pretty enough." "Hip-hop hardman" Russel is "dark, quiet and thoughtful ... and hates Murdoc." For a two-dimensional band, they appeared to have considerably more personality than the majority of pop acts on the market. And that, for Damon in particular, was largely the point.

"The whole pop aesthetic is more and more about personalities and you can get carried away with that and end up being let down," he said in an interview with *Metro*. "Humans are such fragile creatures and the whole nature of celebrity screws you up. Look at all the manufactured bands in the world. Even those that claim not to be are, in some way. Bands such as Coldplay are a little bit too clean to be real. Then there's Westlife, A1... Gorillaz is about trying to destroy that and take it further, to manufacture something with real integrity. It requires a leap of faith."

There was another plus to the four characters fronting the music. It allowed Damon to experiment with hip-hop, reggae and some of the rhythms and textures picked up on his World Music travels. Some of these stylings – had they been presented in the flesh by Damon himself or indeed Blur – may well have attracted derision. Blur's Alex James had already referred to the singer – who now listed his culinary speciality as "ackee and saltfish" and his favoured recent record purchase as 1970s Angolan music – as "the blackest man in West London."

The full reggae-fied simian assault was launched in March 2001 with an extensive, virtual world website and a live show at The Scala, a former cinema in London – among the audience was ex-Clash bassist Paul Simonon. A full size screen was put back in the venue as Albarn and his fellow musicians performed behind it. "Show yourselves!" one punter cried. The audience and press were impressed, albeit to the point of bafflement, and the view from *The*

Daily Telegraph was typical: "Much of the animation was not far removed from the elaborate backdrops seen previously at gigs by the Chemical Brothers or Orbital, except here it was given prime position. Gorillaz raised good questions about what we expect from a concert – who wants to look at ugly blokes playing guitars anyway?" The paper suggested that the whole thing may be little more than a post-modern prank by Albarn and his west London playmates, something that was hardly dispelled with the release of the skanking lead single 'Clint Eastwood'. The desire to maintain the illusion of Gorillaz as a real entity went to considerable lengths, with a detailed fictional band history that even went to the trouble of inventing a made-up debut gig at the 'Camden Brownhouse' in December 1999, which ended in a fictional riot. When pressed, Damon insisted that he was acting as the band's spokesman, as shown during an interview with Radio 1's Steve Lamacq to promote the single.

Lamacq: Where did the idea come from? Is it something which has been there for ages and ages?
Damon: Jamie and I were living together, sharing a flat, and they came to a party where, actually I think Murdoc did with 2D ... two-dimensional people at a party, they stand out, don't they?
Lamacq: Oh yeah, very much.
Damon: And we got talking to them, and then we all kind of came up with the idea it'd be great to have an animated band.
Lamacq: Why?
Damon: Because, everything seems so manufactured these days, even the kind of, well, the kind of tradition that I come from, indie, even that's manufactured now, you know? So, I think we just felt that, let's just sort of play everyone at their own game, and make something better, that's manufactured, that's actually good.
Lamacq: Have you seen some of yourself in 2D?
Damon: Well, the funny thing is, my daughter, whenever she sees the video says "Daddy" to 2D.
Lamacq: What about, now obviously being involved with the virtual band, the other band ...
Damon: Yeah, I mean, they're not *virtual*, they exist, you know?

I mean, have you heard the record?
Lamacq: I've heard the record.
Damon: Well, that *exists* doesn't it?

As far as Damon was concerned, he barely existed in the context of the Gorillaz's eponymous debut album. All tracks are credited to 2D/Murdoc/Russel/Noodles and the various 'real life' collaborators who guest on them. Damon's name is in the fine print as an additional vocalist appearing courtesy of EMI. From the off 'Re-Hash' – all sweet sliding acoustic chords, basslines *a la* Clash and clitter clatter drums – this innovative record is a winner. It has all the looseness of *13* with a world-view extracted from Damon's travels. It doesn't sound like Damon Albarn perhaps because there's vocal distractions from Miho Hatari, singer with New York group Cibo Matto. '5/4' and 'Tomorrow Comes Today' skip through on a similar vibe with each track's vocal a little more 'Albarn-esque' than the last. 'Tomorrow Comes Today', with Damon's beloved melodica and a subterranean bass sound sums up the vibe – it's an easy listen ... dinner party dance music – and is in danger of sliding by unnoticed. Things get a little muddier with 'New Genious (Brother)' with its murky, soundtrack, falsetto vocal and old school scratching; then it's 'Clint Eastwood', the album's first stab at rap. Damon's too wise an owl to fall for doing it himself; San Francisco rapper Del Tha Funky Homosapien does the honours brilliantly. 'Man Research (Clapper)' is all squeaks and random generator noises as Albarn's vocal stays in the upper register; those looking for the kind of insights into the state of Damon's mind and domestic situation available on *13* will be disappointed. This track, like all the others, uses words in largely the same way as 'oohs' and 'la la's'. Words are here for texture, punctuation and rhythm, not for soul-bearing. Remember the good old days when Blur used to provide an ultra-short punk song to cleanse the palate? There's one here too. Just to make this clear, it's even handily called 'Punk'. 'Sound Check (Gravity)' kicks in with a serious 'Guns of Brixton' bass only to be outdone for the following track, 'Double Bass', an instrumental mood piece with an ultra-posh spoken word drop in by Albarn.

'Rock the House' has the unlikely combination of John Dankworth and Del Tha Funky Homosapien thanks to its sample from the veteran jazzman's score for Joseph Losey's modish 1960s movie *Modesty Blaise*. '19-2000' is also rich on collaborations, with Miho Hatari joined on vocals by Talking Head Tina Weymouth. The second Gorillaz single release, the song was a handy No.6 hit for the cartoon funsters. 'Latin Simone (Que Pasa Contiga)' is the most 'World Music' track on offer, with a vocal by the late Ibrahim Ferrer, the Cuban performer who found fame in the film *Buena Vista Social Club* in his 1970s. Albarn takes the back set, supplying background 'aahs'. Synth skank 'Starshine' and the lover's rock 'Slow Country' keep up the reggae quotient – it's a nonsense to classify this as a hip-hop album – until we return to soundtrack territory with 'M1 A1' which samples John Harrison's score for George A. Romero's 1985 zombie movie, *Day Of The Dead*, and upsets the dinner party vibe again with its pinging rock drums and squally guitars. 'Dracula' is the revved up faster version of 'Clint Eastwood' that's since become more familiar than the super slow version and the album tails out with 'Left Hand Suzuki Method' which is '19-2000' revisited; if anything it contains even more cool shoeshine than the version earlier in the album.

This is music making on an international scale – it was produced in London, America and Jamaica – and has far more to do with 'Mali Music', *Ravenous* and *Ordinary Decent Criminal* than *13* or *Blur*. Even if it is fronted by a group of cartoon monkeys, it just *works*. Not everyone knew exactly how or why, but it worked nevertheless. Even those directly involved struggled to make sense of it: "Hip-hop has a lot to do with story-telling and therefore it has that with cartoons," producer Dan the Automator – aka Dan Nakamura – told *The Guardian*. "With hip-hop you get to say a lot more words than you do in a rock record. You can paint a picture." If it was no more than a post-modern prank, it was a highly effective one and Damon's plan to be incognito hadn't distracted from the music one bit. "You'll never see who the musicians are because it doesn't matter," Albarn offered to *CDNow*. "It's funny. There's no actual proof that I'm on the record at all. People just assume it's my voice. And you assume that you are talking to me. But it always strikes me that using the telephone or the internet is a similar kind of mind-fuck as driving down a road and assuming that no one is going to crash into you."

Such a high risk project – pop star hides behind cartoon characters to produce accessible World Music album – could have been taken out into the car park and given a righteous critical kicking. Amazingly, it wasn't. *L.A. Weekly* labelled it as, "hands down, this is one of the best-produced albums of the year." *Rolling Stone* saw it as, "inspired by the punky reggae parties of *Sandinista!*-era Clash, tracks like the dub-rap-rock mutation 'Clint Eastwood' and its catchier two-step Rasta remix bring back the exuberance missing from Blur's last album, *13*, while running with its anything-goes avant-aesthetic." It would have been difficult for Damon to find a duff review of the project, but there were conscientious objectors: *Village Voice* offered this: "It's what you might expect from a bunch of musos playing with Cubase or ProTools: sampled loops, Brixton dub, trip-hoppy tangents. U.N.K.L.E.'s bratty nephew, really, though the album sounds like the group locked the metronome on 'heavy funk groove' – chugging and satisfying at first, it feels exhausted by the fifth or sixth track." Regardless of the few dissenting voices, the album was critically lauded and – crucially – note how all of the above are American publications.

Several events of 2001 would also have a direct and indirect impact on the fortunes of Damon, Gorillaz and Blur. In June, Tony Blair was returned to 10 Downing Street with the lowest turn out of voters since 1918. Since keeping his distance from the Blair government in the 1990s, Albarn had become increasingly disenchanted with the apathy of the UK electorate and an apparent lack of ability or desire on behalf of other performers to tackle political issues. Both these problems seemed to be thrown into sharp relief by one unlikely source that year. First, *Popstars* in February had shown the other side of using a made-up band to sell an awful lot of records. Damon was appalled, but as ever it brought out his competitive streak. "It's quite timely," he said of *Popstars* when interviewed by *Metro*. "[It's] almost part of this weird zeitgeist in pop, but at the opposite extreme to what we're trying to do. I bet we sell more records in the end." Hear'Say, the group created for the ITV show, sold a million copies of their debut single 'Pure And Simple'. This feat was outdone by the next big reality winner Will Young, who hit big with *Pop Idol* which came on air in October of the same year. Nearly nine million people voted in the pop battle of

Young and his arch rival Gareth Gates – turnout in the 2001 election had dropped to dismal 59 per cent. More people voted for Will and Gareth than for the Tories.

The terrorist attacks on New York on September 11, 2001, had undoubtedly focused the world's attention on the religious and ideological gulfs that had opened up across the world, but at that stage it remained to be seen whether it would invigorate any response from voters. Attention was soon shifting to Iraq and claims that it was purchasing uranium from Africa with a view to furnishing itself with so-called 'weapons of mass destruction.' Politics and popstars. A mix that Albarn had resisted in the past – his 'inner Sting' as he once described it – was a mix that Damon would find increasingly difficult to ignore.

With Gorillaz's 'Rock The House' charting at a useful No.18 in November 2001 and the album starting to open up territories that had previously been resistant to Blur's charms – even the Germans were buying it – things couldn't be going better for Gorillaz. For a cartoon collective playing zombie hip-hop funky ska, they'd been chillingly effective and tellingly successful. They would even have the pleasure of having the album nominated for a Mercury Music Prize, be designated as the bookie's favourite, only to peevishly withdraw from the competition. Satanic bass man Murdoc was given the task of band spokesman, explaining why they were pulling out: "Mercury award? Sounds a bit heavy, man! Y'know sorta like carrying a dead albatross round your neck for eternity. No thanks, man! Why don't you nominate some other poor Muppet?" he said in a statement. The award ended up with PJ Harvey. Gorillaz were then promptly nominated for six MTV Awards – notably with not a murmur of protest from Murdoc or anyone else connected with the band. When it was possible for interviewers to get a statement out of Damon as himself – and not as some form of Gorillaz spokesman – he was vague to the point of evasive on the subject of Blur. "It's sort of part of my life still, you know," he said when pressed about his 'day job' on Radio 1. "I've been working on a lot of other stuff ... I've done this record in Mali which is coming out fairly soon. Blur ... I've been writing songs, I've got loads of songs. I sort of hang out for a couple of hours and I go in and record in my little studio at home for a couple more hours each night. So, I dunno, I've got about fifteen songs now, I've got enough for a record but I wanna keep working on that. I think, what I can say is that we'll definitely be putting out a couple of singles this year. I like the idea of putting out singles with Blur at the moment, and not albums."

Unsurprisingly, as the buzz around Gorillaz grew, so did the rumours about the status of Blur – and particularly that of their mercurial guitarist Graham Coxon. On September 20, 2001, Blur came out of the shadows to play an unusual gig at the Hilton Hotel on Park Lane. With the addition of a female keyboard player and backing vocalist, the band performed 'Beetlebum' and 'Song 2' at a music industry bash to honour their manager Chris Morrison, who'd previously worked with everyone from Thin Lizzy to Dead Or Alive. Albarn made a short speech from the stage: "This is a very brutal business we're in and anyone who has lasted deserves credit. Chris has definitely got us through a lot of weird things."

Morrison's ability to deal with weird things that year was being severely tested by Graham Coxon. During the Gorillaz campaign, the guitarist was battling personal issues on several fronts. "2001 was a funny year for me," he understated to Q magazine. "I was in two different mental hospitals in March and then November. There were problems with booze and depression." Coxon began toying with yet another solo album – his fourth in as many years. By the time it was released, however, he was an ex-member of Blur. The final crashing chord of 'Song 2' – played from the stage of the Hilton Hotel – would be his last live noise as a member of the band.

CHAPTER 16

GRINDING TO A HALT?

Blur – all four of them – initially returned to the studio for a week in March 2002, reconvening in May for more recordings, this time for just four days. And then, suddenly it seemed, Coxon was gone. "Our manager Chris Morrison told me my services weren't required anymore," Coxon informed Q magazine. "It was something to do with my attitude. Although I felt I was going about my work honestly, perhaps they mistook honesty for attitude. There is a total problem with honesty and communication in Blur at times."

Although rumours of Coxon's status swirled around London throughout the summer, it wasn't until September that the guitarist confirmed what had happened. In a cat and mouse interview to promote his latest solo album – *Kiss Of Morning* – with veteran music journalist Phil Sutcliffe, he revealed that he had been ousted from the group. Much was made of one track on Coxon's album – 'Song For The Sick' – in which the guitarist wishes death on a character called 'Taylor' ... a 'fuckin' fake' who stabbed him in the back. Coxon insisted that there was no connection between Taylor and any members of Blur – the break was based on purely professional differences. No big bust ups. No screaming matches. No punches thrown. Fair enough. The series of photos to accompany the piece are of Coxon spotting his way out then clambering over a wall, next to the inevitable heading "*The Great Escape*". "They certainly can carry on without me," Coxon told Sutcliffe. "When we started we needed each other an awful lot, but now sometimes I don't think it matters who is involved as long as there are songs and sounds to make. I have no idea if anyone's taken over from me."

Initially, no one did replace Coxon. Technically speaking, that remained the case. The key was diplomacy, with kind and measured words being the order of the day. "I've known him since he was 12, so I would sincerely hope that at some point we'll be talking again, otherwise that's a lifetime friendship wasted," Albarn graciously said to the *NME*. "Graham just genuinely wants to pursue a far more low-key life in every aspect – the way he records, where he lives, how he conducts his life. He's been through a very tough time, and hopefully he's coming out the other end now." Drummer Dave Rowntree – in a surprising claim made to technical musician's website *OTWS* – played down the guitarist's departure: "[Coxon had] kind of absented himself for the past two or three records, so it was business as usual. We didn't make much of a play of it at the time, as you can imagine, because we were still hoping we could patch things up. My best guess is that now there are only three of us, there's one less name for people to have to remember and that's going to make it slightly easier for people to see the band as three individuals." Despite the apparent bluntness of Rowntree's words, a door was left open. A door that would remain resolutely unclosed for the forseeable future. "None of this precludes us getting back together with Graham at some point in the future," said the drummer. "Who knows whether that will happen?"

Some fairly good money was on Albarn going solo. With notable timing, just after the aborted sessions with Coxon, came the release of *Mali Music*, the final result of Albarn's musical travels with a melodica two years earlier. The heavy broadsheet press were largely supportive but music journalists were slightly cynical; John Robinson in the *NME* suggested that the album was a vehicle for proving Albarn's adaptability and suffered from being too "right on" in its use of the Mali musicians. "The album feels ever-so-slightly like a compromise. Obviously determined not to have the whole thing come across as a tawdry bit of cultural tourism, Albarn is painstakingly faithful to much of the material he recorded. Which is fine, of course, but his largely hands-off approach deprives us of what might have been a more engaging fusion of the parties involved." To be fair, *NME* perhaps wasn't the album's natural constituency. World music magazine *fRoots*, on the other hand, definitely was and journalist Jamie Renton had this to say: "Apparently the aim was to create a musical travelogue of Mali, but it's one filtered through a particular laid-back west London sensibility. Albarn mainly contents himself with orchestrating the whole thing and playing simple melodica melodies, with just the occasional understated vocal thrown in. All in all, *Mali Music* is pulled off with just the right mix of respect and inventiveness."

Going through the London session tapes that Coxon had taken part in before his departure, a couple of days' worth of work was deemed usable. What followed was a 'first-come, first-served' series of sessions, with British engineer and producer Ben Hillier overseeing a grab bag of ideas created with whoever was available. "If you're there, you get to play on it, if you're not, you miss out," was how Hillier described it. "Everyone was really hungry to play on the record. If Damon wasn't there and we wanted to record a vocal, then Alex would sing, or if Alex wasn't there then Damon would be desperate to get on the bass. It was quite competitive but really exciting. Everyone had this real drive to play." Damon took on the daunting task of filling in for Coxon on guitar and the prospective sound of the album was further morphed with input from The Dust Brothers – Michael Simpson and John King – who'd already worked with everyone from Beck to Hanson – as well as Norman 'Fatboy Slim' Cook and a return fixture for William Orbit.

In a now familiar 'Damon technique' in times of trouble, a change of scenery was in order, this time Morocco. Recording for the first post-Coxon album was shifted to North Africa. "The whole country is mesmeric," Damon enthused to *The San Francisco Chronicle*. "I went on a recommendation from some of my fellow musicians in Mali who were playing one of the sacred festivals they have in Morocco every year ... We settled down very well and basically lived there for a month and a half. I was writing lyrics and singing in olive groves. It was a very elemental record. There was no sort of restrictions. It was just how it sounded like in the middle of the desert."

How it *felt* there on the other hand was extremely hot. The sessions took place in August in baking Marrakesh heat, with the temperature limiting how much work could be done during the day. Everyone involved were also hit with food poisoning courtesy of the local cuisine. "We all lost about a stone and no-one could be more than twenty minutes away from the nearest toilet," says Hillier, recalling the time Blur discovered that *Moroccan Life Is Rubbish*.

"It was 200 yards to the house where the toilets were and we had a bike outside and every now and then you'd see someone legging it back to the house." Similar to the London sessions, there was a feeling of 'anything goes': Dave Rowntree idly tapping a beat on flightcases being wheeled off a truck was recorded as was Damon jumping up and down in an old truck parked outside, which made a satisfying squeaking noise. Cook flew out for five days and worked on three tracks, managing to find a use for Damon's squeaky truck jumping.

When time ran out in Morocco, the band decamped to Devon, where Albarn had bought a farm. The gear was packed up and shifted to a 200-year-old barn where final parts were recorded and the album was mixed. An early taste of things to come – eagerly awaited by those concerned about the involvement of Cook and the potential for a move into dancier territories – was the self-released single 'Don't Bomb When You Are The Bomb', a virtually guitarless slice of Krautrocking electronica. Damon was quick to head those 'Blur Go Dance' headlines off at the pass. "It's definitely a rockin' record," he told *NME*. "It goes from punk rock to hip-hop to prog rock. Two tracks we've already finished doing with Norman are amongst the most rock-oriented tracks we've ever done. Neither of us wanted to play on [his] past glories. He's a devotee of The Clash, and I love The Clash, and that was where our tastes met." In the end, Cook's named appeared on only two tracks on the album, with Blur and Ben Hillier receiving the lion's share of the credit along with the production assistance of London in-house producer Jason Cox.

Back in London, Albarn's political aspect – something he had tried to keep away from his musical persona – was coming to the fore. In January, he was seen on the streets of Westminster voicing his concern about growing storm clouds of war over Iraq. As he stood with protesters sporting 'No War For Oil' placards, he was an obvious target for reporters looking for a famous face to 'sex up' the story. "There has always been a sense of unease about this war and as it gets closer I think that is manifesting itself on the streets," Damon told the BBC. "I feel that it is something that I was brought up with, that war is never an answer. In this particular instance I don't think emotionally the country has any stomach for it. I don't think we have been consulted as a democracy. It is the wrong war."

Albarn said he believed Saddam Hussein was "a monster who is the creation of the West anyway, so if we are going to depose him, we need to look at the elements in the West that created him."

Just before the album's release, there was a reminder of how things used to be. The good old days of knees-ups and punch-ups were brought back with the release of the documentary feature film, *Live Forever*. Touted as 'Britpop: The Movie', the film had started life as a documentary about Oasis and the rise and fall of Creation records before developing into a larger piece about the mid-1990s British music explosion with Blur vs Oasis as the central motif. Deciding he would only proceed if he got the involvement of The Big Three – Blur, Oasis and Pulp's Jarvis Cocker – John Dower's film is nostalgic and surprisingly non-post-ironic. It's also very funny, with hilarious offerings from the Gallaghers, Cocker and side players like Louise Wener of Sleeper. "I'm not going to be the guy who goes and makes the film about Iraq or Afghanistan, I'm just not that sort of film-maker. I guess I have that English thing of wanting to take the piss slightly. This was a real *Carry On* moment for British popular culture – *Carry On Britpop* – it felt like a slightly ludicrous time. I did become immediately nostalgic for these great characters. Only in this country could we turn a battle of the bands into a pantomime class war." Noel Gallagher manages to sum up the film, the movement, the pages of newsprint written, John Harris' *Last Party* book and the whole Blur vs Oasis malarkey in one crisp statement during *Live Forever*, when asked on camera by Dower about Oasis being deemed the working-class heroes compared to Blur's more middle-class status. "I worked on building sites," states Gallagher, clearly enjoying every moment, "that fundamentally makes my soul purer than theirs." Interestingly, Damon's interview takes place in what appears to be a working-men's club. Gallagher's is in a baronial throne room. "Damon was the first person who agreed to be in the film," says Dower. "He said to me, 'Pitch me the film.' So I pitched him the film and he said, 'Do you know, it's the perfect time to make this film, I really want to do it.' And he was really enthusiastic. And then on the day of the interview he turned up in a very strange mood, I was slightly thrown by him ... but it made for a good interview!" Damon comes across rather oddly in *Live Forever* and his contributions aren't particularly funny, intentionally or not. "I'm not a film-maker who stitches people up... I have nothing to hide," recounts John Dower. "Then just before the film came out, his people started to ring up saying Damon needs to come in for editorial approval ... and the day he came in to look at it, he was in a completely different mood, he was very bouncy and he said, 'I want to do my interview again!' I told him that's not fair on the other people in it. 'Okay, I'll just watch it.' He watched it and he was really big about it. He said, 'I'm true to myself and I like what you've done, I get a kicking off the Gallaghers but nothing new there!'

As preparations were underway to release Blur's new album – now named *Think Tank* – and perhaps to draw a line under the Coxon issue, an announcement was made about the guitarist's 'replacement'. Only it wasn't to be a replacement at all. Former Verve guitarist Simon Tong – who'd been writing and rehearsing with borderline Northern supergroup The Shining – was unveiled in the first week of March at an industry event in London held by Blur's new label, Parlophone. The event was away from prying eyes and a carefully worded statement made clear that Tong was there to help the band out for live performances only – he wasn't the new Coxon. He'd already been rehearsing with Damon, Alex and Dave. 'He's a lovely bloke and he's fitting in,' was the drummer's assessment to industry website *OTWS*. "He's done the impossible, really. He's come into what could have been a very awkward situation with a bunch of people who all knew each other and have done this for years and he's fit in perfectly." Damon was inclined to play down Tong's role a little at the time, making everything appear very casual, perhaps to avoid fans putting too much pressure on Tong and his role within Blur. "He's just been basically learning old stuff and playing together and trying to get some kind of sound together that is our own," the singer told *Under The Radar*. "Cause it's the most depressing thing, I think in the world, if you try and recreate the past and fail. So it's best just to sort of really have an attitude of, 'Well, this is how it sounds now so let's really get involved in how it sounds now and feel comfortable with that.'"

Tong was not represented on Blur's sixth album – *Think Tank* – which was released in May 2003. Graham Coxon was, along with Norman Cook, William Orbit, that squeaky truck in Marrakesh and some underwater cymbals. A big, unmade bed of an album, *Think Tank* is easier to admire than it is to like. Opener 'Ambulance' has synth washes, honking sax effects, shimmying backing singers but not much by way of a tune. It's as cool and knowing as the album's Banksy sleeve – and just as difficult to relate to. 'Out Of Time' is safer ground, with Damon's simple guitar riff, beautiful vocal and a Moroccan middle eight, its poignancy was focused by a video featuring life on board an American aircraft carrier. Released as a single, it was a good solid No.5 chart placing for a lovely song. The Norman Cook propelled 'Crazy Beat' ruffles things up a bit with its squelchy vocal effects, descending punk chords and frankly rum lyrics, before the summery swoon of 'Good Song'. This track features the simplest, wolf whistle of a guitar motif that's liquid sunshine over a lazy, croaky vocal from Damon. Gorgeous. Another single from the album, accompanied by a wistful two colour animated video by artist David Shrigley, it earned the worst chart placing at 22 that the band had managed since 'Sunday Sunday' in 1993. So there you go. 'On The Way To The Club' has the kind of dubby take that wouldn't have gone amiss on the *Gorillaz* album with a jaded lyric that's reflective of *Death Of A Party* and a Kraftwerk keyboard workout. The drug heavy 'Brothers and Sisters' explores similar themes and has Damon stating that we're all drug-takers and then proceeding to list most of the options open to us, as if he's chairing a Narcotics Anonymous meeting. Its waspy synths, hand-claps and lack of tune aren't easy on the ear ... and that's probably the idea. 'Caravan' is a lo-fi ambient croon from Damon before 'We've Got A File On You' is that punk rock moment – albeit with a sense that it's being shouted from a minaret. One minute palate cleanser duly delivered, 'Moroccan People's Revolutionary Bowls Club' comes along like a North African version of Manic Street Preachers' 'La Tristesse Durera' with unattractive keyboard settings; all very clever and worldly but a listener needs to be romanced as well as impressed. 'Sweet Song' – aided by William Orbit – does just that and is sploshed with the same liquid sunshine as 'Good Song', as Damon sings of a sweet contentment despite his own failings and those of others. The longest track on offer is 'Jets', a plodding piece with brushes, minimalist tune and more weird keyboard plinks – the synths seem to be on hand right through the album to counter the lack of Coxon's sonic oddness. 'Gene By Gene' is a looped up Norman Cook job featuring that squeaky Moroccan truck and cymbals being abused by Dave Rowntree and Ben Hillier. "I told Dave that if you hit a cymbal and lower it into a bucket of water it pitch-shifts," says Hillier. "So we got an old fish tank and filled it up with water and spent all day hitting cymbals and lowering them into the water, sampling them and making loops. Gongs too — anything we could hit and lower into water. Norman made a loop out of Damon's squeaking sounds which fitted with the cymbal sounds and it turned into a tune." Tucked at the back of the album is the track that bears the name of Graham Coxon alongside the remaining members of Blur. Billing itself as a ballad for the good times, 'Battery In Your Leg' features John Lennon piano stabs scrubbed down with familiar Coxon noise washes; it's stirring stuff and you have to fight the feeling that it's one of the album's strongest tracks. That would be just too obvious wouldn't it?

With that thought in mind, it would be expected that the press would be getting a good run up to give the album a critical kicking. They'd had a good career, the most popular member had left ... easy target. Amazingly, that wasn't to be and the reviews were so glowing you could toast a crumpet on them. *Uncut* had it down as, "the sharpest, most imaginative and downright listenable album of Blur's career to date ... a grown-up alt.rock album of breathtaking potency and invention." "Against the odds," reckoned *NME*, "*Think Tank* is a success, a record which might not mean much to Strokes fans but which shows Blur's creative spark is undimmed even while their stomach for the pop fight fades." *Mojo:* "Invigorating and intriguing, as hummable as it is inventive ... it's also possibly the best thing Blur have done." Praise indeed; so much so it was nice to have a note of dissent. One was provided by Graham Coxon in June. Prompted by a reader in *Q* magazine's ever cheeky 'Cash For Questions' section, where music fans are coerced into asking artists things that the journalists don't have the nerve to ask, the guitarist was asked what he would have done to improve *Think Tank*. "Chucked the computer out and actually worked on making music instead of playing with Lego electronics," he offered. "And written songs." In retrospect, he's spot on.

The album was released as the first thrust of the invasion of Iraq was underway, spurring Albarn into attending protest rallies and questioning his fellow artists about where they stood. "We've all had to stomach a type of horror which we maybe thought we'd never experience in our lifetime, and it's now become a part of everyday life," he told *NME*. "So I would have thought the responsibility of any open-minded artist would be to try to make some sort of sense out of the chaos we're all involved in. I don't know where the Michael Stipes of the world have gone."

By way of contrast to the gruelling tour schedules of the past, *Think Tank*'s live schedule was initially more geared towards its media profile, with showcase performances on ITV's *CD:UK* and the BBC's *Jonathan Ross Show*, an MTV special filmed in Camden and special 'secret' performances for fans and journalists in France, Germany and Spain. When the live work kicked in, there was a five-night stint at London's Astoria before the festival circuit beckoned in America, Japan and the UK. In September, the Blur wanderlust of old reappeared and the band played two dates at the Gorbunova venue in Moscow.

When the album was left off the shortlist for the Mercury Music Prize that year, the band were oddly miffed. "I don't need a fucking twat panel to tell me it isn't as good as M People," was Alex James's pithy assessment of the situation. Damon kept his own counsel, perhaps wisely after he had jerked around with the Mercury panel in his Gorillaz guise. They had to console themselves with getting Q magazine's 'Album of the Year' instead. With so many plaudits, 2003 ended with a rare critical stumble for Damon. Billed as a "journal of no-fi demos recorded in hotel rooms during Blur's US tour", the *Democrazy* album was a 'brave to the point of foolish' idea to release a disc of "ideas in progress" on the Honest Jon's label. "I wanted people to have an insight into the music-making process ... to unveil it. Literally, me and a guitar in a series of hotel rooms." It did not get a warm reception from critics. *The Guardian* said it was, "occasionally brilliant and frequently irritating beyond belief. It is packed with interesting ideas, but is founded in an appalling self-importance. It is, you are forced to concede, a record not unlike its author." And that was one of the better reviews. *NME* asked, "What illuminating revelation do we learn from the half conceived, cotton-mouthed rubbish that constitutes *Democrazy*? In full: 'Thank Christ

Blur usually finish writing their songs before they sell them, otherwise they'd be shit.'" The winner for worst review must surely be *Dot Music* with the following: "On the evidence of *Democrazy*, the wrong self-indulgent flake got fired from Blur."

The negative reviews were still ringing in Damon's ears as Blur did a final tour of the UK to round off the year. On December 12, they played at the Bournemouth International Centre. They performed a mixed set – including the Coxon track 'Battery In Your Leg' – before finishing with 'The Universal'.

At the time of writing, this is the last time that Blur have played live.

CHAPTER 17

DEMON DAYS

If there's one thing likely to fire the willingness to succeed of someone like Damon Albarn, it's a bit of competition. And some good old-fashioned music industry gossip. These were things he was more than familiar with by this stage of his career but he was about to receive more than his fair share on both fronts.

March 2004 saw the release of an astonishingly good single by Graham Coxon – 'Freakin Out'. A hideously catchy slice of new wave pop with a finger-achingly fast riff, it was an absolutely clear signal that the previously troubled guitarist had more to his solo canon than odd, metallic folk. Lyrically, Coxon stated he had nothing to fear and nothing to prove. Odd that – given that scrawled across the inner sleeve of the Coxon-less *Think Tank* was the message, 'I Ain't Got Nothing To Be Scared Of.' The critics loved the single and were wowed by the album that followed, *Happiness In Magazines*. "The best Graham Coxon imaginable," said *Q*. *Uncut* judged it, "his most accessible work since *Parklife*." *The Guardian*, tellingly, called it, "a great lost Blur album." Maybe, just maybe, there could be another Blur album, just like the old days?

The Blur rumour that really got people's attention appeared not on a fan website or a music magazine but in a daily tabloid. *The Mirror's* 3am gossip column – normally the natural home of wayward popstars and drunken soap actresses – boldly claimed that Coxon was headed back into Blur. Well, at least the headline did. A furious Coxon took the trouble to ring *Designer Magazine* – only Coxon would choose such a publication to rebuff a story in a British red top – to set the record straight. But while pointing out that, actually, he was about to start working with former Blur *producer* Stephen Street, he managed to make matters worse by confirming that he had met up with the other members of the band. "It wasn't like a secret meeting; it was just that we didn't tell anybody," he told the magazine. "It's nobody's business, but it doesn't mean there are any secrets. It was quite nice meeting up because we went through a lot together and we haven't really seen each other to communicate one-to-one for quite a long time. There was quite a lot to say to each other. It's good to see each other every now and then and I think we'll see each other now and then in the future, but I think that's really to mend stuff emotionally more than anything else." From here on in, the foundations were laid for the 'Coxon Returns To Blur' rumour mill ... and business would be brisk over the next two years.

Meanwhile, Damon Albarn was heading for an ominous anniversary – could it really be nearly ten years since Blur picked the most famous fight in rock and the Great Battle of Britpop was fought? But there would be no celebrations to mark one of the daftest moments of the 1990s. Oasis were treading water after another dry album, 2002's *Heathen Chemistry*. Still a hefty live draw and a tabloid favourite, the former rivals' careers could not have been more different. Damon Albarn and Oasis were world's apart – further than they'd ever been – and the last thing Albarn wanted to do was remind people about the events of 1995. Instead, he donned a disguise – a familiar, slightly hairy mask to ensure that 2005 would not be just a year of nostalgia. "The further I can retreat the better," he told *The New York Times*. "Something happened to me which made me distrust the cult of the personality in music. I don't for one second think that realistically I can completely and utterly become anonymous, because people like to know who's doing what they're doing. But when you look in a kind of book of folk music or written music, and the personality of whoever wrote it comes through in the music, there's not a picture of them next to it, is there? There's just the notes. That's the reason for music."

Gorillaz – seen by many as a one-off prank, albeit a globally effective one – were shaping up a return to the fray. As work began on a new album, the question was asked: what would a follow-up album be like? "It sounds like someone has taken the first record and coloured it in," was how 'frontman' 2D summed up the situation. That task could be said to have been achieved by producer Danger Mouse –

otherwise known as New York musician and producer Brian Burton. The Anglophile Burton – another cartoon fan as his pseudonym suggests – had lived in London in the early Noughties where he got his first musical break, but burst onto the international scene via his mixing of The Beatles' *White Album* with rapper Jay-Z's *The Black Album* to create the internet sensation *The Grey Album*. The project caught the attention of a worldwide audience on the internet, not to mention a gaggle of lawyers and also one Damon Albarn of west London. 2D also claimed that the new album would be called *We Are Happy Landfill*, but that's what happens when you allow a gap-toothed animated simian to be your spokesman. Wisely, 2D was overruled and the subsequent album was given the name *Demon Days;* it would prove to be a creative pinnacle for the Gorillaz project, both as a recording and a live experience – as well as a serious contender for the position of career highlight for Damon Albarn.

Released in the spring, *Demon Days* was a critical winner – the cultural opposite of Albarn's last outing with *Democrazy*. Wide ranging with a broader roster of collaborators and a greater mastery of technology, it's a better record than *Gorillaz* on virtually all counts. *Uncut* would judge it to be, "a dazzlingly clever record – great beats, brilliant production, top tunes and some of Albarn's best singing" ... praise in any language, simian or otherwise. The album would go straight in at No.1 in the UK, France, Switzerland and Honk Kong, enter the charts in the Top Five in Argentina, Australia, Belgium, Germany, Ireland, Slovenia, Austria, Denmark, Norway, Canada, Iceland, Italy and Japan and prove a Top Ten smash in America. Any final doubts that Albarn was anything other than an international contender would be banished for good.

From the intro – called 'Intro' – there's enough to keep in touch with the last album – another sample from a George A. Romero film if nothing else, this time *Dawn Of The Dead* -while taking the concept one step further. It's a borderline concept album, as the characters roam a post-apocalyptic world populated by kids with guns, lawless cops and most frightening of all, Shaun Ryder of Happy Mondays. The beats of the first real track, 'Last Living Souls', are crisper and the bass smoother and more fluid than before. The guitar work has more musicality than the last Blur album too, probably down to the presence of Simon Tong. The computer tools have been mastered and the ride is a slicker one with all the tracks of a manageable length and more or less jam free. 'Kids With Guns' explores a theme that runs through *Demon Days* – everything's going to shit unless we do something about it, with the terrible days of the title here to serve as a warning. 'O Green World' sports some Oriental themes alongside its bleeping, calculator tones that would prove useful in Albarn's upcoming experiments, before 'Dirty Harry' stakes an early claim as the album's stand out track. It's got a kiddie chorus, Kraftwerk synth runs, cellos and not that much Albarn. Then 'Feel Good Inc' comes along and outdoes it. Damon is brimming with such confidence he even offers a borderline rap before being comprehensively outdone by De La Soul, as they shimmy across a bassline that's a first cousin to Rick James's 'Superfreak'. The 'After the Armageddon' feel was bolstered by a superb video featuring the 'band' surveying a bombed out world – in every sense – from the safety of their windmills and towers. In a beautifully packaged book that followed the album, called *Rise of the Ogre,* 2D explained what the song and the visuals were all about: "I think Gorillaz built a tower around themselves that they couldn't get out of; of excess and debauchery. The video is based on this feeling."

Most of the stuff attributed to the cartoon characters is errant nonsense, but in this case 2D sounds uncannily like a post-Britpop Damon Albarn. The lead single from the album, 'Feel Good Inc' was a No.2 UK hit and got to No.14 in the US charts, proving beyond all doubt that this was no prank, this was British music on a global scale. Wise scheduling means that 'El Manana' and 'Every Planet We Reach Is Dead' slip by easily while you're still getting over the two previous tracks before the heavy rap from UK-born, US-raised rapper MF Doom. His presence – or Daniel Dumile to use his given name – puts a nice extra layer on proceedings as he is also a real guy masquerading as a cartoon character, Marvel Comics' metal faced villain Dr Doom. 'All Alone' pulls out the stops for classy collaborations with Roots Manuva and Martina Topley-Bird up front and Albarn relegated to backing vocals. Strictly speaking there's no punk rock moment here, but the closest is 'White Light' – it's really short, features a fuzztone guitar and makes no sense, so most of the Albarn trademark boxes are ticked. Then, gloriously, Shaun William Ryder comes on board with 'Dare' a tune so catchy that even the task of having to look up Ryder's nose for a large part of the video couldn't stop it reaching No.1 in the UK. 'Fire Coming Out Of The Monkey's Head' offers useful clues towards Damon's next offerings on a simian theme – the opera *Monkey* – but it's the closest thing on offer to a duff track with a pretentious storyteller voiceover from actor Dennis Hopper. Shuffle forward to – of all things, a Beach Boys pastiche – 'Don't Get Lost In Heaven' and just as you start thinking the album should have been cut at 'Dare', there's a return gig for the London Community Gospel Choir from Blur's 'Tender' to provide the title track and the whole album with a skanking outro. As is often the case with Damon's work, he leaves us on a hopeful high and the promise of better things to come. Just as it was about to drop to four stars, the 'Demon Days' track grabs one back and Albarn provides a five star experience. Reviews *glowed*: *NME,* who by rights should have been slagging Albarn off in this stage of his career said, "Before you even consider the sonic and melodic innovation paraded through the album, there's so much crammed into each of these fifteen songs (without any one of them sounding overproduced or cluttered) that repeated listening is a must." The *Los Angeles Times* decided that, "It's Albarn's evocative words, compelling if understated melodic sense and subdued vocals that are the emotional centre, transcending the gimmick even more than on the first Gorillaz album." "First impressions could not be more wrong," said *The Guardian,* "*Demon Days* goes boldly against the current trend for brash immediacy and instead repays time and effort on the part of the listener." Getting into the spirit of the situation, *Mojo* played their critique just right: "funky, playful but sinister like the best children's stories."

Presenting such a sinister story live would always be a challenge and various methods had been used in the past to parade Gorillaz in front of an audience. The summer 2005 Gorillaz tour of US radio stations wasn't likely to fool anyone. Such a visual project was wasted in such an environment. In terms of visual trickery, the peak was reached at the MTV Awards in Lisbon in November 2005. Billed as the 'world's first 3D hologram performance' – Gorillaz would be named as 'Best Group' too – images of the band were beamed onto the stage using a projection technique called the Musion Eyeliner System, which allowed 2D to walk onto the stage at the ceremony, high five a few of the audience, grab the microphone and launch into 'Feel Good Inc' while Murdoc plays along – bass note for bass note – in his underpants. Then up pop the *real* De La Soul. A treat for the eyes and a wonder of technology and creative graft. But the heart and soul of Gorillaz – and possibly Damon Albarn's finest hour – was to be found at the very same time as the MTV extravaganza, with a series of live performances at the Manchester Opera House. As part of a pre-cursor to the Manchester International Festival, a delightful conceit for the gigs to take place over a five night period was constructed. It would be a tribute to Gorillaz, performed by Damon Albarn and Company. Albarn and Hewlett even wheeled out Murdoc to explain the concept. "The way I look at this gig is kinda like the Pope giving his blessing to another Parish," was the official statement given by the pant-flashing bass player. "Gorillaz whole-heartedly condone these Manchester concerts and I'm sure musically it'll be top-notch, especially with the original guests. You should look at it like a great orchestra performing the works of, say, Beethoven. These gigs will be the only 'Gorillaz Approved' renditions we ever allow, so catch it while you can." Total nonsense, of course ... yet more genius.

The stage of the Opera House is not the biggest in the world – it's not even the biggest in Manchester – so space was tight for the singers, guitarists (including Simon Tong), drums and percussion, DJs and string sections that accompanied Albarn. Playing in front of seven screens that threw out such bright colours that the main musicians were rendered as virtual silhouettes, Albarn was clearly identifiable at an upright Joanna, thanks to the familiar profile offered by his retroussé nose ... and because he was centre stage. It got tighter still as a series of guests joined the ensemble – Neneh Cherry was up first for an ominous version of 'Kids With Guns' and had to dance on the spot through lack of space. Somehow they managed to squeeze thirty kids from two schools in Wythenshawe – a notoriously tough area of Manchester that has long enjoyed the honour of being the biggest housing estate in Europe – for 'Dirty Harry.' As the kids whooped it up and sang of needing a gun to keep themselves from harm, some of the audience got up to follow the groove ... but were forced back into their seats by the Opera House's security staff. De La Soul – managing to be on two stages in separate countries at the same time – Ike Turner, MF Doom and Roots Manuva all followed; fantastic each and every one, but none quite equalled the burst of pleasure around the theatre that the kids generated when they all begin to shimmy in unison. The playing, sound reproduction and Albarn's singing were all first class – this was no improvised gang show; this was a world-class musical performance. But when Shaun Ryder appeared, Manchester was back in the house to mess with the slickness a touch; the bouncers really started to struggle and several people were ejected from the building. "Scumminoop, scumminoop, scumminoop ... it's DARE!" Bottle in hand and lollipop in mouth, Ryder stopped the show from getting too *showbiz*. Things chilled out when Dennis Hopper (on tape) intoned 'Fire Coming Out Of The Monkey's Head' and there was genuine poignancy when Ibrahim Ferrer appeared in video form for 'Latin Simone' – he'd died three months earlier aged 78.

Demon Days was a truly special event. You could dance to it, fight a bouncer to it and shed a tear to it. It was quite a show. "Extraordinary," was *The Daily Telegraph*'s view. "Top performers have struggled for decades to find a comfortable marriage between sound and vision, but here they were perfectly matched. There was a coherence behind the whole presentation – the colour- changing panels of light that threw many of the performers, including Albarn himself, seated mostly at the piano, into semi-silhouette; the subdued lighting; the look of the thing. It just worked." "Doesn't so much re-invent the album as underline what a remarkable piece of work it is, a kaleidoscope of disparate musical influences held together by a very singular vision," was *The Guardian's* take; local team the *Manchester Evening News* gave it the full five stars: "The show demonstrated that the group has cast off at least some of the shackles of anonymity to bring their spectacular second album to life. It's a decision the talented Mr Albarn won't regret."

In fact, the talented Mr Albarn would allow this extraordinary show out of its cage again ... then he did what he's done in the past. He stopped it in its tracks. The full ensemble – including a real life Dennis Hopper – staged *Demon Days* at the legendary Apollo Theatre in Harlem in April the following year. Albarn was clear that he was doing it for the challenge as there was no money to be made. "It involves hundreds of people being very dedicated," he told *Q*. "We work with a stadium-sized crew for what is a very small theatre. It's financial suicide." *Demon Days* in Harlem – despite the graphics being a no-show on the first night – was a triumph. The notoriously picky showbiz bible, *Variety* said, "the full-scale presentation proved most engaging when the flesh-and-blood performers were capable of getting in sync with their animated duet partners ... a three-sheets-to-the-wind Shaun Ryder (late of Happy Mondays and Black Grape) earned extra credit by doing his best to morph into a cartoon character himself, fashioning himself as an odd hybrid of W.C. Fields and Mister Magoo for an unsteadily undulating 'Dare'."

It was all such a triumph that Damon decided it would perhaps be wise to go out at the top. Despite plans for a tour along the lines of the MTV performance and even a Gorillaz film Damon decided it was the end. "At the moment, we're like, that's probably the last album we make," he told the BBC's *6 Music* backstage at the Apollo. "I don't think we could make a better album than *Demon Days* really, for what this is and how it works." That night he went off to celebrate the show's success with supermodel Kate Moss and Paul Simonon, formerly of The Clash.

Demon Days had got to the parts that other Albarn projects just couldn't reach. "*Demon Days* had a real point to being made," he reflected to *The Independent,* as the sales figures pushed past *six million.* "I really wanted to create a piece that was a provocative reflection on the world I see out there. I'm surprised we've managed to get so successful considering how bleak it is."

Point proven. With the second Gorillaz album, Damon had financially and creatively outstripped his rivals. And then some. That should do the trick – a job well done, dust your hands off and take a break. Yet astonishingly, just weeks before *Demon Day*s was even released, Damon Albarn had gone back into Studio 13 to don yet another disguise: this time a black top hat. Accompanied by a pensioner, a replacement guitarist and a 'south London thicko', he had somehow managed to create an entirely new persona accompanied by a new set of songs and a new direction. With all that creative energy to spare, you'd think that he'd have enough left

Damon Albarn

over to at least come up with a name for it.
    Apparently not.

CHAPTER 18

THE GOOD, THE BAD AND THE PUB

There's a cheery welcome to be had from the website of the Pig's Nose Inn – plus a hint of how the pub would find its own place in music history and in the story of Damon Albarn.

Hi! We are Peter and Lesley Webber who own The Pig's Nose Inn, East Prawle, Kingsbridge, Devon. The pub is the most southerly pub in Devon and was once a smugglers inn that dates back 500 years. It overlooks the sea and village green. We sell real ale straight from the barrel and also provide a scrumptious varied menu with the help of Carlo, our amazing Italian chef. There is an adjoining hall where we hold live music events.

The band that would perform in the adjoining hall – the latest in a baffling array of guises over and above his 'lead singer of Blur' persona – helped Damon reconnect with the place that had previously provided him with so much lyrical and musical inspiration. The place that he'd felt uncomfortable about revisiting on record since the heady days of *Parklife*: London, England.

The roots of the new project went back a fair way. Tony Allen, Nigerian-born drummer, songwriter and pioneer of Afrobeat music – where jazz meets more traditional highlife sounds – was an unusual early recruit to what was initially an Albarn solo project. The veteran player, impressed by being name-checked in Blur's 'Music Is My Radar' single, invited Albarn over to Paris where he was playing a gig, with a view to some onstage collaborations. Enjoying himself and drunk on high octane rum, Albarn was too refreshed to do much good. "I just could not find the beat at all!" he recalled to *Time Out*. "It was terrible. And about halfway through, I just wandered over and started hugging Tony while he was drumming. Funnily enough, though, we made some kind of bond there. He just laughed, he could see that I'd just got carried away with how exciting it all was, and he invited me over to Nigeria." Accompanied by *Demon Days* producer Danger Mouse, Damon headed for Lagos; sessions took place – enough for an album – but Damon felt his mojo was elsewhere. Simon Tong was also on board and had accompanied Damon on the Lagos sessions. "We recorded in an old Decca studio that had been built in the 1960s," recalled Tong during interviews recorded for a DVD to accompany a special edition of the eventual album. "I don't think anyone had cleaned it since, it was absolutely filthy. Nothing worked, we had to take every bit of equipment we needed. We had quite a big band, we did some really good stuff." As an honorary member of Gorillaz, Albarn had shown great loyalty to Tong, perhaps by way of a thank you for taking on the potentially fraught job of filling in for Graham Coxon in Blur.

It was Albarn's producer who suggested that the best idea might actually be to relocate back home in London. Since the days when Albarn had effectively killed off Britpop – and stung by criticisms of his writing as being one part Martin Amis to one part Dick Van Dyke – reflecting London life on record ... reflecting *English* life ... was deemed out of bounds. He'd spilled the guts of his shattered love-life on *13,* shared his concerns for the world on *Demon Days,* but write about life in the capital? Gor blimey mate, leave it *aaaht.* "I started to feel embarrassed about being articulate," he told *NME* a decade after the self-imposed embargo on London commentary, "I felt out of touch with what was going on."

The answer wasn't to be found in Lagos ... but much closer to home in Ladbroke Grove. Paul Simonon – former bass player with The Clash but now concentrating on painting – had been at the audience for the first Gorillaz gig at the Scala in 2001, keeping an eye on the talent. Damon Albarn had been keeping an eye on Simonon for considerably longer. "I'd been a massive Clash fan since school. The first album I ever bought was Adam And The Ants' *Kings Of The Wild Frontier,*" he bravely admitted to *NME.* "After that it was [The Clash's] *Combat Rock.*" Damon met Simonon face to face at Joe Strummer's wedding reception in Ladbroke Grove in 1995. When Albarn started forging plans for a new, three dimensional band, he called Simonon – London personified – only to discover that the bass player lived just two streets away. "I get asked to do a lot of things and 99 times out of a hundred I say no," Simonon told *Scotland on Sunday*. "I prefer to stick to my painting. But when Damon asked me, I said yes. I really like his music and I knew he'd refused to go to 10 Downing Street when Blair invited him. I thought, 'That's my sort of person.' It's the first time I've made a record without any stress."

Fortunately for Damon, Simonon had picked up a bass two months earlier after playing at a friend's birthday party in the company of fellow ex-Clash man Mick Jones and Primal Scream's Bobby Gillespie. It gave him 'the taste for it' again. "We spent a lot of nights drinking and discussing our experiences," Simonon recalled to *Time Out*, "talking about how strange it is that in this part of town, what were once slums are now back to being one-family Victorian houses, but next door is a council estate that was Victorian houses that were knocked down. That weird eco-system where the rich are there, the poor are there and on the weekend they meet up." If Joe Strummer was always seen as the brains of The Clash, then Paul Gustave Simonon was perceived as the beauty. Cutting a stern, yet glamorous figure through the punk years, his image is preserved in millions of homes the world over on the cover of the *London Calling* album, which featured Pennie Smith's photo of him smashing his bass onto the stage in New York in 1979. He was also a talented artist and a musician beyond The Clash with his Latino rockabilly reggae outfit Havana 3AM, an early trailblazer for World Music. "I was the dark horse," he told *Melody Maker* in the late 1980s. "I think they [journalists] thought I was an idiot. A thicko from South London." His looks would add a scuffed up cool to the look of Damon Albarn's new venture. This was only added to when he turned up to group photo session with a busted nose and a black eye. Damon must have been delighted. The photographer was ... Pennie Smith.

Key sessions for the new band were recorded between the summer and autumn of 2005, the last was just a few weeks after the end of Gorillaz's *Demon Days* run in Manchester; whoever juggles Damon's schedule deserves a medal. The Albarn solo idea was heading towards a collective album. Tong described the early sessions that the band took part in to *Pitchfork:* "We just sort of played. We tried the songs in lots of different ways, and we weren't afraid to just scrap a whole recording session, or scrap a song and try something completely new. It was just a matter of keeping that sort of magic, and capturing the essence of each tune. Damon would come in with some songs and we would just kind of play around and experiment, but we recorded everything right from the beginning. It pretty much stayed that way all the way through, to keep it fresh and slightly demo-ey." Things were kept quiet and the project – to be called The Good, The Bad And The Queen – would stay under wraps for the best part of a year.

In early interviews, there was an insistence that The Good, The Bad And The Queen was a project title, not a band name. "I suppose when we were seventeen and we were a bit insecure and we needed a sense of identity, having a name was useful," Simonon shrugged when asked about the lack of band name by London's *Time Out* magazine. "It's a bit embarrassing being in a gang when you get to our age," Albarn added by way of further clarification. Not giving a name to the band was also a useful distraction from the knee jerk criticism that was levelled at the project before anyone had heard a note – that this was a *supergroup* – still a rock 'n' roll war crime in many people's eyes and for others an affront to someone who used to swing a bass in The Clash. "Usually supergroups are just super-rubbish," countered Simonon, firmly. "I can't think of a single one that's been inspirational. I mean that's part of the reason punk happened, because all the so-called 'super-groups' weren't communicating to anyone except themselves."

Albarn – with his farm in Devon – decided the county was far enough away from the potentially prying eyes of the capital to provide a gentle live debut for the project at the aforementioned Pig's Nose. The band's debut – with Albarn still insisting that the band had no name – was on October 20, in front of an audience of 150. "It's good," mused Simonon at the gig. "It's the birth, and the egg has broken. It was great," Albarn explained to *NME.com*. "We've done a lot of rehearsal and none of us have taken it for granted even though we've done a lot before. You know that everyone has performed in front of 100,000 people, so they're not there to prove anything, they're there to really make sure the music is as good as they can get it." The pub also provided Albarn with a visual trademark to go with the project. One that would stick. "Yes, the top hat ... in the back of the pub, they had a 'dressing-up' box and it was in that. I just put it on for laughs and people said, 'Oh, it looks really good.' I kind of got stuck with it. I think it helps with the mood of the story." The Pig's Nose outing was followed by similar low key affairs in Exeter and Ilfracombe, the latter being in a newly cool coastal town where Damien Hirst was busy 'doing a Reykjavik' by opening a bar and restaurant. All were essentially a warm-up for the band's London debut at the Camden Roundhouse on October 26. Damon told the audience they intended to play the whole of the proposed album in order ... Oh, and 'The Good, The Bad And The Queen' was the name of the album, not the band. With nothing familiar to get a grip on – no chance of a 'Guns Of Brixton' or a 'Parklife' tonight – the atmosphere in the venue was tense and the audience were often heard chatting during the songs, trying to get a grip on what they were hearing. The testiness leaked onto the stage too. At one point, Albarn turned on the band for playing like "shit" insisting, "we can play better than this." At the time, Allen was asked by *Pitchfork* about whether he was happy to take orders – or even a bollocking – from someone like Albarn. "I must respect him, because two captains can never be in one ship," was Allen's seasoned reply. "There must be one captain leading the boat, so that the boat can reach its destination. We must all drop our egos at the door."

Reviews for the show were mixed though on balance it's fair to say that Damon got away with it. "The Good, The Bad And The Queen may never achieve the commercial heights of Gorillaz, even Blur,[but] there's a sense that this project has a higher purpose." predicted *MusicOHM*. Taking note of Albarn's onstage outburst, *NME* noted that it "gives more ammunition to those who think he's too uptight to be genuinely great – but between strops and audience murmurings there was enough to suggest that in The Good, The Bad And The Queen, Damon has defied the haters and pulled it off again." *The Guardian* was far from convinced. "Sounds like a polished second chapter to Albarn's 2003 fractured solo offering, *DemoCrazy*. Despite the gang mentality – they play for themselves, often turning inward to face Allen – this is never more than an interesting one-man band." The wider public got to see what the fuss was about in December when the outfit played three songs on BBC2's prestigious *Later* programme, fronted by Jools Holland, as a teaser for the forthcoming album due in the New Year. When the album was finally released – some 18 months after the initial recording sessions and with Danger Mouse on synths, percussion and most importantly on production – there was a chance to hear what the eclectic mix would produce: "I wanted to make a scary, sad but ultimately optimistic record," said Albarn just prior to its release. In a way, he succeeded.

Although its cover image dates back to London in the mid-19th century, many of Paul Simonon's drawings that are scattered inside the album's packaging are of more recent additions to the capital: alcopops and cctv cameras, parking meters and satellite dishes ... essential elements of modern city dwelling to some, unnecessary evils to others. London, it would appear, is very much in the eye of the beholder. It was, to use one of the many and varied descriptions that Albarn brought into play when asked about this set of songs, a "narrative of moods". As he had done in the past (especially with his dedicated spin of *13* being 'The Justine Album'), Damon set out his stall early: this was 'The London Album', now that he felt comfortable commentating on the characters and situations inspired by the capital once again. "I've been holding back on writing an album like this ever since *Parklife*. I just felt so burned by everything that happened around Britpop and felt I wasn't mature enough to cope with the ridiculous stage I found myself on. It seriously wasn't worth it. I'm not saying these new songs have the immediacy of *Parklife* and I'm not trying to compete with it. But I definitely feel it's a worthy successor," was how he explained himself.

Opener 'History Song' actually tells us more. Lyrically it may have connections with *Parklife*, but sonically we are in *Think Tank* territory, baggy (in a comfy sense rather than a Stone Roses vibe) and late night, with a half bottle of rum to hand and a fag on the go. Spanish guitars rub up along clattering yet quiet drums, a skanky bass and organs from the box marked 'The Specials' as Albarn sets the scene: if you don't like this place, then you will by the end of the next forty minutes. Tune is sacrificed to tone, which is cosmopolitan. '80's Life' sets off like a 1950s doo-wop and largely stays that way with a barber shop protest song about living through a war that's unlikely to come to an end in the near future – or unlikely to come to an end at all. 'The Northern Whale' uses the true story of a whale that swam up the Thames in January 2006 and captured the imagination of the public. Britain seemed more concerned about the fate of the mammal than of wider issues at the time of the incident, which Albarn uses to lyrical effect over an odd mix of buzzy synths, bar room piano vamps and a chorus that's surely influenced by the Jagger and Richards song 'As Tears Go By', made famous by Marianne Faithfull. "There are myths that when a strange creature arrives in the city, it tells people something about their society," Damon explained to *NME*. "The fact that the whale died says it all." Britain had relaxed its drinking laws to allow 24-hour consumption a week before one of the key recording sessions for the album and this is reflected in 'Kingdom Of Doom', where Albarn despairs at a country boozing away while war rages on – in his mind whether it's a bottle of beer or a bottle-nosed whale, we're easily distracted away from the real issues. "You can drink all day, shop all day, watch telly all day and then you add that line, 'the country's at war', at the end of a sentence and it's a different world." he explained to *Time Out*. "Even the news is consumerist. Life wouldn't be normal at the moment unless every night there was someone getting blown up in Iraq. That is the whole crazy thrust of the not-so-hidden agenda of politics over the last five years. It relies on that picture being there, in bars or stations, in shops, you catch a little bit of this chaos on the TV, while you're looking at that new pair of trainers. They work together in a weird way." 'Herculean' was the single lifted from the album, albeit very swiftly as it was released and deleted within 24 hours. It would be a downbeat track by most people's standards but here it's positively uplifting. Again, there's a reference to the new drink laws, with the 'medicine man' available '24-7' in a town where the canal and the gas works live alongside the morning call for prayer, a diverse town that is greater than the sum of its parts. "There are a lot of people running around saying [the album is] all about West London and it's about this and about that, it's not really," Simonon told *Isolation*. "There are geographical references, which are important to us. We are all affected by global warming and if we haven't, we will be, there are things that are brought up as subject matter on the album that affect everybody, so it's not just about London, or west London in particular. It's sort of like a musical post card." 'Behind The Sun' puts its cheap sounding keyboards against lovely piano tones and strings and overlays a virtually constant theme of a police siren as Albarn yearns for the simpler days of the past. In 'The Bunting Song' he gets explicit – all England wants you home, states the singer – as the clouds of conflict darken over a London that doesn't seem to care too much about the war and even its own soldiers, not least because an escape to the countryside beckons. Why put out the bunting to welcome them home, when it's unlikely they will return? There's more warnings of war in 'Nature Springs', but the danger is mainly environmental as the seas rise and threaten our very way of life – it's a pleasure to listen to Tony Allen's drumming here as he seems to go in several directions at once before meeting up with himself at the end of the song. 'A Soldier's Tale' – despite it's title – is opaque about its lyrical intentions – Damon says it's about a fear of technology - but the strings slide and swell over a simple Simonon three-note riff and an early morning vocal from Albarn. If there's potential for a *Parklife* moment, it hovers around the jazzy spy theme 'Three Changes' with its tales of violence, guns and estates on a 'little island' as Damon's accent teeters close to Pearly King territory. It's still a great track, with Simonon stomping around the tune accompanied by Tong's clipped guitar. 'Green Fields' – a re-imagining of a tune Albarn had contributed to Marianne Faithfull's 2005 album *Before The Poison* – sums up the mood of the record in one go; a Beatles-esque lament which name-checks the Goldhawk Road, war and tidal waves as this green and pleasant land is concreted over. It also gives a nod to a key source of inspiration for the whole piece: Martin Amis's sprawling novel, *London Fields*, charting a selection of the city's inhabitants and their individual failings as a mysterious conflict threatens their way of life. Hefty finale 'The Good, The Bad And The Queen' rounds off the cycle; the denizens of the city finish their tasks – be it idling or industry – preparing to do it all again the next day. It's a heady mix and even the bohemian Simonon struggled to sum the album up. "It's got spaghetti western in there, bit of reggae, bit of rock 'n' roll ... bit of everything really. What we've actually come up with is something that's actually quite folk orientated ... that's how I would classify it ... as being sort of tough folk music."

There's much to admire on *The Good, The Bad And The Queen* but it has another similarity with *Think Tank* as well as a comfy, loose sound: it appeals greatly to, but sometimes misses, the heart. You admire its skill, dedication and inventiveness but you wouldn't necessarily feel impelled to rescue a copy if fire was threatening your CD collection. That said, the heavier end of the critical fraternity weighed in heavily in the album's favour. *Observer Music Monthly* rated it as, "one of the most surprising and magical records for which Damon Albarn has ever been responsible." *The Guardian* went further: "You're left both marvelling at the album itself, and considering what a unique figure Albarn cuts. If you doubt it, try to imagine the result if any of Britpop's other major players had assembled a supergroup and made an anti-war concept album. Now take your fist out of your mouth." "*The Good, The Bad And The Queen* is a noir-ishly understated suite of songs," stated *Mojo*, "further testament to its chief author's need to keep on moving." Of all the reviews, *NME* probably hit the nail on the head: "For all its weird beauty, this is very much Damon's record – much more so than Gorillaz. Or indeed, Blur."

Without a 'normally released' lead single and little airplay, the album still reached No.2 in the UK charts – propelled by Albarn fans, critical support and the merely curious – and made the Top 50 in the American *Billboard* chart. The band dutifully played a mid-sized North American tour taking in Toronto, New York, Washington, Austin, New Orleans and California. The success – via sales and the admiration of the press – raised questions about where the project would go from here. "Who knows?" shrugged the ever laid back Paul Simonon. "Damon's going to be off doing other work and I've got some painting to catch up on ... everybody's got their own work. It's quite healthy really, as opposed to a situation where we're just all on this bus and it keeps going until it decides to crash."

Something though, had got lost in the exotic mix of Damon Albarn's adventures in World Music, *Demon Days*, *The Good The Bad And The Queen* and the plans he had for his next guise. Something that many people had forgotten about in the rush and push of critical acclaim and record sales.

Blur.

Remember them?

"I'm really committed to Blur," Albarn told *Q* magazine as he waited to go onstage at the Apollo Theatre in Harlem to perform

Damon Albarn

Demon Days back in 2006. "But I'd really like it to be four people again. I hated playing old Blur songs without Graham on the *Think Tank* tour. Am I saying no more Blur records unless Graham comes back? No. But it's got to be something really brash and stupid. There are real problems to be overcome before I feel right about it."

CHAPTER 19

BACK FOR GOOD?

It's a rum old crowd outside Manchester's Palace theatre for a muggy Tuesday night in June 2007. There are Indie Cindies and Billy Britpops, with their man-bags and gladrags along with a smattering of celebs ... *Hi De Hi* actress Sue Pollard, anyone? There's even a few opera buffs. They're here to see *Monkey: Journey to the West*. The reason that the audience filing into the Palace is so atypical is that this is the first ever performance of an opera with music composed by Damon Albarn. He'd been dropping hints and references to the project during the previous year – and had somehow managed to create the piece while fulfilling his role in The Good, The Bad And The Queen. Now, here it was. "This is a very different thing for me," says Albarn. "For the first time in my life I'll be able to hear my music played – properly – because obviously I've always been in the middle of it."

Inside the theatre, there's confusion as the bizarre ticketing arrangements cause gentle anarchy for those here to witness Albarn's opera debut. The show is part of the Manchester International Festival and was initially billed as a preview when tickets went on sale. The show was then changed to a public technical rehearsal as it was decided *Monkey* wasn't ready to be seen as a fully formed entity. So anyone who'd bought a ticket was given a refund. And everyone who subsequently wanted to see the show was offered a freebie. The Palace is packed – but then again it's not often you get a free night out in Manchester.

The story dates back to 16th century, but anyone of Albarn's generation will know it best from the seriously loopy, imported TV series shown on the BBC in the late 1970s. It tells of an arrogant, bollock-scratching Monkey with a hair-trigger temper, imprisoned for 500 years after rebelling against Heaven and claiming himself to be the equal of Buddha. He's then sent on a quest to find holy scriptures to make amends for his wicked ways. "It's been a real spiritual journey for everyone involved," Albarn told *The Sunday Times*. "If we fail at this, it will set a lot of things back ... if it works it could be absolutely extraordinary." Albarn's opera version of *Monkey* that unfolds on the stage of the Palace may be ridiculously ambitious ... but it works.

Damon, along with Gorillaz collaborator Jamie Hewlett and opera and film director Chen Shi-Zheng, provided a show like no other, filling the stage with jugglers, dancers, martial artists, plate spinners, amorous pigs, ethereal monks and flying starfish. As the dialogue and lyrics kicked in, a slight groan went out across the stalls as some of the audience realised ... *ah – it's all in Mandarin*. A flickering LED display fizzled into life just below the level of the stage.

Live subtitles. Brilliant.

As soon as *Monkey* had begun – with animated sequences filling the entire stage before live actors take over – it grinds to a halt. A babble of English and Chinese voices crackled across the PA system as technical staff tried to iron out the first of the night's hitches and glitches. A tall man in the stalls leapt out of his seat and ran up the aisle to the mixing desk. He would do this some twenty times over the space of the next two hours. Frankly, it's rather annoying. Then you realised: the hyperactive theatre-goer in a Fred Perry shirt was Damon Albarn. He would get out of his seat as many times as he wanted to; he was *willing* the show to succeed ... and he was willing the man at the mixing desk to succeed in very strong and forceful terms indeed.

Musically, there was little that can be classified as typically Chinese. The were buzzes and beeps of electronica, repetitive codas that Michael Nyman would have been proud of and even Brechtian stomps. "You really don't want to be pastiching Chinese music," noted Albarn in *The Sunday Times*.

Given the scale of what's on offer, the problems are surprisingly few and far between. Performer Fei Yang, playing the eponymous Monkey, takes a few unscripted swoops with his wire work – at one stage bashing into the crotch of an onstage female acrobat. The stage is so full and the visuals so intense and exciting that, as you leave the theatre, there's a danger that the last thing the audience will be talking about on the way home is Albarn's music. But this time he is genuinely part of a *team*. The preview goes down well – not exactly a storm but Pollard for one is on her feet at the end. Cast and crew go for the traditional post-mortem. Tweaks are suggested and implemented, cuts are discussed and declined, safety suggestions are made and readily taken on board.

When the reviews come in, they are overwhelmingly positive. "It's lavish, dazzling and entertaining," stated the *Manchester Evening News*. "Albarn's inventive music plays wittily on the tension between the ancient and the new, and, although it's a long way from Blur or even the Gorillaz, it's by no means inaccessible." "I don't know much about Chinese opera, but I know what I like," offered Andy Gill in *The Independent*. "Ninety minutes of fascinating music by Damon Albarn, in which Oriental and Occidental forms are skilfully combined. The traditional Chinese elements – brittle wooden percussion and finger cymbals, astringent lute and violin sounds – are blended with Western beats, orchestral ostinatos that recall Philip Glass, the whine of bowed saw, fairground and oompah music, sombre brass passages, sprinkled throughout with moments that trigger memories of a vast range of musical touchstones, from Harry Partch and Laurie Anderson to Gregorian chants. What more could you want? Indeed, what more could they have crammed into this enchanting show?" A note of caution, though, came from Alfred Hickling in *The Guardian*: "Albarn has certainly extended himself, encompassing a vast, brashly amplified melange of Chinese percussion, esoteric electronica (including an Ondes Martenot), and a blaring contraption of his own invention known as a Klaxophone. Yet, surprisingly for someone with Albarn's melodic gift, there are no arias, thematic development or even much in the way of a memorable tune. Ultimately, *Monkey* is a cartoon opera in the same way that Gorillaz is a cartoon band, which makes it difficult to empathise with the characters on an emotional level." Richard Morrison in *The Times* brushed such thoughts aside, noting, "The sense of something new and exciting being created from the melding of many disparate styles – pop and classical, Western and Eastern, visual and aural. The audience, about fifty years younger on average than the usual opera crowd, loved it."

Had Albarn taken a firm and perhaps final step away from his past? Now approaching forty, he is no longer the tracksuit-topped Mockney waving an ice cream in the 'Parklife' video. He is a musician capable of turning his hand to opera – the musical field that has claimed the scalps of many a foolhardy rocker in the past – and succeeded. Creatively, commercially and critically. From the stage of the Palace Theatre in Manchester, the Britpop years had been comprehensively put to bed. Just in case there's any doubt, the point was made coolly apparent the following day. Rising from his hotel bed after the *Monkey* preview, Damon would have flicked on the TV to see a familiar face amid very unfamiliar scenes. Tony Blair stepping down as Prime Minister. The first rock 'n' roll PM, the first British political leader to know how to handle a Stratocaster and the politician who courted the Britpop stars of the day for his own ends, had left the building. He told the House of Commons this: "I wish everyone, friend or foe, well. And that is that. The end."

But was it?

No sooner had the Blair years ended, it seemed like we wanted them to start all over again. Nostalgia isn't what it used to be; if nothing else because it takes considerably less time to arrive than in the old days. They used to wait at least twenty years before the ache for something long gone became so great that a desire to revive it became overwhelming. Now, we're more impatient. By 2007, nothing seemed quite so appealing as the 1990s. Many current bands in the UK had appropriated key aspects of Blur's sound from the previous decade. Unfortunately, some of the aspects chosen weren't necessarily the best to go for. Acts like The Fratellis, The Pigeon Detectives and The View had certainly adopted some of Blur's more 'knees up Mother Brown', musical hall tendencies. Hard-Fi have taken on the suburban angst and Fred Perry frustration of *Parklife*. The Kaiser Chiefs stylings – synth versus guitar with a story to tell – attracted the wrath of Albarn himself. The Leeds band's second album, *Yours Truly, Angry Mob* was dubbed "empty" and "messy" by Albarn, who compared it unfavourably to Blur's *The Great Escape*. The fact that the Kaisers' second single from the album – 'Everything Is Average Nowadays' – had a title that sounded like it was deliberately inspired by *Modern Life is Rubbish*, seemed to make things worse. To be fair, the obvious Blur reference points seemed endless. "I don't give a shit what Damon says," was the measured response given to *The Daily Star* by Ricky Wilson, lead singer of the Kaiser Chiefs. "It's one man and his opinion. Of course we tried hard – it's our second album. He can say what he likes."

During the opening week of *Monkey*, as politicians jostled and pundits predicted the next political move after Blair had stood down, the music industry was fizzing with teasing talk of its own. The buzz was about big reunions from 1990s superstars. When the announcements came, there was excitement in two very different camps. Take That started the tidal wave of nostalgia with a colossal reunion tour – minus Robbie Williams – and followed it up with a surprisingly accomplished new album. They subsequently broke all records and completed what has been dubbed by some as 'the greatest comeback in British pop history.' This opened the floodgates for various reformations, some good, some bad and some very, very ugly. Twenty-something women everywhere were digging out their Union Jack hot pants with the news that the Spice Girls were back – their winter 2007 Wembley show sold out in *39 seconds*. Joining them on the comeback trail were the All Saints, East 17 and from the pages of the music weeklies, The Verve, Richard Ashcroft's Britpop outsiders citing "the love of music" as their main reason. The only missing member was Simon Tong – he was too busy playing with The Good, The Bad And The Queen. It was almost like a time portal had been opened with a direct link to the 1990s and plenty more were ready to step through it: Shed 7, Dodgy, Northern Uproar and Kula Shaker also hit the comeback trail and all had their own justifications for doing so. For Shed 7's Rick Witter, it was all about the hits – no new material, thanks – for old and new fans. Kula Shaker's Crispian Mills had his own take: "Everyone got tarred with the Britpop brush," he said to *Metro* on the band's return. "But now, ten years later, we can be judged in our own right."

The clever money had been on the big returning band being ... Blur. A series of dropped hints and coded references had been trickling out from various members of the band. Ever the tease, Alex James was the chief culprit, while on the promotional trail for his autobiography, *A Bit of a Blur*. "We're all heading into the studio this summer. Graham's coming too. [We're] gonna see if they've still got it ... if not, I think we'll just call it a day." Coxon himself told James he was "up for a bit of a jam", his spokesman told *Pitchfork*: "There's a lot of rumour and conjecture around about Blur at the minute, but I can tell you that nothing concrete has been planned."

But then Dave Rowntree, fresh from a failed bid to become a local councillor in the Marylebone ward in London, confirmed that time had been booked. "There is a week in the diary," Dave Rowntree told *NME*. "But it's a very small thing – it could either be a seed or a full-stop." The paper became a sort of message board for Blur, each adding their own take on the matter week on week. "I've made a couple of solo albums and now I'm in a really collaborative frame of mind. I'm leaving this year open for collaborations, to do a lot of writing and practical domestic stuff ... I didn't want to plan anything this year in case anything big came about." When Albarn learned of Coxon's tentative thumbs up, he weighed in with this: "If he's in a collaborative mood, then he should collaborate with his oldest mate. Simple as that."

Despite their decommissioned state, Alex James believes that Blur will never actually split up – even if they never tour or record again. "I think we are kind of stuck together forever one way or another. There will always be Blur somehow or other, I think." But recommissioning Blur could, quite possibly, be the worst thing that Damon Albarn ever does. It could provide a nightmare conclusion to the fable of his charmed life. The talismanic luck seemingly provided by the necklace that he wears – that gift from his mother when he was aged six – might finally run out.

To many, Albarn has always seemed to want things both ways. He wanted to pick fights with other bands yet not be seen as the bad guy; he was keen to shed Blur's teeny following yet still maintain sales and venue capacities; he wanted to dabble in world music, soundtracks and opera but not be seen as pretentious. Annoyingly, for his critics at least, in most cases he *has* had it both ways. But reforming a once glorious band with genuine credibility ... now that's a tricky one.

But Damon Albarn is a man who doesn't seem too perturbed by what people think of him. Recall him chastising the orchestra during the sessions for *Ordinary Decent Criminal* ... in front of the rolling *South Bank Show* cameras; remember him putting a flea in the ear of his band at the Roundhouse in London, before a packed audience; bring to mind him taking the sound engineer to task during the first performance of *Monkey* as theatre-goers squirmed slightly in their seats. He doesn't suffer fools gladly, nor does he seem to have much patience with talented people who put a foot wrong.

His run in with Oasis – brought to life so amusingly in John Dower's film *Live Forever* – actually benefited the Burnage boys more than anyone. At the time they were nowhere near as popular as Blur and the fight Damon picked with them bordered on pop chart bullying. Yet, the row bolstered the fortunes of Oasis considerably. It was a masterstroke of marketing though and although the row happened in the last century, yet we're still talking about it today. Would a spat between Hard-Fi and Kaiser Chiefs raise such a kerfuffle these days? Absolutely not. The fame he initially craved kicked back at Damon Albarn – and before he found calm in Iceland, he admits it left him in a mess. "I was in a state of constant agitation for nearly two years," he told *Rolling Stone*. "I had heart palpitations, and I thought about death virtually daily. I had a real physical sense that the off button was going to be switched at some point very soon, and that was very upsetting to me, because as a teenager and as a child, I was very relaxed and happy." Damon's former partner – and such a vital player in this fable – Justine Frischmann, says that Damon endured three months of not being able to sleep or stop crying during the *Parklife* period. "But once he got over the shock of the fact that he was actually getting what he wanted," she told Q magazine, "it was pretty plain sailing for him."

Albarn has taken as much as he has given out over the years – the blows from Noel and Liam Gallagher have been low and crude, but the slings and arrows of Brett Anderson of Suede have been wielded like a stiletto. When Anderson once heard that Albarn had publicly accused him of taking heroin, this was his response to the claims in *NME*: "I find that objectionable," said Anderson, "especially when made by a talentless, public schoolboy who's made a career out of patronising the working-classes." Ouch. But of course, Damon is no more a public schoolboy than Anderson or either of the Gallaghers. If he's been privileged in any way, it's through being on the receiving end of the kind of happy, creative childhood that most people only dream of. That's not his fault nor should it be anything he is criticised for. The bedsit poet as the only type of songwriter capable of creative prowess is a clichéd and tired stand-point.

The journey from his idyllic roots to soaking up applause for his first opera has been unlike any other in British rock. Technically, creatively and socially he just seems better at it than anyone else. A great deal has happened since those first forays into synth pop and his inaugural live performance with Seymour back in 1988. But from the word go, things seem to have gone in Damon Albarn's favour. "It was great. It was perfect," he recalled to *Select* about that first ever gig. "I felt, *this is something*. It was literally just an old train shed in this low-key museum that we hired out. The audience sat in a tube train carriage. We used my dad's old strobe light from the 1960s. We were drunk, but in a good way, it was very innocent, pure." Everything seems to come very easily to Albarn and his muse. Yet, paradoxically, no-one doubts the puritanical work ethic that backs up his immense creativity – a powerful combination. That seems to annoy his detractors more than anything. Suburban pop paranoia, World Music, hip-hop and reggae, soundtracks and opera. It all seems to flow unabated. "I still get writer's block sometimes but I have learned not to worry about it. If I get it, I just go off and do something else, work on something different, then come back to it later."

The Britpop generation he so easily outstripped seems an age away now. The stuff of nostalgia and memoirs. Alex James's *Bit Of A Blur* is essentially a list of all the daft things he did and who with. He's now a married, sober cheese farmer. For a darker note on the same theme, there's *All That Glitters* by Powder singer Pearl Lowe, a grim trawl through the drugs, backstabbing and drugs of the Britpop years. For some, Britpop was a laugh and an excuse to try one on ... for others, it was a life wrecker.

Despite its constant associations with politics, Blair and the end of the century, Britpop was a strangely *apolitical* affair. The political voice that Damon Albarn eventually found – which came to the fore when he was at his most anonymous in the guise of Gorillaz – continues to grow. He's lent his name to a campaign against the introduction of ID cards, comparing the British Government's attempts to control people with paperwork to similar practices in

Nazi Germany. His opposition to the UK Government's replacement of the Trident nuclear weapons system saw him donate a song – '5 Minutes To Midnight' – to the cause. The piece was performed by the 50-piece Sense of Sound choir in March 2007 on board the Greenpeace boat Arctic Sunrise while it was docked in the Thames. Again, Damon is using his fame to influence others. "I think people shouldn't care what other people say when they're talking about these issues," he told *NME*. "Peer pressure is the worst kind of censorship: you can't talk about issues because it's not cool. Rubbish, we all have to engage." The pop star as political mouthpiece dilemma is an awkward hurdle to vault – something Damon is acutely aware of. He's no hothead stumbling into causes and issues. He knows the risks and how performers can come across in such situations. As mentioned, it's a question of fighting his "inner Sting". As Damon himself once admitted, it's not easy to be taken seriously when you're a pretty boy. "Sting came up to me at some awards ceremony and said, 'You know what, you remind me of me when I was young.' It was the most horrifying thing that ever happened to me. I go running every morning now and my mantra is, 'I must not turn into Sting.'"

In direct contrast to his reputation in some quarters as a single-minded visionary, the skill and judgement that Albarn has shown perhaps more than any other during his career is his ability as a *collaborator*. From Graham Coxon to Chen Shi-Zheng, he has shown an unerring sense of who to pinpoint for his own work and who to jump on board with for theirs. This has created an output of such volume, quality and variety it shames his contemporaries. This is a man unafraid of hard work. "Sometimes I'll be watching TV and get irrationally angry with myself," Albarn once told *Q*, "because I'm wasting time." The latest in the collaborative roll call is Kano; Albarn has contributed vocals to *London Town*, the UK rapper's 2007 album which also features Kate Nash and Craig David. Damon also launched his own stage at 2007's Glastonbury Festival – Albarn's line up on the Park stage included African musicians such as Tinariwen alongside Hard-Fi, Terry Hall and The Magic Numbers. Meanwhile the expected swift end to The Good, The Bad And The Queen that many predicted simply hasn't happened. The project won 'Best Album' at the 2007 *Mojo* awards and they continued to play live through the summer festival season of 2007 and into the autumn. It seems to be a collaboration that's just too good to put aside.

And finally ... that day in the studio for the Blur boys to get back together? It never happened. Instead, it turned into a nice meal for all four former members of the band that came to symbolise all things Britpop – the mid-to-late 1990s summed up in four faces. A chance to catch up. Talk about the old days. That makes it sound fairly final, doesn't it? The person who appears to have put the kibosh on the whole affair is the same person who stepped in and killed Britpop; the one who stopped the über-successful Gorillaz in their simian tracks; the man who may or may nor continue with The Good, The Bad And The Queen.

Damon Albarn.

"It doesn't feel right," he told Q in the autumn of 2007, when asked why he was backing away from bringing back Blur. "It feels like a disingenuous thing to do, on my behalf."

That, it seems fair to say, is probably the end of the matter for the foreseeable future.

The return of Blur could be such a step backwards. Particularly when there are so many forward steps yet to be taken: "In music, as soon as you think you've discovered one code, you're immediately faced with a thousand other codes," Albarn told the *Manchester Evening News* in 2007. "Music is infinite and that's why, for me, it's a life-long journey."

DAMON ALBARN DISCOGRAPHY

A complete and comprehensive discography of every track that Damon Albarn has contributed to during the course of his various band, solo and collaborative projects is a sizeable job in itself. This discography is intended to give the key highlights and some indication of the copious volume – and eclectic style – of Damon's recorded output.

Blur - Singles

She's So High (Food/EMI) 1990

There's No Other Way (Food/EMI) 1991

Bang (Food/EMI) 1991

Popscene (Food/EMI) 1992

For Tomorrow (Food/EMI) 1993

Chemical World (Food/EMI) 1993

Sunday Sunday (Food/EMI) 1993

Girls and Boys (Food/EMI) 1994

To The End (Food/EMI) 1994

Parklife (Food/EMI) 1994

End Of A Century (Food/EMI) 1994

Country House (Food/EMI) 1995

The Universal (Food/EMI) 1995

Stereotypes (Food/EMI) 1996

Charmless (Food/EMI) 1996

Beetlebum (Food/EMI) 1997

Song 2 (Food/EMI) 1997

On Your Own (Food/EMI) 1997

M.O.R. (Food/EMI) 1997

Tender (Food/EMI) 1999

Coffee & TV (Food/EMI) 1999

No Distance Left To Run (Food/EMI) 1999

Music Is My Radar (Food/EMI) 2000

Out Of Time (Parlophone/EMI) 2003

Crazy Beat (Parlophone/EMI) 2003

Good Song (Parlophone/EMI) 2003

Blur - Albums

Leisure 1991
She's So High/Bang/Slow Down/Repetition/Bad Day/Sing/There's No Other Way/Fool/Come Together/High Cool/Birthday/Wear Me Down

Modern Life Is Rubbish 1993
For Tomorrow/Advert/Colin Zeal/Pressure On Julian/Starshaped/Blue Jeans/Chemical World/Intermission/Sunday Sunday/Oily Water/Miss America/Villa Rosie/Coping/Turn It Up/ Resigned Commercial Break

Parklife 1994
Girls & Boys/Tracy Jacks/End Of A Century/Parklife/Bank Holiday/Badhead/The Debt Collector/ Far Out/To The End/London Loves/Trouble In The Message Centre/Clover Over Dover/Magic America/Jubilee/This Is A Low/Lot 105

The Great Escape 1995
Stereotypes/Country House/Best Days/Charmless Man/Fade Away/Top Man/The Universal/ Mr Robinson's Quango/He Thought Of Cars/It Could Be You/Ernold Same/Globe Alone/Dan Abnormal/Entertain Me/Yuko & Hiro

Blur 1997
Beetlebum/Song 2/Country Sad Ballad Man/M.O.R./On Your Own/Theme From Retro/You're So Great/Death Of A Party/Chinese Bombs/I'm Just A Killer For Your Love/Look Inside America/Strange News From Another Star/Movin' On/Essex Dogs

Bustin' + Dronin' 1998
CD1 -Movin' On/Death Of A Party/On Your Own/Beetlebum/Essex Dogs/Death Of A Party/Theme From Retro/Death Of A Party/On Your Own/CD 2 (Live)

Popscene/Song 2/On Your Own/Chinese Bombs/Movin' On/M.O.R.

13 1999
Tender/Bugman/Coffee & TV/SwampSong/1992/B.L.U.R.E.M.I./Battle/Mellow Song/Trailerpark/Caramel/Trimm Trabb/No Distance Left To Run/Optigan 1

Blur: The Best Of ... 2000
Beetlebum/Song 2/There's No Other Way/The Universal/Coffee & TV/Parklife/End Of A Century/No Distance Left To Run/Tender/Girls & Boys/Charmless Man/She's So High/Country House/To The End/On Your Own/This Is A Low/For Tomorrow/Music Is My Radar

Think Tank 2003
Ambulance/Out Of Time/Crazy Beat/Good Song/On The Way To The Club/Brothers And Sisters/Caravan/We've Got A File On You/Moroccan Peoples Revolutionary Bowls Club/Sweet Song/Jets/Gene By Gene/Battery In Your Leg

Gorillaz – Singles

Clint Eastwood (Parlophone/EMI) 2001

19-2000 (Parlophone/EMI) 2001

Rock Da House (Parlophone/EMI) 2001

Tomorrow Comes Today (Parlophone/EMI) 2002

Feel Good Inc (Parlophone/EMI) 2005

Dare (Parlophone/EMI) 2005

Dirty Harry (Parlophone/EMI) 2005

Kids With Guns (Parlophone/EMI) 2006

Gorillaz – Albums

Gorillaz 2001
Re-Hash/ 5/4 /Tomorrow Comes Today/ New Genious (Brother)/Clint Eastwood/Man Research (Clapper)/Punk/Sound Check (Gravity)/Double Bass/Rock The House/19-2000/Latin Simone (Que Pasa Contigo)/Starshine/Slow Country/M1 A1

Demon Days 2005
Intro/Last Living Souls/Kids With Guns/O Green World/Dirty Harry/Feel Good Inc/El Mañana/Every Planet We Reach Is Dead/November Has Come/All Alone/ White Light/DARE/Fire Coming Out Of The Monkey's Head/Don't Get Lost In Heaven/Demon Days

The Good, The Bad And The Queen Singles

Herculean (Parlophone/EMI /Honest Jon's) 2006 (deleted)

Kingdom Of Doom (Parlophone/EMI /Honest Jon's) 2007

Green Fields (Parlophone/EMI /Honest Jon's) 2007

The Good, The Bad And The Queen Albums

The Good, The Bad And The Queen 2007
History Song/80's Life/Northern Whale/Kingdom Of Doom/Herculean/Behind The Sun/The Bunting Song/Nature Springs/A Soldier's Tale/Three Changes/ Green Fields/The Good, The Bad And The Queen

Soundtracks

Ravenous (EMI Soundtracks) 1999

Ordinary Decent Criminal (Icon/Atlantic Records) 2000

101 Reykjavik (EMI Soundtracks) 2001

'World Music'

Mali Music (Honest Jon's/Parlophone/EMI Records) 2002

Democrazy (Honest Jon's) 2003

Album Collaborations

Elastica (Elastica) 1995
Trainspotting 1996
Random 1997
Laugh (Terry Hall) 1997
20th Century Blues (With Michael Nyman) 1998
The Menace (Elastica) 2000
Deltron 3030 2000
This Is Where I Belong – The Songs of Ray Davies 2002
Home Cooking (Tony Allen) 2002
100th Window (Massive Attack) 2002
The Hour Of Two Lights (Terry Hall/Mushtaq) 2003
Before The Poison (Marianne Faithfull) 2004
London Town (Kano) 2007

REFERENCES

The following magazines were very helpful: *Puncture, Guitar Player, Option* and *Hot Press*. Exceptional articles on Blur which provided us with an essential insight include 'The Secret Life' in *Q* (1/95), The Stud Brother's *Melody Maker* piece entitled 'The Empire Strikes Back' (25/9/93) and Stuart Maconie and David Cavanagh's 'The Compleat Blur' in *Select* (7/95 and 8/95). Also *Esquire Q* and music365.com. As well as chronicling Blur, *Q* has been there to tell the tales of those around the band – key interviews by John Harris (Justine Frischmann) Phil Sutcliffe (Graham Coxon) and the enquiring natures of the magazine's readers (Cash For Questions) were all of great help and interest. *Esquire* also ran several lengthy and excellent pieces. Publications as diverse as *Mojo, Select, The Face, National Geographic, Manchester Evening News* and *Grazia* also played their parts along with websites such as MusicOHM.com, music365.com, The Bulb and SoundtrackNet as well as the tireless work done by fansites detailing the work of all Albarn's interests and projects. *Time Out*'s piece on The Good, The Bad and The Queen by Eddy Lawrence was a key early scene setter as was Andrew Smith's article on Monkey in the *Sunday Times*. Not forgetting *LA Weekly, The Guardian, The Observer, Red* and of course *NME*. Bookwise there's *Suede: Love and Passion* by David Barnett, *The Last Gang in Town* by Marcus Gray and *The Blair Years* by Alastair Campbell ... you need to read them all to get the full picture.

ALSO AVAILABLE

FROM

INDEPENDENT MUSIC PRESS

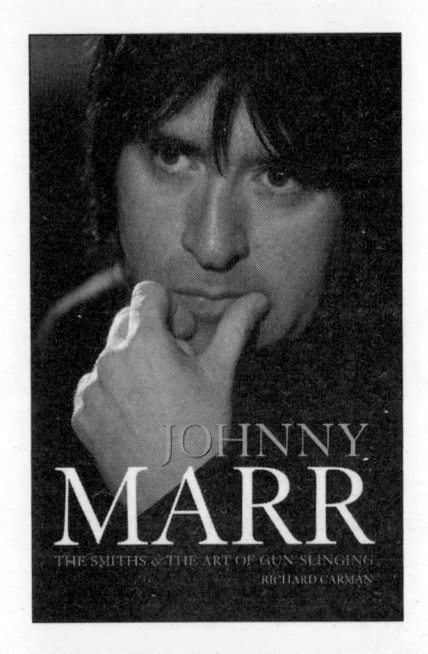

JOHNNY MARR: THE SMITHS & THE ART OF GUN-SLINGING
by Richard Carman

The Smiths were the best British band since The Beatles. Their shimmering, muscular, guitar-driven pop remains the barometer for everyone who looks back at the 1980s with affection. In a decade that arguably produced more poor pop music than any other since the 1950s, The Smiths shone like a beacon and inspired a generation of indie guitar bands, and their influence continues undiminished to this day. After The Smiths, Marr continued to inject beautiful, sophisticated guitar into some of the best music of the period: The Pretenders, Kirsty McColl, Billy Bragg, The The and Talking Heads all benefited from his incendiary input. More recently with his band Johnny Marr & The Healers, Johnny remains as influential and important as ever. This is the first full-length biography of Johnny Marr, looking beyond world of The Smiths and into the solo career of Britain's most influential guitar player of the last two decades – a tale coloured by exclusive interviews with people such as key Smiths insider Grant Showbiz, Billy Bragg and David Byrne. A must-read for anyone who cares about The Smiths as well as great rock or pop.

ISBN 0 9549704 8 9   208 Pages   Paperback, 8pp b/w pics   £12.99   World Rights

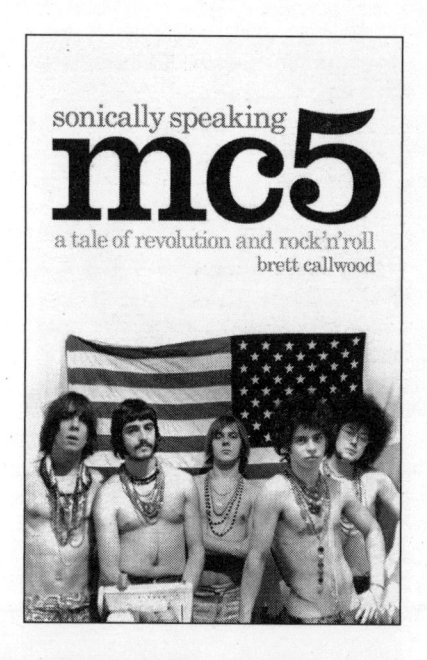

MC5: SONICALLY SPEAKING – A TALE OF PUNK ROCK AND REVOLUTION
by Brett Callwood

The first in-depth biography of the group, Sonically Speaking charts the career of this most seminal of bands, as well as unravelling what became of the members after the break up of the MC5. For this definitive book, author Brett Callwood travelled to Detroit and Los Angeles to track down and interview the three surviving founder members of the MC5 in-depth. He also spoke at length with other key players in this remarkable tale, such as former manager John Sinclair, artist Gary Grimshaw, former White Panther Pun Plamondon, Leni Sinclair, Jackson Smith – the son that MC5's Fred had with Patti Smith – and Russ Gibb, manager of the legendary Grandee Ballroom, among others.

ISBN 0 9552822-2-5 224 Pages Paperback, 12 b/w pics £12.99 World Rights

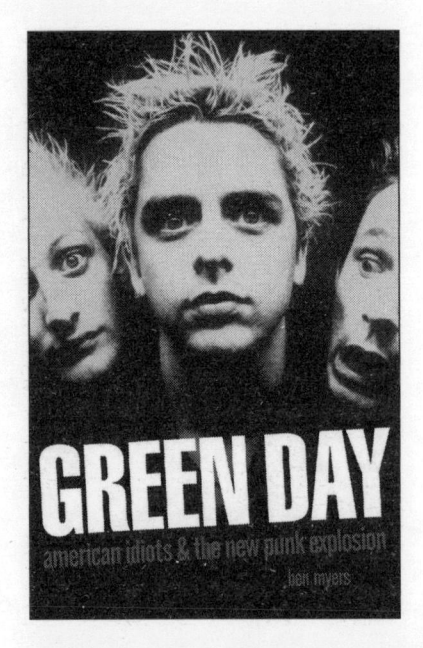

GREEN DAY: AMERICAN IDIOTS AND THE NEW PUNK EXPLOSION
by Ben Myers

The world's first and only full biography of Green Day. Self-confessed latch-key kids from small blue-collar Californian towns, Green Day have gone on to sell 50 million albums and single-handedly redefine the punk and rock genre for an entire generation. Inspired by both the energy of British punk bands as well as cult American groups, Green Day gigged relentlessly across the US underground before eventually signing to Warners and releasing their 1994 major label debut *Dookie*, which was a 10-million-selling worldwide hit album. With the arrival of Green Day, suddenly music was dumb, fun, upbeat and colourful again. Many now credit the band with saving rock from the hands of a hundred grunge-lite acts. In 2004 Green Day reached a career pinnacle with the concept album *American Idiot*, a sophisticated commentary on modern life - not least their dissatisfaction with their president. Myers is an authority on punk and hardcore and in this unauthorised book charts the band members' difficult childhoods and their rise to success, speaking to key members of the punk underground and music industry figures along the way.

ISBN 0 9539942 9 5   208 Pages   Paperback, 8pp b/w pics   £12.99   World Rights

I SWEAR I WAS THERE: THE GIG THAT CHANGED THE WORLD
by David Nolan

On June 4, 1976, four young men took the stage of a tiny upstairs hall in Manchester for a gig that, quite literally, *changed the world*. In front of a handful of people they played one of the most important live sets of all time. Alongside Woodstock and Live Aid, the Sex Pistols performance at the Lesser Free Trade Hall has been named by critics as one of the most pivotal performances in music history ... not necessarily because of the quality of the music – but because of the effect the music had on the audience.

Members of Joy Division and New Order, the Smiths, the Fall and Buzzcocks were there that night as well as Tony Wilson. The truth behind that gig – plus the Pistols repeat performance six weeks later and their first ever TV appearance – has been shrouded in mystery for thirty years. Until now, everyone's been happy to print the legend. For the first time, here's the truth. Featuring previously unpublished photos and interviews with key players and audience members.

ISBN 0 9549704 9 7   208 Pages   Paperback, 40 b/w pics   £12.99   World Rights

Visit our website at www.impbooks.com for more
information on our full list of titles including books on:

Bernard Sumner, MC5, Bruce Dickinson, Slash,
'Skins', 'Scooter Boys', Dave Grohl, Muse, The Streets,
Green Day, Ian Hunter, Mick Ronson,
David Bowie, The Killers, My Chemical Romance,
System Of A Down, The Prodigy and many more.

www.myspace.com/independentmusicpress